C0-AUG-287

DISCARDED

The New Economic Analysis of Multinationals

NEW HORIZONS IN INTERNATIONAL BUSINESS

Series Editor: Peter J. Buckley
Centre for International Business,
University of Leeds (CIBUL), UK

The New Horizons in International Business series has established itself as the world's leading forum for the presentation of new ideas in international business research. It offers pre-eminent contributions in the areas of multinational enterprise – including foreign direct investment, business strategy and corporate alliances, global competitive strategies, and entrepreneurship. In short, this series constitutes essential reading for academics, business strategists and policy makers alike.

Titles in the series include:

The European Union and Globalisation
Towards Global Democratic Governance
Brigid Gavin

Globalization and the Small Open Economy
Edited by Daniel Van Den Bulcke and Alain Verbeke

Entrepreneurship and the Internationalisation of Asian Firms
An Institutional Perspective
Henry Wai-chung Yeung

The World Trade Organization in the New Global Economy
Trade and Investment Issues in the Millennium Round
Edited by Alan M. Rugman and Gavin Boyd

Japanese Subsidiaries in the New Global Economy
Edited by Paul W. Beamish, Andrew Delios and Shige Makino

Globalizing Europe
Deepening Integration, alliance Capitalism and Structural Statecraft
Edited by Thomas L. Brewer, Paul A. Brenton and Gavin Boyd

China and its Regions
Economic Growth and Reform in Chinese Provinces
Edited by Mary-Françoise Renard

Emerging Issues in International Business Research
Edited by Masaaki Kotabe and Preet S. Aulakh

Network Knowledge in International Business
Edited by Sarianna M. Lundan

Learning in the Internationalisation Process of Firms
Edited by Anders Blomstermo and D. Deo Sharma

Alliance Capitalism and Corporate Management
Entrepreneurial Cooperation in Knowledge Based Economies
Edited by John H. Dunning and Gavin Boyd

The New Economic Analysis of Multinationals
An Agenda for Management, Policy and Research
Edited by Thomas L. Brewer, Stephen Young and Stephen E. Guisinger

The New Economic Analysis of Multinationals

An Agenda for Management, Policy and Research

Edited by

Thomas L. Brewer

Faculty, Georgetown University McDonough School of Business, Washington, DC, USA

Stephen Young

Professor and Director, Strathclyde International Business Unit, University of Strathclyde, Glasgow, UK

Stephen E. Guisinger

Formerly Professor of International Management, University of Texas, Dallas, USA

NEW HORIZONS IN INTERNATIONAL BUSINESS

Edward Elgar

Cheltenham, UK • Northampton, MA, USA

© Thomas L. Brewer, Stephen Young and Stephen E. Guisinger 2003

All rights reserved. No part of this publication may be reproduced, stored in
a retrieval system or transmitted in any form or by any means, electronic,
mechanical or photocopying, recording, or otherwise without the prior permission
of the publisher.

Published by
Edward Elgar Publishing Limited
Glensanda House
Montpellier Parade
Cheltenham
Glos GL50 1UA
UK

Edward Elgar Publishing, Inc.
136 West Street
Suite 202
Northampton
Massachusetts 01060
USA

A catalogue record for this book
is available from the British Library

Library of Congress Cataloguing in Publication Data

The new economic analysis of multinationals: an agenda for management, policy, and
research/edited by Thomas L. Brewer, Stephen Young, Stephen E. Guisinger.
    p. cm. — (New horizons in international business series)
    Based on a symposium held in 1998.
    Includes bibliographical references and index.
    1. International business enterprises — Management. 2. International business
    enterprises. I. Brewer, Thomas L., 1941– II. Young, Stephen, 1944– III.
    Guisinger, Stephen E. IV. New horizons in international business.

HD62.4.N483 2003
338.8′8 — dc21   2002037943

ISBN 1 84064 154 1

Typeset by Cambrian Typesetters, Frimley, Surrey
Printed and bound in Great Britain by MPG Books Ltd, Bodmin, Cornwall

Contents

Figures

Tables

Contributors

Thomas L. Brewer, former Editor of the *Journal of International Business Studies*, and Associate Professor, McDonough School of Business, Georgetown University, Washington, DC, USA

Peter J. Buckley, Professor of International Business and Director of the Centre for International Business, University of Leeds (CIBUL), UK

Mark C. Casson, Professor of Economics, University of Reading, UK

Richard E. Caves, Nathaniel Ropes Professor of Political Economy, Department of Economics, Harvard University, Cambridge, Massachusetts, USA

John H. Dunning, Emeritus Professor of International Business, University of Reading, UK, and Emeritus Professor of International Business, Rutgers University, USA

Edward M. Graham, Senior Fellow, Institute for International Economics, Washington, DC, USA

Stephen E. Guisinger, formerly Professor of International Management, University of Texas at Dallas, USA

Sylvia Ostry, Distinguished Research Fellow, Centre for International Studies, University of Toronto, Toronto, Canada

Alan M. Rugman, Leslie Waters Chair of International Business, Kelley School of Business, Indiana University, USA and Thames Water Senior Research Fellow, Templeton College, University of Oxford, UK

Alain Verbeke, Professor of International Business and Public Policy, Solvay Business School, University of Brussels (VUB), Belgium, and Associate Fellow, Templeton College, University of Oxford, UK

Louis T. Wells, Jr, Herbert F. Johnson Professor of International Management, Harvard Business School, Cambridge, Massachusetts, USA

Stephen Young, Director, Strathclyde International Business Unit, University of Strathclyde, UK

Dedication

This book is dedicated to the memory of Professor Stephen Guisinger, a good friend and collaborator, who died in Dallas, Texas on 3 July 2001. He inspired and co-edited the symposium in the *Journal of International Business Studies* on 'Multinational Enterprise and Economic Analysis' (volume 29, number 1), on which this book is based.

Steve enjoyed a distinguished career as a scholar and teacher of international business, and he was active in governmental policy-making circles as a specialist in foreign direct investment issues and business–government relations. His publications included articles in *JIBS* in 1989, 1991, 1992, 1995 and 1998. He had recently begun working on an international business textbook based on his analytic framework emphasizing the interactions of firms with their political–economic environments. He worked with numerous doctoral students in his career, and was always a strong supporter of them during and after their studies. Perhaps less known to members of the AIB were his professional activities on government policy issues – for instance, as a frequent consultant to the World Bank on foreign direct investment issues, particularly in Asia. He was also directly involved in drafting the Asia Pacific Economic Cooperation (APEC) code on foreign direct investment.

Steve had been robust – and energetically looking forward to the future – until a few days before his death. Many of us will continue to be inspired by his example.

Introduction

This book is based on a symposium that appeared the *Journal of International Business Studies* in early 1998. The stimulus for the symposium was the appearance in 1996 of Richard Caves' *Multinational Enterprise and Economic Analysis*. Caves' book is one of several that could be used as the starting point in an inquiry into the future of research on international business. John Dunning's *Multinational Enterprise and the Global Economy* and Peter Buckley's and Mark Casson's *The Future of the Multinational Enterprise* are other books that immediately come to mind, and there are others as well. However, Caves' book had a unique feature: the 1996 book was the second edition, appearing fourteen years after its predecessor in 1982. The two editions thus permit the reader not only to gauge the stock of economics research available on the multinational firm in the early 1980s but also to know how one eminent scholar in the field has appraised the flow of studies over the decade or so that followed. The topical and methodological distribution of studies in this flow segment, we believe provides signals as to where researchers and journal editors were placing their bets on scholarly work.

The symposium was thus conceived as a way for recognized scholars in the field of international business to use Caves' work as a benchmark in order to focus attention on two questions. First, have any important strands of research slipped through Caves' net? Secondly, where would these scholars place their bets on the topics and research methods that will yield the highest returns to research over the next two decades? We invited Professor Caves to add his own insights on scholarly roads 'less traveled' – but roads which could make a significant difference on our understanding of international business.

Each participant in the symposium selected one or more chapters from Caves' book to use as a starting point for his or her essay. Readers will perhaps turn first to essays dealing with topics related to their own special fields of interest. It would be a mistake to stop there, however, all readers should be able to find passages in each essay that will cause them to pause and ask themselves: 'Can I apply this concept to my own work?' Or better yet, 'Here is a new topic where I can exercise my theoretical or methodological or other comparative advantage.' At the very least, serious scholars should peruse the articles' bibliographies, which reflect trends in the international business literature.

The themes of the chapters can be summarized in relation to types of foreign direct investment, which of course is the distinguishing feature of MNEs. Thus, in Table I.1 the grouping of the central ideas of the essays in one

Table I.1   The evolving research agenda: illustrative topics

Levels of analysis	Maturing	Emerging
Firms	Hierarchies	Network alliances Teams Ambiguous boundaries Employee empowerment Corporate culture Internal entrepreneurs
Transactions	Foreign direct investment trade as substituted transactions costs	Foreign direct investment trade as complements
Foreign direct	Greenfield ventures Market access Atemporal	Mergers and acquisitions Production efficiency Ongoing exit Options path dependency
Products	Goods	Services
Industries	International competition	Global concentration Strategic transactions Non-cooperative games
Countries	Home or host to multinational enterprises	Home and host to international enterprises National innovation systems Standards competition
Subnational area		Regional clusters
International regions	North–South/East–West	Multiple overlapping
General	Shallow integration Economics alone Exogenous Reductionism Efficiency	Deep integration Multi-disciplinary Endogenous Complexity Equity distribution

place has an inherent heuristic value, for it facilitates a consideration of the question: Are there common themes, gaps, and important interdependencies that provide fruitful topics for further analysis? The summary in Table I.1 is thus a catalog of some of the ideas, concepts, frameworks, and theories found in the articles. Following our emphasis on change, we have chosen to group these ideas as contrasts wherever possible. To stress the notion of growth and evolution, we have assigned ideas to the categories 'old' and 'new.' To be sure, these are our impressionistic judgments – not those of the chapters' authors, and not the result of a systematic, quantitative content analysis. We hope this juxtaposition of ideas provokes productive discussions in faculty offices and conferences, and stimulates a useful new thought process in individual researchers.

The volume ends with a concluding chapter by Stephen Young and Thomas L. Brewer in which they provide a summary and overview of both Caves' work and the chapters in the book, together with an extended discussion of the multinational enterprise and public policy.

Stephen E. Guisinger
Thomas L. Brewer
Stephen Young

1. Research on international business: problems and prospects

Richard E. Caves

The field of international business slices across the grain of areas of study in business administration. Strategy, finance, marketing, organizational behavior, human-resource management: each has its domain of decision making within the firm and its stock of models, frameworks, and research procedures for addressing them. International business designates not a class of decisions but a group of firms that face decision making problems beyond those that confront single-nation businesses or encounter the same problems transformed by their international context. Strategy issues become distinctive because the multinational enterprise (MNE) serves product markets balkanized by transport costs, government restrictions, and/or differences in tastes and production conditions. Financial decision making becomes ensnared with exchange-rate variation and differences of custom and law in national commercial and investment banking practices. Marketing struggles with differences in national tastes and distribution systems. The firm's human-resource policies must adapt to national differences in culture that affect managerial hierarchies, national traditions and practices that constrain employee compensation and evaluation practices, and particularly differences in trade union organization and blue-collar wage-setting practices. The choice of organizational structure must reconcile the conflicting pulls of geographic and product-line heterogeneity.

We can study MNEs' responses to each of these classes of decision problems colored by national boundaries and differences, deriving lessons for business (and public) policy. Yet the heterogeneity of the problems, coupled with the diverse approaches and research methods of business administration's subfields, exert centrifugal forces that scatter the research results and make it difficult to capture their potential intellectual spillovers. The whole resists being more than the sum of its parts, and the researcher well acquainted with one set of parts incurs the far-from-home traveler's costs of learning the other parts.

International economics slices across the sector-based organization of other fields of economics (industrial organization, labor, public finance, financial institutions and markets), and faces the same problems of coherence and integration as the study of international business. Nonetheless, economic analysis enjoys a great advantage in its unified theoretical view of market processes and allocative decisions, which supplies a map that can indicate the road(s) leading from any condition or disturbances to any outcome that they might influence. In the case of the MNE, the most traveled boulevard is transaction-cost analysis of the 'firm. vs. market' problem: that is, why some allocation decisions are made through spot transactions or arm's-length contracts, while others are internalized within business organizations. The transaction-cost approach treats the MNE as one species of multi-market firm. It helps us to frame any questions about the MNE's decision making in a manner consistent with the logic of why organizational links between internationally decentralized business units outperform their interaction through arm's-length markets. Of course, a framework that characterizes MNEs' decision making in any given domain should also show how their decisions are interrelated. This approach to MNEs' behavior, parading under various banners (notably John Dunning's OLI framework), seems serviceable for organizing our knowledge about the MNE. It sustained my recent effort to comprehend and summarize the last fifteen years of research on the MNE without conspicuous breakdowns (Caves 1996).

GENERAL PROBLEMS

While research on MNEs is a thriving business, it faces certain problems of procedure and inference that do not always get the respect they deserve from researchers. Several of these merit attention before we consider the specific stock of unexploited research opportunities.

Isolating Effects of Policy Choices

A core problem of quantitative research on international business (indeed, the qualifier 'international' may be dropped) lies in the basic job specification handed to the researcher on business administration. The 'business normative' goal is to advise managers on the best choice for some business policy. A natural research strategy is to draw a suitable sample of firms that have made different choices for that policy and estimate the value of the outcome or performance level associated with each decision. The resulting estimate of each choice's effect will be unbiased if the decision makers make their choices 'in the dark', randomizing their strategies so that they are uncorrelated with the structural opportunities surrounding the business (that is, random 'treatments' applied to experimental 'plots').

Of course, managers try to improve on random choices and make the best decision contingent on the constraints and opportunities facing the firm, and their efforts tend to trip up the researcher who would 'second-guess' the policy choice. Policy A might be the best for a firm stuck with an inferior set of opportunities; policy B may be a viable but not ideal choice for a firm blessed with good opportunities. The investigator who does not control for the firms' different opportunities concludes that policy B beats policy A, whereas the short-changed firms are those that chose B. The more canny researcher tries to duck the problem by employing controls for differences in the decision maker's opportunities by means of a set multivariate models of the determinants of performance. That move will often not suffice, however, because the policy choice is dependent on, and hence correlated with, the indicators of the business's opportunities, making it unlikely that the researcher can estimate their separate influences precisely. In statistical estimation multicollinearity inflates standard errors and, in practice, makes the results frustratingly sensitive to small changes in the measurement of the variables and/or specifications of the model. Independent of this problem, any random disturbance or uncontrolled structural condition that affects both choice of policy and performance will bias the estimated effect of the policy on performance. Solutions to these problems do exist: for example, a two-pass procedure in which the researcher first relates the sampled businesses' policy choices to their opportunity sets. That yields a prediction of how apt each choice was, given the decision maker's opportunities and the average choice pattern of all decision makers in the sample. The second step is then to test whether policies that appear well matched to the firm's opportunities outperform those that are mismatched.[1] This design unfortunately is hard to implement in research on international business, where firms' opportunity sets are hard to define and characterize accurately and likely to be highly heterogeneous. The design also depends, of course, on firms not doing *too* good a job in making the observed choices. If no mismatches occur in the observed sample, the researcher hits a blank wall, because the differential effect of superior over inferior policy choices by identically situated firms cannot be observed; that is, all business decisions are correct, but the researcher has no way to test and confirm this.[2]

This problem of isolating the effects of policy choices is certainly not specific to international business, but it proves particularly vexing for researchers of MNEs. The source of the trouble is exposed by the basic transaction-cost model of the MNE, which predicts that foreign direct investment will be launched to exploit the differential quality of the firm's proprietary assets. Proprietary assets are largely intangible, and it is hard to measure what we do not see. Moreover, what matters is generally not the absolute quality of the firm's assets, but their differential advantages over those of other firms (single-nation rivals or other MNEs). One must measure not just 'charm', but 'charm differentials'.

The researcher often has significant leverage against this problem at the research-design stage where controls are being established. In a matched-pairs design it may be possible to select control firms that (from their assets or actions) appear to possess opportunities closely similar to the treatment firms'. Care can also be taken to ensure that treatment firms which made particularly bad policy choices do not fall out of the sample.

Uncertainty, Winners and Losers

A second general problem with research on MNEs lies in the uncertainty of their investments and the turnover of their activities. That foreign direct investment is a risky business is implied by the transaction-cost model. It characterizes the potential foreign investor as a single-nation enterprise whose management possesses as 'birthright capital' common knowledge of conditions, customs and laws at home. When the firm ponders a foreign investment, it must incur costs to acquire a suitable amount of that same knowledge about the potential host market. Such information is costly, so the firm rationally limits its intake. However, that limitation trades off the cost of information against the cost of ignorance: an increased chance that its foreign investment will be blighted by some shortcoming that shrivels its profitability and perhaps forces abandonment. We therefore expect foreign investment to appear especially risky, even before taking account of such intrinsic risk sources as exchange-rate variations and hostile foreign governments that are a lesser or nonexistent affliction for domestic investors.

Dead business units tell no tales, and much quantitative research on MNEs shows some degree of 'survivor bias' in addressing only those firms that have enjoyed enough success to sustain their international operations. Some research designs can clear themselves of any charges of distortion from survivor bias, but others cannot. Consider some business strategy that we observe to yield higher than normal profits for the firms employing it. Can we safely advise potential adoptees that the strategy is a sure bet? Not without checking whether another set of firms adopted the same strategy unsuccessfully, ran fatal losses, and hence disappeared off the screen. Indeed, a standard economic model holds that risk-neutral firms, with equal access to some risky market and well informed about the distribution of its profits and losses, will on average earn only normal profits from the investments; that is, the stream of entrants will regulate itself, swelling when the average-success entrant earns positive profits, drying up when it runs losses. The winners' excess profits will offset the losers' deficits, leaving the overall average expected return in equilibrium 'normal profits'.[3]

If research on international business can slip by neglect of unsuccessful risk-takers, it can also err by assuming that exiting firms and business units are failures. This problem is well illustrated by, and pertinent to, research on international joint ventures, alliances and other such projects that involve cooperation among independent enterprises. Investigators who observe high turnover rates in these projects have commonly taken them as proof of governance difficulties or other infirmities of the organizational form. An important consideration, however, is that such projects are frequently intended to pursue some special purpose or 'one-shot' opportunity. Each investment has an expected cash flow that, however safe or risky it may appear, possesses only a limited longevity. The partner firms in the venture, by contrast, can be regarded as portfolios of such investments. Their life expectancies much exceed their individual specific joint projects, even if the single-firm and joint-venture projects are drawn from populations with the same underlying distribution of returns. Thus, research in international business can be thrown off-track by the assumption that terminated businesses are always failures, when they might be wrapped-up successes.

Several lessons flow from these considerations of riskiness. First, it appears to be an under-researched issue in international business, with ample room for studies that document the variability of outcomes and not just their mean. Secondly, it is important to recognize survivor biases in selected samples of firms; these cannot always be avoided, but they can be recognized and sometimes even exploited. Thirdly, in drawing lessons from apparent failures, it is important to credit the victims with intended rationality where appropriate: did they really miss a trick, or did they get a bad draw on a fair bet?

Longitudinal Data

Another general problem with research on international business lies in the cost of constructing databases. A database is of course the classic public good with a marginal resource cost to subsequent users much below that of the original assembler. Some branches of both business and economic research enjoy access to rich common-use databases: finance, of course; labor economics; and recently, research on taxation of international business. Lacking, however, are longitudinal databases to track the sequences of foreign direct investments undertaken by MNEs. One recalls fondly Raymond Vernon's Harvard Multinational Enterprises Project (HMEP), which sustained such a data set tracking large US MNEs from their earliest days up to 1975 (Curhan et al. 1977). This source nourished much of our foundation stock of knowledge about MINEs.

Although no broad and comparable database is kept current nowadays, the time may again be ripe. In a number of countries the primary government census records on establishments and firms have now been organized into public-use longitudinal databases, and these have sustained flourishing programs of new research that contribute bountifully to the fields of industrial organization, labor economics and macroeconomics. In most countries, these databases apparently do not conveniently distinguish foreign subsidiaries, or units of domestic firms that also have investments abroad, from the run of domestic firms. Canada is a notable exception, however, and research by Baldwin (1995, esp. chapter 11 and 13) demonstrates the value of being able to follow foreign subsidiaries over time, especially in comparison with domestically controlled rivals. Due to disclosure prohibitions the information lurking in these longitudinal databases cannot easily be linked to longitudinal profiles of MNEs of the HMEP variety, but researchers should be alert to the possibility of a new start in this direction.

SPECIFIC AVENUES OF RESEARCH

What specific research projects hold promise for enriching our knowledge of the MNE? An attempt to produce such a roster has the marks of a fool's errand. Research opportunities share many properties with twenty-dollar bills on the sidewalk. If they are not counterfeit, they do not stay long in place, and anyone who proffers information on their whereabouts has either poor eyesight or a hidden motive. None the less, the twenty-dollar bill metaphor has its limitations: the hunch that a site promises high returns to research effort brings one only to the threshold of devising a way to seize and style some opportunity. The suggestions offered here about research opportunities with a promising payout in various areas are entirely personal and carry no guarantees.

Bases for Foreign Direct Investment

Research on the bases for profitable foreign investments has well documented the role of proprietary assets, that is, intangible capabilities of the firm that function as proprietary public goods. In previous research these assets have been proxied in an adequate if indirect way by outlays on R&D and sales promotion. Many recent foreign investments, however, seem to fit the proprietary-assets model awkwardly. The products of the steel, glass and cement industries exhibit no classic signs of affinity for foreign investment. The relevant proprietary assets may be the implicit contracts between suppliers and large customers located abroad, reflecting the foreign investor's ability to manage the logistics of continuous supply and adaptation to the customer's needs rather than general product-embodied assets (for example, Adams 1997). An investigation of foreign direct investment in 'commodity' industries might focus on differences between sellers in customer contract and supply procedures as a basis for explaining the occurrence of foreign investment.

Also, firms in some industries find that their skills in differentiating products, secure in the domestic market, do not travel well to markets abroad, making profitable foreign investments depend on other (for example, logistical) factors; the major home appliance industry seems to be an example (Feder 1997).[4]

Another under-explored basis for foreign investment is managerial capability that is market- or industry-specific. Consider foreign investments by US electric utilities in British regional electricity distributors. Product-embodied attributes and better service to extant overseas customers clearly fail as explanations. Could managerial experience with operating in a multi-seller market, even under a heritage of tight regulatory constraint, be the answer? The affirmative is strongly suggested by the focus of recent US foreign direct investment in Europe on deregulated sectors that have previously seen little multinational activity (Javetski 1996), although the payout to these investments remains to be seen (Frank and Rose 1997). Another salient pattern is the recent popularity among European airlines of recruiting top executives with experience in the competitive, unregulated US airline industry. Another site for investigating the essence of MNEs' value-creating activities is the service sector. Both general proprietary assets and goodwill of customers with far-flung activities provide likely explanations. Less obvious is the process by which the MNEs' underlying service capability gets transferred abroad while remaining proprietary to the firm (see Grosse 1996).

A third type of puzzling international linkage is foreign investment in supplier or customer firms abroad. Such links are not new and are classically explained by examples of the internalization of buyer–seller relations ill-served by arm's-length long-term contracts. Vertical foreign direct investments and alliances, however, may have other explanations that merit researchers' attention. A classic explanation for vertical integration into a market is that, due to regulation or oligopoly behavior, the intervening price is elevated substantially above marginal cost. By either starting or acquiring a business selling the overpriced product or service, a buyer can retrieve this margin on transactions with the newly acquired partner. Long-distance telephone services are widely thought to be thus overpriced outside the United States (and indeed inside as well, on the view of MacAvoy [1996] and others). Could international telephone mergers and alliances be driven by this 'business stealing' motive? Or does the classic explanation of optimizing service to large business customers remain sufficient? Vertical foreign investment is also encouraged by new developments in the governance of supplier–customer relations occurring in those US manufacturer–retailer markets in which integrated computer and logistics systems mechanize the placement and delivery of orders. To researchers familiar with the hazards of governing intricate arm's-length market relationships, the viability of these intimate relations in the face of hold-up opportunities and haggling costs comes as a surprise. If they do indeed represent an advance in firms' ability to manage intricate supplier–customer relations at arm's length, they may lower incentives for vertical foreign direct investment, even while they augment incentives for horizontal foreign investments to exploit the capability of managing such relationships.

The fashionable word 'globalization' is too easily invoked in an agenda for research on MNEs, but it does correctly target several areas of research interest. The tendency of growth in countries' flows of international trade in goods and services to exceed the growth of gross domestic product is one key symptom of globalization. MNEs contribute through increased intracorporate trade following internationally decentralized production of components and product-line items, itself presumably due to economies of scale and specialization large enough to warrant the associated increase in international transportation and communication costs. This process of intracorporate globalization does not seem to be very well documented, or its determinants identified (but see Andersson and Fredriksson 1996). The prevalence of trade expanding forces makes the trend plausible, but the rise of 'flexible manufacturing' and technologies for minimizing inventory-holding costs cut against it. The trend also raises interesting problems of governance and coordination; for example, Birkinshaw's (1996) study suggests a surprisingly large amount of decentralization of product-mandate decisions within the MNE.

The integration into the international economy of the former centrally-planned economies and of rapidly developing (and liberalizing) 'third-world' nations opens a rather different link between the MNE and globalization processes. The economic disequilibria that afflict these economies offer many opportunities for 'enterprise' in the transfer of proprietary assets, skills and experience developed in mature industrial markets. The question is not whether these provide opportunities for foreign direct investors but what type of opportunity will exert the dominant pull. The very disequilibrium conditions in these economies may raise the importance of local knowledge, however, which puts foreign investors at a disadvantage. And there may be concerns of the old 'obsolescing bargain' type about sinking investments that could become hostages following major shifts (reversions) of public policy. How these several vectors of forces exert their pulls on foreign investors is a question of major interest.

MNEs and Competitive Processes

The older literature on MNEs is gravid with stories of their involvement in international cartels' operations. Although international price-fixing conspiracies are certainly not unknown nowadays, one senses that the encounters between MNEs and competition policy have shifted to a different arena. Consider the international horizontal mergers that have occurred in waves in successive international product markets. First of all, these waves pose a substantial explanatory task. Economic theory shows that horizontal mergers for market power are not an automatic route to higher profits for the combining firms: if the erstwhile competing firms raise prices and their international competitors follow suit, yes; if the industry competes by setting quantities or capacities, the combining firms tend to shrink while their rivals expand, and the merger will likely be unprofitable (Deneckere and Davidson 1985). The tendency for international horizontal mergers to bunch within an industry might be attributed to market-power motives if indeed one combination raises the expected profitability of others. That explanation seems less likely, however, than one attributing to the combined firm a strategic or contingent advantage: commanding a widened range of assets in-place around the world and ready for fast response to future unexpected disturbances, notably including aggressive moves by important competitors (Caves 1991). Such investments in strategic options tend to provoke reactive mergers among international rivals. This explanation for intra-industry merger waves faces an obvious competitor: that some common opportunity to exploit scale economies has revealed itself to all rivals. From casual examination of affected industries, exogenous scale-economies shifts are far from obvious and the strategic-options story appears to fit the facts. It raises concerns for both business and public policy that mergers occur not because the combined assets can in general be managed more efficiently, but because they promise greater ability to fend off raids on the corral in the form of rivals' pre-emptive moves. A careful investigation of this hypothesis would be welcome.

MNEs' role in competitive processes intersects with the issue of turnover, discussed previously. Some foreign investments augment market competition, because the MNE is likely to be the firm best equipped to surmount barriers to entry into a market. Entry barriers that generate excess profits for successful incumbent firms create an incentive for outsiders to attempt entry, even if the attempt might fail. Recent research on business turnover suggests that entry barriers may lower the success rate of entrants more than they reduce the gross number of would-be entrants (for example, Lieberman 1989); entrants into such markets may well fail as often as those into markets where competitors are numerous and earn only normal profits. Where foreign investors tend to head the queue of potential entrants, they become hostages to fortune and may face high failure rates. The same hazard confronts foreign investors who cluster in particular host localities and time periods, for whatever reason. One wishes that the researchers who studied bunching in foreign investment (initiated by Knickerbocker 1973) had checked for a negative association between concentrated entry and success.

Turnover and riskiness in foreign investment have been under-studied partly due to deficient data, but partly also due to the myopic habit noted above of associating shutdowns and sell-offs of foreign subsidiaries with failure. With foreign investment increasingly made through acquisitions of established business units, MNEs operate in a broad market for business-unit control in which the most general reason for divesting a foreign subsidiary is that someone will pay more than the capitalized value of the cash flows it yields to the current owner. This condition is potentially independent of whether the current owner profits on its investment, and of whether the unit has experienced some negative profit shock. Research on the turnover of foreign subsidiaries could fruitfully place it in the context of this 'job-matching' process in the market for corporate control, through which business units pass into the hands of managers who expect to wring more value from them. The same imperative applies to research on the turnover of joint ventures and other inter-firm collaborations: termination may mean that a profitable, but temporally limited, business opportunity has been brought to a close, and not that some negative shock has occurred. For that matter, an activity may be continued not because it yields positive profits on the original investment, but because that investment was sufficiently sunk for continuation to be more profitable than exit.

Financial Flows and Business Behavior

Some finance-oriented research on MNEs focuses on macroeconomic variables and relationships, some on MNEs' participation in, and effect on, capital and foreign-exchange markets, and some on the interplay between MNEs' real activities and their financing. The last seems to offer particularly rich opportunities for reaching current research frontiers. One research line springs from the question of how MNEs adapt to changes (actual and expected) in foreign-exchange rates. For example, Blonigen (19971) recently pointed to a previously unnoticed mechanism linking FDI to exchange rate movements: when the US dollar depreciates against the yen, the proprietary assets of a potential US target firm become more valuable to a Japanese acquirer (who can use them to produce more yen-denominated profit in the Japanese market) relative to a competing American acquirer (who by assumption uses them to gain profits in depreciated dollars). He confirmed the prediction that Japanese firms make more acquisitions in US industries (relative to acquisitions by US domestic firms) when the dollar depreciates. Furthermore, this factor is additional to the mechanism proposed by Froot and Stein (1991) of a wealth effect stemming from the increased purchasing power over US assets of yen-denominated corporate liquidity when the yen appreciates.

This contribution flags a number of issues for further investigation. First, it provides a sort of test that FDI via acquisition is asset-seeking by the acquirer, rather than asset-exploiting.[5] Asset-seeking foreign investment has been much discussed, but few sharp tests have been devised to distinguish it (compare Wesson 1993). Secondly, it implies that international acquirers whose profits are strongly aligned with their home currencies (Japan was Blonigen's astute choice) behave differently from acquirers with internationally diffused profit opportunities. Thirdly, the Froot-Stein mechanism, although supported by substantial empirical evidence, takes an odd view of corporate behavior (its wealth effect is more plausible for household than for a value-maximizing enterprise), and it would be attractive to learn whether other corollaries of a corporate wealth effect are confirmed. For example, casual observation suggests that another determinant of foreign MNEs' acquisitions in the United States may be the profitability or liquidity of their existing US subsidiaries. Such a wealth effect (which might be tax-related) seems to call into question the view that centralized management of funds in the MNE reallocates liquidity globally to equalize marginal returns on investment projects wherever they are undertaken.[6] Fourthly, the Froot-Stein mechanism suggests a dilemma for the managers of foreign direct investments that are motivated by portfolio diversification or some other wealth-related objective of the ultimate beneficial owner. The management of foreign direct investments for portfolio objectives is potentially at odds with their management to maximize their real returns, both in terms of the specific decisions taken and the types of managerial skills recruited to take them. The poor returns apparently earned by numerous large Japanese direct investments in US real estate during the 1980s both highlight the problem and suggest research avenues.

One financial decision of MNEs studied only sporadically is the extent of local borrowing undertaken by foreign subsidiaries. It holds interest from several viewpoints. It provides a route of arbitrage between countries with differing costs of debt capital, thus affecting the degree of integration of international capital markets. Existing research has suggested that local borrowing serves to hedge the MNE's exposure to exchange-rate movements. That raises the question of trade-offs between this and other forms of hedge; it also touches on the extent and rationality of corporate aversion to exchange-rate risks. Finally, local borrowing by a subsidiary may substitute for the supply of equity funds by the foreign parent. Equity transfers appear rather strongly influenced by tax factors, and so local borrowing is bound up with the MNE's strategy for minimizing its global tax burden.[7]

If local borrowing raises the question of risk-avoidance versus expected-value maximization by the MNE, so does the financial leverage chosen at the enterprise level by MNEs and domestic companies. Burgman (1996) reaffirmed the finding that MNEs choose lower leverage than their domestic rivals, even though the business risk of their cash flows is also lower.

Burgman did not reject foreign-exchange risk as a determinant of MNEs' choice of lower leverage, but in general his multivariate analysis of leverage determinants yielded a bounty of puzzling coefficients. The issue remains open.

Development and Technology Transfer

The processes of globalization mentioned previously raise questions about the consequences of foreign investment in an increasingly integrated trading world. In the developed countries the effect of foreign investment (and trade) on wages in regularly questioned: is outbound foreign investment 'exporting' jobs? Is inbound investment 'importing' them? Most economists have little time for the rhetoric of job creation, accepting the view that aggregate employment levels are affected little if at all by such forces. Effects on real wages and returns to human capital, however, are an important issue. On a strictly neoclassical view, FDI arbitrages capital toward cheaper sites of production, of which unit labor costs are an important determinant. Foreign investment attracted by lower real wages tends to raise them in the recipient country and correspondingly reduce them in the sending country. Some aspects of globalization, however, call that substitution process into question. Insofar as MNEs vertically disintegrate their production processes, locating each stage in the lowest-cost international location and shipping intermediates and components among their branches, each firm's demands for labor at various production sites become complements: to increase its global throughput, it must expand at all locations. Recent research (Brainard and Riker 1997; Riker and Brainard 1997) seems to confirm this complementarity in MNEs' effects on labor demand between more and less developed countries. Strong substitution, however, continues to prevail among countries at a given development level.[8] Clearly, more research at both the aggregate and the firm (MNE) level is warranted.

The changes currently under way in the transition and developing economies provide an attractive site for research. One notes their contrasting initial conditions: the predominance of large, but inefficient, state enterprises (or their privatized successors) in the transition economies; the fragmentation and protection common in the developing countries. These settings pose different challenges for foreign investors, and there may be interesting contrasts of strategy to observe between them. Research at this micro level has its counterpart in broader investigations of the characteristics of host countries (or of country/industry cells) that explain the volumes of foreign direct investment that they attract. Substantial progress has been made identifying the effects of public policies (for example, laws governing intellectual property), and more remains to be done.

The spillover effects of foreign investment on the host country's industry or locality have long attracted interest, although only in recent years have researchers gained access to suitable data. At least two attractive lines of research come to mind. First, while much has been accomplished in research on technology transfer and diffusion (see Basant and Fikkert [1996] for a recent example), some aspects of our knowledge remain thin. What we know about the costs of transferring technologies internationally and the costs of imitating, a multinational competitor's technology rests on much-cited, but indisputably thin, bodies of survey evidence; one would welcome their revisitation. Secondly, some forms of spillover from FDI may have eluded research. Casual evidence such as Carroll (1994) suggests that FDI can contribute importantly to a host's commercial infrastructure, such as business information systems and communications networks. The investor (foreign or otherwise) is likely to capture a good deal less than the social benefit of investments that reduce transaction and information costs for many agents in the local economy. Interest attaches to both the aggregate extent of such spillovers and the degree to which foreign investors can manage their subsidiaries to limit spillovers or capture some of their benefits.

With the global rush toward relatively unregulated market organization of the economy, one almost feels nostalgia for the strategic issues associated with the 'obsolescing bargain' between the MNE and the host government. The game-theoretic representation of the problem is now well understood, and we have some descriptive information on how MNEs and host governments have arrived at incentive-compatible contracts in which the government (sovereign and therefore unable formally to bind itself) incurs or sponsors the cost of a project's sunk components. It would be interesting to have more information than we do on the prevalence and terms of these contracts. In particular, casual evidence suggests that host governments can, through a period of 'responsible' behavior (perhaps associated with constitutional changes), attract foreign natural-resource investors without benefit of such contractual protection. MNEs seem more willing to assume rational self-interested behavior of governments, in which case dire need for transferred resources becomes itself a bond against defection. Incentive-compatible contracts seem important in some settings, reputations in others (see Sullivan 1995; Moffett 1997), and evidence on the prevalence of, and trade-off between, these mechanisms would represent attractive new knowledge.

Alliances

Research on corporate alliances hardly needs pump-priming, and we have many tests of hypotheses about the sources of revenue productivity in various types of alliances and the determinants of their chosen governance arrangements.[9] Apart from attracting widespread business and public interest, alliances provide a rich opportunity to test certain aspects of modern contract theory. Consider the distribution of control between two parties to a joint venture (JV), or other such alliance: they can share 50–50, or control can rest in one party or the other. It has been widely recognized that the party retaining control is likely the one contributing to the JV resources that are subject to appropriation or degradation. However, other angles are also available. Following Grossman and Hart (1986), consider two parties to a potential JV who differ in their access to information relevant to the JV's payout arriving after the deal has been struck, at which time the better-informed party has an advantage in diverting the JV's benefit to itself. In the incentive-compatible contract the better-informed party obtains control of the JV, but it must pay its partner up-front an amount that reflects the controller's expected capture of the project's profits. This model seems capable of testing on certain classes of JVs.

Alliances may also cast up interesting problems for contract theory. Consider the role of trust in alliances, studied recently by Johnson et al. (1996) and Aulakh et al. (1996). Trust is thought to evolve in repeated interactions between parties. However, in the theory of finite games, a well-known result is that cooperation cannot be sustained (trust will be violated) as a repeated game comes to its end. How does this square with the apparent accumulation of trust in alliance relationships? Can the parties create valuable reputations for cooperation, or offer other hostages sufficient to induce their rational good behavior? Or are the deals in which trust arises forms of 'infinite games' in which everybody thinks the probability of further interactions is high? In the latter case, trust may be nothing more than the learned minimization of communication failures in a stable multi-period interaction. In the former, it may cast up some novel behavior for consideration in the theory of contracts.

NOTES

1. For an attempt to deal with this problem in the context of judging the effectiveness of firms' product-market diversification choices, see Caves, Porter, and Spence (1980), Chapter 12.
2. The problem has been presented here in simple substantive terms, but it is readily translated into issues of econometric procedure.
3. This problem is recognized here and there in the literature on industrial economics. Lippman and Rumelt (1982), for example, point out that entry barriers surrounding an industry need not generate net excess profits when account is taken of those who try unsuccessfully to leap the fence.
4. Perhaps related to an enhanced role for managerial capability as a basis for foreign investment is casual evidence suggesting that foreign investment follows not from the firm's domestic successes, but from negative shocks to the domestic market that leave it with underutilized managerial and other capacities (Glain 1997).
5. Blonigen (1997) found no exchange-rate effect on Japanese acquisitions in US non-manufacturing sectors, such as wholesale and retail trade, where acquisitions are more likely asset-exploiting rather than asset-seeking.

6. In his recent survey of the effects of taxes on MNEs' behavior, Hines (1996) noted that research has failed to integrate tests of tax effects with the careful modeling and measurement of non-tax determinants of such decisions as a subsidiary's reinvestment of its profits.
7. Hines (1996) noted this role of local borrowing in his useful survey of the empirical literature on the effects of tax policy on MNEs.
8. Early research on offshore processing and procurement (such as Jarrett 1979) implied this result in the determinants it exposed of the extent of disintegration by industry and host country.
9. See the 1996 symposium 'Global Perspectives on Cooperative Strategies' in *Journal of International Business Studies*, **27** (5).

REFERENCES

Adams, Chris (1997), 'Steelmakers scramble in a race to become global powerhouses', *The Wall Street Journal* (26 August), pp. A1, A11.

Aulakh, Preet S., Masaaki Kotabe and Arvind Sahay (1996), 'Trust and performance in cross-border marketing partnerships: a behavioral approach', *Journal of International Business Studies*, **27** (5): 1005–32.

Andersson, Thomas, and Torbjörn Fredriksson (1996), 'International organization of production and variation in exports from affiliates', *Journal of International Business Studies*, **27** (2): 249–63

Baldwin, John R. (1995), *The Dynamics of Industrial Competition: A North American Perspective*. Cambridge: Cambridge University Press.

Basant, Rakesh, and Brian Fikkert (1996), 'The effects of R&D, foreign technology purchase, and domestic and international spillovers on productivity in Indian firms', *Review of Economics and Statistics*, **78** (2): 187–99.

Birkinshaw, Julian (1996), 'How multinational subsidiary mandates are gained and lost', *Journal of International Business Studies*, **27** (3): 467–95.

Blonigen, Bruce A. (1997), 'Firm-specific assets and the link between exchange rates and foreign direct investment', *American Economic Review*, **87** (3): 447–65.

Brainard, S. Lael, and David A. Riker (1997), 'Are US multinationals exporting US jobs?' Working Paper No. 5958, National Bureau of Economic Research.

Burgman, Todd A. (1996), 'An empirical examination of multinational corporate capital structure', *Journal of International Business Studies*, **27** (3): 553–70.

Carroll, Paul B. (1994), 'Foreign competition spurs Mexico to move into high-tech world', *The Wall Street Journal* (5 July), pp. A1, A9.

Caves, Richard E. (1991), 'Corporate mergers in international economic integration', in Alberto Goveniana and Colin Mayer (eds), *European Financial Integration*, Cambridge: Cambridge University Press.

Caves, Richard E. (1996), *Multinational Enterprise and Economic Analysis*, 2nd ed. Cambridge: Cambridge University Press.

Caves, Richard E., Michael E. Porter and A. Michael Spence (1980), *Competition in an Open Economy*. Cambridge, MA: Harvard University Press.

Curhan, Joan P., William H. Davidson and Rajan Suri (1977), *Tracing the Multinationals: A Sourcebook on US-based Enterprises*, Cambridge, MA: Ballinger.

Deneckere, Raymond, and Carl Davidson (1985), 'Incentives to form coalitions with Bertrand competition', *RAND Journal of Economics*, **16** (4): 473–86.

Feder, Barnaby J. (1997), 'For white goods, a world beckons', *The New York Times (New England Edition)* (25 November), pp. D1.

Frank, Robert, and Matthew Rose (1997), 'A massive investment in British cable TV sours for US firms', *The Wall Street Journal* (17 December), pp. A1, A 11.

Froot, Kenneth A., and Jeremy C. Stein (1991), 'Exchange rates and foreign direct investment: an imperfect capital markets approach', *Quarterly Journal of Economics*, **106** (4): 1191–217.

Glain, Steve (1997), 'A whole new wave of Japanese exports is headed westward', *The Wall Street Journal* (14 November), pp. A1, A6.

Grosse   Robert (1996), 'International technology transfer in services', *Journal of International Business Studies*, **27** (4): 781–800.

Grossman, Sanford J., and Oliver D. Hart (1986), 'The cost and benefits of ownership: a theory of vertical and lateral integration', *Journal of Political Economy*, **94** (4): 691–719.

Hines, James R., Jr. (1996), 'Tax policy and the activities of multinational corporations', Working Paper No. 5589, National Bureau of Economic Research.

Jarrett, J. Peter (1979), 'Offshore Assembly and Production and the Internalization of International Trade Within the Multinational Corporation: Their Causes and Effects on US Manufacturing Industry Wage and Profit Rates', Ph.D. dissertation, Harvard University, Cambridge, MA.

Javetski, Bill (1996), 'Old world, new investment', *Business Week* (7 October), pp. 50–51.

Johnson, Jean L., et al. (1996), 'Setting the stage for trust and strategic integration in Japanese–US cooperatives alliances', *Journal of International Business Studies* **27** (5): 981–1004.

Knickerbocker, Frederick T. (1973), *Oligopolistic Reaction and Multinational Enterprise*, Boston: Division of Research, Graduate School of Business Administration, Harvard University.

Lieberman, Marvin B. (1989), 'The learning curve, technology barriers to entry, and competitive survival in the chemical processing industries', *Strategic Management Journal*, **10** (5): 431–47.

Lippman, S. A. and R. P. Rumelt (1982), 'Uncertain imitability: an analysis of interfirm differences in efficiency under competition', *RAND Journal of Economics*, **13** (2): 418–38.

MacAvoy, Paul W. (1996), *The Failure of Antitrust Regulation to Establish Competition in Long-Distance Telephone Services*, Cambridge, MA: MIT Press.

Moffett, Matt (1997), 'Multinational miners really dig Brazil', *The Wall Street Journal* (22 January), p. A10.

Riker, David A., and S. Lael Brainard (1997), 'US multinationals and competition from low wage countries', Working Paper No. 5959, National Bureau of Economic Research.

Sullivan, Allanna (1995), Western oil giants return to countries that threw them out', *The Wall Street Journal* (9 March), pp. A1, A6.

Wesson, Thomas J. (1993), 'An Alternative Motivation for Foreign Direct Investment', Ph.D. dissertation, Harvard University, Cambridge, MA.

2. Models of the multinational enterprise

Peter J. Buckley and Mark C. Casson

INTRODUCTION

The appearance of a major work of survey and synthesis, which goes into successive editions (Caves 1996), is a clear sign that a subject has reached maturity. Maturity can sometimes indicate stagnation, however, and so the question naturally arises as to whether stagnation has set in to international business research. Caves' second edition is an encyclopaedic work, but it is very much like the first edition in its general structure. Only the details have been modified in the light of recent research.

This paper argues that any impression of stagnation is misleading: rather than quibble over a number of minor details of Caves' exposition, it makes a single substantive point. It identifies a new research agenda for modelling multinational enterprises (MNEs) which is not fully reflected in Caves' work. This agenda has emerged over the last ten years. It is difficult to recognize because its various components have not yet coalesced. It is nevertheless unfortunate that Caves has failed to emphasize its significance in his recent revision of his book.

MODELS OF MULTINATIONAL ENTERPRISES

The new agenda emphasizes dynamic issues. It highlights the uncertainty that is generated by volatility in the international business environment. To cope with volatility, corporate strategies have to be flexible, and flexibility can be achieved by several means. New dimensions of corporate strategy therefore have to be recognized. Efficient information processing is crucial to cope with the resultant increase in the complexity of decision making. This has important implications for the organizational structure of the MNE, and for the motivation of its managerial employees. The new agenda spells out these implications in a rigorous fashion.

The traditional agenda of Caves takes a more static view of international business. It focuses on:

- the nature of firm-specific competitive advantage;
- the choice of location of production; and
- the determination of the boundaries of the firm.

The classic application of the traditional agenda is on the foreign market entry decision. This agenda recognizes change, but interprets it as a sequence of independent one-off events, rather than as a continuous systemic process. Thus, entry into any given market is analysed independently of entry into others, and each entry strategy tends to be evaluated in terms of its immediate effects rather than in terms of the new opportunities to which it may ultimately lead. The market entry issue will remain important; it has, indeed, received new impetus from the recent wave of foreign direct investment (FDI) into Central and Eastern European markets (Hood and Young 1994). But the models of market entry developed in the 1970s remain too static to address the crucial issues of the 1990s because they fail to take proper account of volatility.

This does not mean that static analysis is obsolete. Static analysis is much simpler than dynamic analysis, and for this reason the traditional static approach is a natural preliminary to the new dynamic one. A dynamic model always contains a static model as a special case, and the properties of this special case provide important clues as to whether the dynamic model is logically sound.

The new dynamic agenda focuses on:

- uncertainty and market volatility;
- flexibility and the value of real options;
- cooperation through joint ventures and business networks;
- entrepreneurship, managerial competence and corporate culture; and
- organizational change, including the mandating of subsidiaries and the 'empowerment' of employees.

The stimulus for the new agenda was the end of the 'golden age' of Western economic growth, which came abruptly to an end with the oil price shock of 1973–4 (Marglin and Schor 1990). Lags in recognizing and interpreting the symptoms of this change caused its impact on academic literature to be delayed. The event marks a watershed in the post-war growth of Western MNEs. The intensification of international competition in the late 1970s had dramatic adverse effects on corporate profitability in the West. The focus of corporate strategy switched from entering new foreign markets to defending existing ones. International operations were restructured to drive down costs and improve supply responsiveness. Flexibility became the key to international competitiveness in the turbulent 1980s.

Flexibility is the *leitmotif* of the new agenda. It may be defined as the ability to reallocate resources quickly and smoothly in response to change. The significance of flexibility is greater, the greater is the amplitude and frequency of change in the environment. As far as MNEs are concerned, the impact of change is captured by the volatility induced in the profit stream. The volatility of profit that would occur if the firm made no response to change summarizes the impact on the firm of volatility in its environment.

Low volatility characterized the economic environment during most of the 'golden age'. The economic literature reviewed by Caves remains dominated by the experiences of this era. Selecting the most appropriate mode of entry into a foreign market remains the focus of attention. The international rationalization of production receives surprisingly little attention. While flexibility has been the focus of some of the most original research of the last decade, there is little sense of this in Caves' work.

Following a brief review of economic methodology, this chapter examines the factors underlying the end of the 'golden age'. With the aid of theory and the benefit of hindsight, it is shown how international business factors stimulated productivity growth in Asia and eventually undermined the competitiveness of the West. It is argued that the entry of new multinational producers, and a general commitment to continuous innovation, has increased volatility in global markets. It is shown that survival and prosperity in a volatile environment depend upon flexible response. This applies to nation-states, to industrial regions and to individual firms. Flexible firms need to locate in flexible regions of nation-states with flexible economic policies. In this way the forces of flexibility are continuously restructuring the world economy. To understand these forces properly, the traditional 'tool kit' of international business theory, as deployed in Caves, needs to be supplemented with new techniques. The chapter concludes by setting out the kind of economic modeling that is appropriate for building a new dynamic theory with flexibility at its core.

METHODOLOGY: MODELS *VERSUS* FRAMEWORKS

The economic theory of international business attempts to answer practical questions in a rigorous way. This means making assumptions explicit – in particular, specifying the strategies available to each firm and spelling out their details. Strict assumptions are used in order to simplify the analysis as much as possible. Simplicity provides logical transparency and ensures that the results can be easily understood. This is the methodology employed by Caves and adopted in this paper.

Economists invoke the principle of rational action to predict the circumstances under which firms will choose a given strategy. The assumption of rationality is not a piece of misguided psychology, but a response to the practical need for simplicity (Buckley and Casson 1993). When the firm's objective is profit maximization, the choice of strategy is driven by the firm's structure of revenues and costs. This is determined by the firm's environment. The identification of the key characteristics of this environment enables the firm's behavior to be modeled in a very parsimonious way. The predictions of the model emerge jointly from the profit maximization hypothesis, and the restrictions imposed by the modeler on the structure of revenues and costs. Predictive failure of the model is addressed by re-examining these restrictions and not by discarding the maximization principle that is at the core of the theory (Buckley 1988).

This method can be contrasted with an alternative approach in international business which leaves the assumptions implicit and derives propositions from a discursive literature review. This dispenses with formal analysis and relies on synthesis. Unfortunately, a synthesis is no better than the analytical components from which it is built. The more complex the synthesis, the more important it is that each component is sound. The logic of rational action provides just the check on analytical consistency which is required.

The variables entering into the theory do not have to be strictly of an economic nature. The criterion for inclusion is that they are analysed from a rational action point of view (Buckley and Chapman 1996). A good illustration here is the analysis of international joint ventures (IJVs), where economic factors, such as market size, are supplemented by technological, legal, cultural and psychological factors to generate a satisfactory model (Geringer and Hébert 1989).

The development of an economic model is often stimulated by the desire to explain certain 'stylized facts'. The traditional agenda, for example, sought to explain the predominance of US MNEs in high-technology manufacturing industries during the 'golden age'. The new agenda seeks to explain the rise of IJVs after the end of the 'golden age'. Economic models offer a simple, yet rigorous, explanation of facts which other approaches explain in more complicated and more heuristic terms. If economic models did no more than rationalize what everyone already knows, their value would be limited, however. Fortunately, the way in which economic models are constructed means that they do not merely explain the facts which they were designed to deal with, but also provide new predictions. It is their ability to draw attention to phenomena that have not been noticed and to integrate the explanation of these phenomena with explanations of already known phenomena that is a true measure of their success.

It is instructive to contrast the methods of economics with those of strategic management (Porter 1991) and development studies (Lall and Streeten 1977). Porter contrasts 'models' and 'frameworks'. He sees the traditional method of economics as model-building which 'abstracts the complexity of competition to isolate a few key variables whose interactions are examined in depth' (Porter 1991, p. 97). 'The applicability of any model's findings are almost inevitably restricted to a small subgroup of firms or industries whose characteristics fit the model's assumptions' (p. 98). Porter identifies the progress of strategic management with its ability to construct frameworks. 'Instead of models, however, the approach was to build frameworks. A framework, such as the competitive forces approach to analyzing industry structure, encompasses many variables and seeks to capture much of the complexity of actual competition' (p. 98). Frameworks are analogous to expert systems which are tailored to particular industries or companies.

> My own frameworks embody the notion of optimization, but no equilibrium in the normal sense of the word. Instead, there is a continually evolving environment in which a perpetual competitive interaction between rivals takes place. In addition, all the interactions among the many variables in the frameworks cannot be rigorously drawn.

In contrast to Porter's support for frameworks rather than models, Krugman attributes the failure of development studies precisely to its rejection of rigorous models. Despite having identified important themes which are key to successful modeling of development issues – 'emphasis on strategic complementarity in investment decisions and on the problem of coordination failure' – development economists have failed to explain them to academic colleagues and policymakers in a coherent way (Krugman 1995, p. 28).

According to Krugman, 'mainstream economic theory rests on two observations: obvious opportunities for gain are rarely left unexplored and things add up' (1995, p. 74). This formulation is similar to, but subtly different from, the two key principles put forward by Buckley and Casson (1993) – optimization and equilibrium. There is a difference between optimization and being self-interested. Buckley's and Casson's formulation allows for objectives which are beyond self-interest or 'opportunities for gain'. These may include following ethical injunctions and pursuing altruistic sentiments. Similarly, the truism 'things add up' is valid only *ex post*, where it is true by definition. Things add up *ex ante* only in situations of equilibrium – and equilibrium may not always hold. Krugman's justification for this method is that

> what we do when we construct an economic model is to try to use these two principles to cut through the complexities of a situation. And the remarkable thing is how often that succeeds. . . . the basic principles of economics tell us that there is an unexpected order in the outcome, which is quite independent of the details. (1995, p. 75)

A significant strength of Porter's framework is that it postulates continuous incremental change. Its weakness is that it does not analyse the strategic response to change in a rigorous way. The new agenda in economic modeling, being more dynamic than the old, addresses the point about continuous change head-on. Because of its economic logic, rigor is guaranteed. It is therefore not only a natural successor to the traditional agenda, but also a necessary refinement of Porter's work.

It could be argued, of course, that the insights of the new agenda should be simply grafted onto the old agenda, rather than developed in a distinct, but complementary, way. But forcing dynamic considerations into an essentially static context results in loss of simplicity (Buckley 1983). Complex typologies must be developed to distinguish all of the special cases that arise – a process that can clearly be traced in the evolution of Dunning's eclectic theory in response to the growth of IJVs and 'resource-seeking' investment (Dunning 1977, 1993). Once the complexity of the model approaches the complexity of the phenomena that it attempts to analyse, it ceases to function as a model, and becomes simply a description of the situation instead.

THE END OF THE 'GOLDEN AGE'

During the 'golden age' of Western economic growth, trade was liberalized through GATT and through customs unions, such as the EEC and EFTA. US mass production technology was transferred through the internal markets of MNEs. Key European industries were transformed. Cheaper motor vehicles created a more mobile society. Female labor force participation increased. Cheaper consumer durables combined with higher incomes raised aspirations to historically unprecedented levels. Mass consumer demand fuelled demand for branded products, such as convenience foods. The glamor of US affluence made US marketing and advertising skills easy to transfer abroad.

The 'golden age' terminated suddenly with the oil price shock of 1973. Imports of manufactured goods from Japan and the newly industrializing countries (NICs) of South-East Asia quickly began to replace domestic production in Western markets – including motor vehicles, which had been one of the 'engines' of Western growth up to that point. The West woke up to the fact that for some time Asian firms had been systematically absorbing Western technologies and adapting them to local conditions. The full consequences of international technology transfer and trade liberalization were finally being felt.

Traditional international business theory can easily explain how technology transfer to Asia was effected. However, the mechanisms were somewhat more varied than those emphasized by Caves. Technology transfer was effected on government initiative, as well as on the initiative of Western multinationals (Fransman 1995). Licensing agreements and joint ventures were widely used. The domestic partner was often a 'national champion'. Once it had mastered the technology, the champion diffused it to other firms. Diffusion to other large firms was effected through social networking, factory visits and collaborative research. Diffusion to smaller firms was effected through subcontracting arrangements in which substantial training could be involved. Small firms could also play a direct role in pirating technologies that were easy to copy. 'Reverse engineering' was important too. Product designs were easier to imitate than technologies because patent protection was weaker, and 'me too' designs proliferated as a result.

The price advantage of Asian products stemmed from a number of factors. The weakness of trade unions (often as a direct consequence of political measures) maintained wages at competitive market-clearing levels (Mirza 1986). The limited scope of social security gave a strong incentive to work. Government expenditure was concentrated on infrastructure investment, such as roads, ports, airports and telecommunications, which reduced the costs of intermediate inputs, such as transport. Investment in large container terminals cut the cost of shipping to Western markets, for example. Improved domestic communications facilitated 'just in time' production, which economized on inventory costs. Mass production was initiated from the outset to exploit economies of scale to the full. Temporary protection of the domestic market helped to build up demand quickly, and exporting commenced at the outset. A strong desire to save ensured that domestic demand did not crowd out export demand in the long run.

The contrast with the West is clear. During the 'golden age', Western public expenditure was focused on fighting the 'Cold War' and on building a 'Great Society' or 'Welfare State'. Military expenditures and transfer payments to the poor crowded out productivity-enhancing investment. Rising taxes, it is alleged, discouraged work and risk-taking. The concept of a 'corporate economy' (Marris 1979) institutionalized collective bargaining and legitimated union strike-threat power. Wage inflation and 'featherbedding' increased costs – particularly the costs of intermediate inputs such as transport, which were supplied by highly unionized industries.

A similar set of factors explains why technology transfer succeeded in Asia, but failed in Africa. (The Latin American experience lies somewhere between these two extremes.) The deficiencies of European governments were mirrored in their former colonies in Africa. Industrial strategy was based on state-of-the-art technology applied to mega-projects rather than on the diffusion and incremental improvement of established techniques (Ergas 1987). Competition for status between neighboring nations encouraged lavish public expenditure, financed by foreign borrowing, which could not be repaid when projects failed. Foreign borrowing was also used to finance wars, as well as conspicuous consumption by the political elite. Corruption raised transaction costs. Inward-looking protectionist policies distorted domestic prices and inhibited agricultural development. Industry, though protected, failed to reap economies of scale because of the low growth of the domestic market. When Western MNEs retrenched in the 1970s, they therefore retreated from Africa in order to concentrate on defending their markets at home.

The lessons for international business theory are fairly clear. It is not sufficient to focus exclusively on the choice of mode when analysing technology transfer. As Dunning (1997) has emphasized, full account must be taken of location factors, such as the structure of the host economy, the policies of the host government and the nature of local business culture, in explaining the comparative success and failure of FDI.

FLEXIBILITY

Competition from Asia was a visible symbol of a less apparent, but more fundamental change in the business environment, namely a persistent increase in the amount of volatility with which firms have to contend. Volatility has become much greater since the end of the 'golden age'. There are several reasons for this.

The international diffusion of modern production technology has increased the number of industrial powers, and hence increased the number of countries in which political and social disturbances can impact significantly on global supplies of manufactured products. The liberalization of trade and capital markets means that the 'ripple' effects of shocks travel farther and wider than before (Casson 1995, Chapter 4). Ripples are transmitted more quickly too: news travels almost instantaneously, thanks to modern telecommunications. Thus speculative bubbles in stock markets spread quickly around the world. Following the breakdown of the Bretton Woods system, exchange rate fluctuations have created a new dimension of financial volatility too.

As a result, any given national market is now affected by a much wider range of disturbances than ever before. Every national subsidiary of an MNE experiences a multiplicity of shocks from around the world. It is no longer the case that a national subsidiary has to respond to shocks originating in its national market alone. The shocks come from new sources of import competition and new competitive threats in export markets too. While most shocks reveal themselves to firms as competitive threats, new opportunities for cooperation may sometimes be presented as well. The awareness of this sustained increase in volatility has led to a search for more flexible forms of organization.

Increased volatility is not the only reason for greater interest in flexibility. Contemporary culture is very much opposed to building organizations around a single source of monopoly power. The nation-state, for example, is under threat from advocates of regional government. The traditional role of the state, to supply defense, can in principle be effected through multilateral defense treaties in which politically independent regions club together for this specific purpose. The demise of the Soviet bloc, and the subsequent political realignment between its member states, may be seen as an example of this kind of cultural change at work. This distrust of monopoly power may be linked to an increase in other forms of distrust, as suggested below.

The aversion to internal monopoly is apparent amongst MNEs as well. This movement began in the early 1980s when the powerful central research laboratories of high-technology MNEs were either closed down, shifted to the divisions, or forced to operate as suppliers to 'internal customers' in competition with outside bodies, such as universities (Casson, Pearce and Singh 1991). Headquarters' bureaucracies came under attack shortly afterwards, as 'delayering' got under way. The favored form of firm has become a federal structure of operating divisions drawing on a common source of internal expertise, but where each division belonging to the federation is free to outsource expertise if it so desires. As with any trend, there has been a tendency for certain advocates to take it to extremes. Just as the 'golden age' was rife with suggestions that oligopolies of hierarchical MNEs would come to dominate world markets, so the 1990s have spawned visions of the 'network firm' and the 'virtual firm'. A factor common to these visions is a 'fuzzy' boundary of the firm, where the firm fades into the market through joint ventures with declining proportional equity stakes. These arguments for fuzzy boundaries are, unfortunately, often based on equally fuzzy reasoning. Fuzzy boundaries can be configured in many different ways. The new research agenda outlined in this chapter places arguments for fuzzy boundaries on a rigorous basis, and predicts the specific form that fuzziness will take in each particular case.

It is evident that the search for flexibility has a number of important implications for the firm's:

- external environment;
- boundaries; and
- internal organization.

These issues will now be considered in turn.

EXTERNAL FLEXIBILITY: THE NATIONAL COMPETITIVENESS ISSUE

Initial Western reaction to de-industrialization and the plight of the 'rust-belt' heavy industries was concern over competitiveness. There continues to be considerable debate, however, over what competitiveness really means (Buckley, Pass and Prescott 1988). Some economists argue, using the Ricardian concept of comparative advantage, that loss of manufacturing competitiveness is a natural consequence of economic maturity (Krugman 1996). The strength of Western economies no longer lies in manufacturing, but in services. Thanks to jet travel, television broadcasting and other technological developments, an increasing number of services, such as tourism and media entertainment, are readily exportable. Consumer demand for services is income-elastic, moreover, so the long-term prospects for the service sector are good. Furthermore, manufacturing is increasingly capital-intensive, whereas many service industries are inherently labor intensive because they are more difficult to automate. To regain competitiveness, therefore, labor must be shifted out of manufacturing and into services. To eliminate frictional and structural unemployment, this process must be expedited by measures to promote labor market flexibility.

According to this view, Asian countries, being at an earlier stage of industrial development, have exploited labor market flexibility to switch labor out of agriculture and into industry. First-generation workers who have just left the land are often very hard-working, and so, despite their inexperience, this gives a productivity boost to nascent industry. If flexibility can be sustained, workers can be switched from one industry to another – from textiles to semiconductors, for example – as competition increases from other countries following up the ladder of development. It is in this way that Japan has stayed ahead of competition from the Republic of Korea and Taiwan (China). Such has been the speed of Asian development that several economies, including Singapore, Hong Kong and Japan, have already completed the manufacturing phase, and have become major service economies in their own right.

An alternative view of competitiveness emphasizes the firm-specific nature of competitive advantage. There are wide differences in productivity between firms in the same industry, it is claimed. Theories of comparative advantage, framed in terms of a representative firm, ignore this (Thurow 1992). Some firms have major competitive advantages, and others have none at all. The competitive advantages of leading Western firms have been eroded by internal failings, it is alleged. It is not that Western workers have lost comparative advantage in manufacturing, but that Western firms have lost the ability to manage.

The distinction between firm-specific competitive advantage and nation-specific comparative advantages is essentially a question of the period of analysis. Firm-specific competitive advantage is essentially a short-run concept. Firm-specific advantages cannot be taken as given in the long run because they continually obsolesce and have to be regularly renewed (Buckley and Casson 1976). A nation with a comparative advantage in entrepreneurship will be able to renew firm-specific advantages through sustained innovation, but a nation without such comparative advantage will not. An explanation of loss of competitiveness that emphasizes loss of firm-specific advantages is equivalent, from a long-run perspective, to an argument that local comparative advantage in entrepreneurship has been lost. Countries that systematically generate firms with specific advantages are those that have a nation-specific comparative advantage in entrepreneurship.

From this perspective, it is plausible to argue that the West has lost comparative advantage in both manufacturing and entrepreneurship. The first is an unavoidable consequence of economic maturity, but the second is an avoidable consequence of institutional failure and inappropriate business culture. The conflict between the nation-specific view and the firm-specific view is actually a disagreement about whether nation-specific comparative advantage has declined more in manufacturing than in entrepreneurship or less. Those who adhere to the firm-specific view, which probably includes the majority of international business scholars, implicitly believe that entrepreneurial decline is the major problem, and that cultural and institutional changes are required to put it right. The increased volatility of the world economy, and the consequent increase in demand for flexibility, has put Western entrepreneurial failures under the spotlight.

RESTORING COMPETITIVENESS

Western governments have attempted to restore labor market flexibility through legislation. In the United Kingdom, for example, the legal privileges of trade unions (such as secondary picketing) have been reduced, and minimum wage laws relaxed. Qualifications for the receipt of unemployment benefit have been tightened up. Firms have responded in a predictable way. Greater use is made of temporary labor to accommodate peaks and troughs in demand. Full-time workers are expected to work more flexible hours. Work has been subcontracted out to avoid statutory national insurance premiums. The rise in labor-only subcontracting has brought back the 'putting out' system, which was characteristic of the eighteenth century's 'commercial revolution'.

Privatization has been used to promote greater flexibility in the supply of intermediate products to industry. The United Kingdom has privatized 'strategic' heavy industries (steel), public transport (railways and airlines), and utilities (telecommunications, electricity, gas and water). Privatization allows peripheral activities to be sold off and complementary activities to be combined, thereby facilitating significant changes in the scope of the firm. Newly privatized enterprises can acquire other newly privatized enterprises, or enter into joint venture agreements with them. For the first time in the post-war period, large scale involvement by MNEs is now possible in most of the utility industries.

Steps have also been taken to improve entrepreneurship. Business education has been expanded, top rates of income tax have been reduced to encourage risk-taking, and successful business people have been encouraged to play a more active role in public life in order to raise the status of entrepreneurs. Politicians have increasingly promoted the values of competitive individualism and downgraded the values of organic solidarity which characterized the 'Welfare State' (Casson 1990).

Links between universities and business have been strengthened in order to improve the coordination of product development and basic research. This may not directly benefit the nation as much as might have been expected, however. Products researched in one country can be produced in another country, and even exported back to the country where they were researched to compete with local products there. The decentralization of R&D within large MNEs (Pearce and Singh 1992) creates internal markets where this kind of transfer can be easily effected. Thus a US MNE could use a wholly owned research laboratory in the United Kingdom to tap into government-funded research in order to develop a product to be made in the United States for export to the United Kingdom. The profits from the product innovation will also accrue to the United States – an effect that has been stressed, in a somewhat different context, by Reich (1990).

Government measures to improve competitiveness seem to have been reasonably successful over the past decade. However, it should not be forgotten that the reason why some MNEs continue to produce in Europe for the European market has more to do with the common external tariff of the European Community, and the threat that it might increase, than with the location advantages of Europe *per se*. Thus, tariff considerations and substantial job-creation subsidies have played a major role in the attraction of Asian motor vehicle manufacturers to the United Kingdom. Similarly, one of the advantages to foreign firms of producing in the United States is that it is easier to adapt product designs to the market using a local production base.

The fact that Asian firms can successfully produce in the West behind a tariff wall suggests that they possess firm-specific advantages of the type generated by sustained entrepreneurship. One of these advantages appears to lie in *internal* labor market flexibility. There is a tendency in the West to see labor market flexibility as something external to the firm. It is reflected simply in low wage rates. There is less emphasis on firm-specific training, and workers are less versatile than in Asian firms. This is apparent on the shop-floor. On-the-job training is weaker, and attention to quality is lower as a result. Machine down-time is greater because workers cannot fix minor repairs or help each other out when retooling a production line.

In general, Asian firms appear to have taken flexibility more seriously as a production issue. Not only have they invested more in labor versatility, but they have also invested more in equipment for flexible manufacturing systems too. This is reflected not only in their Asian plants, but also in their operations in the West.

FLEXIBLE BOUNDARIES OF THE FIRM: NETWORKS AND JOINT VENTURES

The typical US MNE of the 'golden age' was a vertically, as well as horizontally, integrated firm. In consequence, each division of the firm was locked into linkages with other divisions of the same firm. As Asian competition intensified, there was growing recognition of the costs of integration of this kind.

Commitment to a particular source of supply or demand is relatively low-cost in a high-growth scenario, since it is unlikely that any investment will need to be reversed. It is much more costly in a low-growth scenario, where production may need to be switched to a cheaper source of supply, or sales diverted away from a depressed market. The desire for flexibility therefore discourages vertical integration – whether it is backward integration into production, or forward integration into distribution. It is better to subcontract production and to franchise sales instead. The subcontracting of production is similar in principle to the 'putting out' arrangement described above, but differs in the sense that the subcontractor is now a firm rather than just a single worker.

Dis-integration was also encouraged by a low-trust atmosphere that developed in many firms. Fear of internal monopoly became rife, as explained above. Production managers faced with falling demand wished that they did not have to sell all their output through a single sales manager. Sales managers resented the fact that they had to obtain all their supplies from the same small set of plants. Each manager doubted the competence of the others, and ascribed loss of corporate competitiveness to selfishness and inefficiency elsewhere in the firm. Divisions aspired to be spun off so that they could deal with other business units instead. On the other hand, managers were wary of the risks that would be involved if they severed their links with other divisions altogether.

A natural way to restore confidence is to allow each division to deal with external business units, as well as internal ones. In terms of internalization theory, internal markets become 'open' rather than 'closed' (Casson 1990, p. 37). This provides divisional managers with an opportunity to bypass weak or incompetent sections of the company. It also provides a competitive discipline on internal transfer prices, preventing their manipulation for internal political ends, and bringing them more into line with external prices. There are other advantages too. Opening up internal markets severs the link between the capacities operated at adjacent stages of production. The resulting opportunity to supply other firms facilitates the exploitation of scale economies because it permits the capacity of any individual plant to exceed internal demand. Conversely, it encourages the firm to buy in supplies from other firms that have installed capacity in excess of their own needs.

The alignment of internal prices with external prices increases the objectivity of profit measurement at the divisional level. This allows divisional managers to be rewarded by profit-related pay based on divisional profit rather than firm-wide profit. Management may even buy out part of the company. Alternatively, the firm may restructure by buying in a part of an independent firm. The net effect is the same in both cases. The firm becomes the hub of a network of interlocking joint ventures (Buckley and Casson 1988; 1996). Each joint venture partner is responsible for the day-to-day management of the venture. The headquarters of the firm coordinates the links between the ventures. Internal trade is diverted away from the weaker ventures towards the stronger ones, thereby providing price and profit signals to which the weaker partners need to respond. Unlike a pure external market situation, the partners are able to draw upon expertise at headquarters, which can in turn tap into expertise in other parts of the group.

A network does not have to be built around a single firm, of course. A network may consist of a group of independent firms instead. Sometimes these firms are neighbors, as in the regional industrial clusters described by Best (1990), Porter (1990) and Rugman, D'Cruz and Verbeke (1995). Industrial districts, such as 'Toyota city', have been hailed as an Asian innovation in flexible management, although the practice has been common in Europe for centuries (Marshall 1919). As tariffs and transport costs have fallen, networks have become more international. This is demonstrated by the dramatic growth in intermediate product trade under long-term contracts. For example, an international trading company may operate a network of independent suppliers in different countries, substituting different sources of supply in response to both short-term exchange rate movements and long-term shifts in comparative advantage.

Flexibility is also needed in R&D. A firm cannot afford to become over-committed to the refinement of any one technology in case innovation elsewhere should render the entire technology obsolete. As technology has diffused in the post-war period, the range of countries with the competence to innovate has significantly increased. The pace of innovation has consequently risen, and the threat of rapid obsolescence is higher as a result. The natural response for firms is to diversify their research portfolios. But the costs of maintaining a range of R&D projects are prohibitive, given the enormous fixed costs involved. The costs of basic R&D have escalated because of the increased range of specialist skills involved, while the costs of applied R&D have risen because of the need to develop global products which meet increasingly stringent consumer protection laws. Joint ventures are an appropriate solution once again. By establishing a network of joint ventures covering alternative technological trajectories, the firm can spread its costs whilst retaining a measure of proprietary control over new technologies.

The advantage of joint ventures is further reinforced by technological convergence: for example, the integration of computers, telecommunications and photography. This favors the creation of networks of joint ventures based on complementary technologies rather than on the substitute technologies described above (Cantwell 1995).

Joint ventures are important because they afford a number of real options (Trigeorgis 1996) which can be taken up or dropped depending upon how the project turns out. The early phase of a joint venture provides important information which could not be obtained through investigation before the venture began. It affords an opportunity later on to buy more fully into a successful venture – an opportunity which is not available to those who have not taken any stake. It therefore provides greater flexibility than either outright ownership or an alternative involving no equity stake.

FLEXIBILITY AND INTERNAL ORGANIZATION

In a very volatile environment the level of uncertainty is likely to be high. Uncertainty can be reduced, however, by collecting information. Flexibility was defined above in terms of the ability to respond to change. The costs of response tend to be smaller when the period of adjustment is long. One way of 'buying time' to adjust is to forecast change. While no one can foresee the future perfectly, information on the present and the recent past may well improve forecasts by diagnosing underlying long-term trends. Collecting, storing and analysing information therefore enhances flexibility because, by improving forecasts, it reduces the costs of change.

Another way of buying time is to recognize change as early as possible. In this respect, continuous monitoring of the business environment is better than intermittent monitoring because the potential lag before a change is recognized is eliminated. Continuous monitoring is more expensive than intermittent monitoring though, because more management time is tied up.

Investments in better forecasts and speedier recognition highlight the trade-off between information cost and adjustment cost. This trade-off is particularly crucial when volatility is high. High volatility implies that more information should be collected to improve flexibility, which in turn implies that more managers need to be employed. This is the reverse of the usual recommendation to downsize management in order to reduce overhead costs.

To improve flexibility whilst downsizing management, the trade-off between information cost and adjustment cost must be improved. There are two main ways of doing this. The first is to reduce the cost of information processing through new information technology (IT). The second is to reduce adjustment costs by building flexibility into plant and equipment, through both its design and its location. A combination of IT investment and flexible plant can reconcile greater flexibility with lower management overheads in the manner to which many MNEs aspire.

The information required for strategic decision making is likely to be distributed throughout the organization. It is no longer reasonable to assume that all the key information can be handled by a single chief executive, or even by the entire headquarters management team. It is difficult to know in advance where the really crucial information is likely to be found. Every manager therefore needs to have the competence to process information effectively. Managers need to be able to recognize the significance of strategic information that they acquire by chance, and to have access to senior executives in order to pass it on. In other words, ordinary managers need to become internal entrepreneurs.

Few entrepreneurs have sufficient information to make a good decision without consulting other people, however. In a traditional hierarchical firm, the right to consult is the prerogative of top management. If ordinary managers are to have the power to initiate consultation, and act upon the results, then channels of communication within the firm need to be increased. Horizontal communication, as well as vertical communication, must be easy, so that lower-level managers can readily consult with their peers.

A natural response is to 'flatten' the organization and encourage managers to 'network' with each other. This improves the trade-off between local responsiveness and strategic cohesion (Bartlett and Ghoshal 1987; Hedlund 1993). Unfortunately, there has been some confusion over whether flatter organizations remain hierarchies at all. However, as Casson (1994) shows, the efficient managerial processing of information normally requires a hierarchical structure of some kind. The key point is that the more diverse the sources of volatility, the greater the advantages of widespread consultation. The less predictable the principal source of volatility on any given occasion, the greater the incentive to allow consultation to be initiated anywhere in the organization. In practice this means that an increased demand for flexibility is best accommodated by flattening the organization, whilst maintaining basic elements of hierarchy.

THE COSTS OF FLEXIBILITY: ENGINEERING TRUST

If flexibility were costless, then all organizations could build in unlimited flexibility at the outset. In practice, the greater the flexibility, the higher the transaction costs. For example, the flexibility to switch between different sources of supply and demand (described above) means that relations with customers and suppliers become more transitory than before. Cheating becomes more likely, because the prospect of further transactions between the same two parties is more remote. Direct appeals to the other party's loyalty lose their credibility too.

The same effect occurs when internal entrepreneurship is promoted. Internal entrepreneurs are given more discretion to act upon information that they have collected for themselves, and this increases their opportunity to cheat.

Giving managers a direct stake in the business activities they help to build is one solution. The firm incubates new business units in which particular managers, or groups of managers, have equity stakes. An alternative approach is to appeal to the integrity of managers instead. They are treated well, and in return are expected to be open and honest about what they know.

It is one of the ironies of the 1970s that at a time when personal integrity needed to be high in order to support more flexible organization, it had been allowed to fall very low. The decline of traditional religion, the intellectual cynicism created by two world wars, and the rise of mass consumerism have all been blamed for this state of affairs. Communitarians argue correctly that moral values like integrity are most efficiently engineered at the societal level, through family, church and school. But when these institutions fail, they must be engineered to support specific economic relations instead (Fukuyama 1996). Firms must engineer these values amongst their employees at their own expense (Kotter 1996). Greater flexibility therefore implies greater costs in promoting a corporate culture that reinforces moral values.

INTERACTION OF FIRM FLEXIBILITY AND LOCATION FLEXIBILITY

The desire for flexibility may encourage the firm to produce the same product in several locations so that it can switch production between them as circumstances change. Multiple internal sourcing may therefore be pursued even where some sacrifice of economies of scale is involved. DeMeza and Van der Ploeg (1987), Capel (1992) and Kogut and Kulatilaka (1994) have all emphasized that firms can switch production between alternative locations in response to real exchange rate shocks. The basic idea is that MNEs can combine their superior information on foreign cost conditions with their ability, as owners of plants, to plan rather than negotiate output levels, to switch production more quickly than can independent firms.

This strategy requires, however, that the firm should commit in advance to the locations where it believes it will wish to produce. If it is difficult to foresee where the best locations may lie, then flexibility may be enhanced by subcontracting arrangements instead. Speed of response may be slower, but the range of potential locations is greater. Where short-run volatility predominates, multinational integration may well enhance the value of the firm (Allen and Pantzalis 1996), but long-run volatility may favor the disintegration of the firm instead.

If a firm is seeking flexibility at one stage of production, then it will experience a derived demand for flexibility at adjacent stages of production. This flexibility is conferred by ease of transport to and from all the locations employed at the adjacent stage. Some locations are inherently more flexible in this respect than others because they are at nodal points on transport networks. They therefore have low transport costs to a wide range of different destinations. For example, if production is dispersed, then warehousing of finished product should be at an appropriate hub. Greater demand for flexibility concentrates demand for warehousing at such hubs – for example, Singapore (for South-East Asia) and Lille (for North-West Europe).

An MNE that is seeking flexibility in its sources of supply will wish to choose a location where government policy is *laissez-faire*, so that there are no import restrictions. It may be seeking flexibility in the range of products it produces too. This encourages it to seek out locations with a versatile labor force. Flexibility is also conferred by supplier networks that operate with a high degree of trust. Local production needs to be embedded in an impartial legal system and in strong social networks to ensure that trust is high. An 'invisible infrastructure' of mediating institutions, or equivalently, a large endowment of 'social capital', is therefore a feature of the locations that MNEs committed to flexibility are likely to seek out. Flexibility is not just an element of corporate strategy, but a component of location advantage too. Such location advantage depends crucially on the nature of local institutions and local culture.

FLEXIBILITY AND FIRM-SPECIFIC COMPETITIVE ADVANTAGE

Flexibility also has implications for firm-specific competitive advantage. Skill in recruiting imaginative employees becomes a competitive advantage when internal entrepreneurship is required. Charismatic leadership by the chief executive may promote loyalty and integrity amongst key staff. A tradition of informal and consultative management will facilitate the sharing of information amongst employees. One way of expressing this is in terms of the 'capabilities' or 'competencies' of managers, or the human resources controlled by the firm (Richardson 1960; Loasby 1991). In a volatile environment where flexibility is crucial, the key resources of the firm are those that promote internal entrepreneurship. The firm consists not of a single autocratic entrepreneur, but a team of entrepreneurs (Wu 1988) coordinated by a leader who promotes high-trust communication between them.

It is worth noting that the need for flexibility does not necessarily support the idea of a 'learning organization'. To be more exact, flexibility has important implications for what people in a learning organization actually need to learn. According to Nelson and Winter (1982), learning supports the refinement of existing routines. This is misleading. It suggests that the firm operates in a basically stable environment and merely learns how to do even better what it already does very well. In a volatile environment, however, much of what has been 'learned' from past experience quickly obsolesces. The truly durable knowledge that needs to be learned in a volatile environment consists of techniques for handling volatility. These techniques include forgetting transitory information about past conditions which are unlikely to recur. But while 'unlearning' or 'forgetting' is important, it is often difficult to do. The difficulty of 'unlearning' helps to explain why so many 'downsizing' and 'delayering' exercises have identified middle-aged middle managers as targets for redundancy or early retirement. Such people are believed to find it too hard to forget. The 'knowledge' they acquired as junior managers was very relevant during the 'golden age', but has since become obsolete. Some managers have proved sufficiently flexible to be 'retrained', but others have not. Those who were too inflexible to benefit from retraining have been required to leave because their 'knowledge' had become a liability instead of an asset in the more volatile situation of today.

NEW TECHNIQUES OF ANALYSIS

The key to modelling volatility is to postulate a steady stream of shocks impinging at random on the international business environment. There are exogenous shocks, which are autonomous, and endogenous shocks, which are induced as a consequence of the exogenous ones. The need for simplicity means that many shocks have to be treated as exogenous, even though they are in fact endogenous. The formation of customs unions, the reduction of international shipping costs through containerization, and the breakdown of the Soviet system may all be treated as exogenous random shocks impinging on the global economy. These shocks influence the relative rise and decline of individual nations. This emphasis on the modeling of shocks means that probability theory has a significant role to play in the new research agenda (Dixit and Pindyck 1994). The probabilistic foundations of stochastic processes assume particular significance. There is a close link between the collection of information and the refinement of probability measurement, and another link between optimal forecasting and the concept of a 'martingale' (Dempster and Pliska 1997). These ideas are most extensively developed in the field of financial options, but they can be applied to 'real options' too (Mello, Parsons and Triandis 1995).

Managers of MNEs perceive the growth and decline of individual national economies as the result of random shocks. Increased volatility in the international economy means that there is greater uncertainty than before about the future growth of any particular economy. For example, there is currently considerable uncertainty about the growth prospects of Thailand and other South-East Asian economies. Theories of rational choice under uncertainty (Hirshleifer and Riley 1992) are therefore central in analysing corporate behavior in volatile environments.

Uncertainty can be reduced by gathering information, as noted earlier. Information improves the quality of decision making, but the returns to information diminish at the margin as with any other resource. Efficient search is normally conducted sequentially and stops when the expected value of the next item of information is just equal to its expected cost of collection. The cheapest information is usually obtained second-hand through communication with other people. It can also be obtained as a by-product of other activity. The organization of a firm may be understood as a rational response to the challenge of collecting the right sort of information in the most appropriate way. This is the major insight of the economic theory of teams (Marschak and Radner 1972). The organization effects a division of labor in information processing, and assigns particular managers to particular roles according to where their personal comparative advantage lies. Some are good observers, others are good communicators, whilst the most entrepreneurial types make the best decision makers. They are all slotted into appropriate niches in the organization.

The timing of decisions is absolutely crucial in a volatile environment. The right decision may be of little use if it is taken at the wrong time (Rivoli and Salorio 1996). Committing resources too early to a growing market, for example, means that costs are incurred before adequate revenues can be generated, while deferring until too late means that the market may be permanently lost to competitors (Buckley and Casson 1981). An important reason for deferring investment is that new information may become available later which would lead to a better decision. This is the central point in the theory of options

(Trigeorgis 1996). Investment is often irreversible in the sense that the resources committed are illiquid and cannot be fully recovered later through divestment. Deferring a decision on an irreversible investment reduces the risk that the investment may go ahead on a mistaken assessment of the situation (Campa 1994). The more volatile the environment, the more likely it is to change, and hence the greater the advantage of waiting until all imminent changes have occurred.

It would be wrong to infer, however, that investment is always discouraged by volatility. Investment often leads to the discovery of new information. Suppose, for example, that there are two foreign markets, one of which is known to be similar to the other. Investing in the smaller market involves a smaller commitment than investing in the larger one. A by-product of investment in the smaller market is information about the larger market. This information reduces the risk of investing in the larger one. It therefore pays to invest first in the smaller market, even though the prospects are worse than in the larger one, because the experience gained can be used to improve the later, more important, decision. This idea is central to the Scandinavian model of the internationalization of the firm (Johanson and Vahlne 1977).

In general, the growth of MNEs may be understood as a sequence of investments undertaken in a volatile environment, where each investment feeds back information which can be used to improve the quality of subsequent decisions. In this sense, the expansion of the firm is a path-dependent process (Kogut and Zander 1993). Most expositions of path-dependency assume, however, that the choice of path is essentially myopic, in the sense that decision makers make no attempt to anticipate the kind of information that will get fed back at each stage. This need not be the case, however. An entrepreneurial firm may be able to anticipate how the information that it will obtain in the future depends on the decision that it currently has to make. In this case its managers can exploit the logical structure of this learning process to expand in an optimal manner. The sequence of industries into which the firm diversifies and the sequence of the countries in which it invests represent a rational dynamic strategy of growth.

Similarly, strategic divestment in response to competition may also be seen as a consequence of a rational dynamic strategy. In a volatile environment a rational firm will anticipate the possibility of competition by investing in a manner that takes subsequent divestment options into account. It will make only those investments that it is either unlikely to want to divest, or which will be easy to divest because the sunk costs involved are relatively low. The typical investment will involve assets that have several alternative uses and are easy to sell off to other firms. Since assets of this kind are easy to obtain in the first place, through acquisition, the theory suggests that acquisitions and divestment of highly 'liquid' or 'non-specific' assets are likely to play a major role in flexible investment strategies. This is one reason why acquisitions and divestments became more common at the same time that IJVs became more common too. Both are implications of the strategic pursuit of flexibility in a volatile environment.

The pursuit of sophisticated strategies of this kind requires a great deal of information to be shared within the organization. It is crucial that this information is communicated in an honest manner. Integrity is often assured by repeated interaction, as explained by the theory of non-cooperative games (Kreps 1990). Alternatively, integrity can be assured by cultural engineering (Casson 1991). Cultural engineering within a firm can be effected in two main ways. One is by selecting people who have already been subjected to appropriate cultural influences. This explains why many firms recruit selectively from certain communities, educational institutions and ethnic groups. Cultural homogeneity not only improves internal communication, but standardizes employees on a uniform set of moral values. The alternative is for the firm to recruit people purely on the basis of competence and to standardize the morals through active dissemination of a corporate culture. The first strategy allows the firm to 'free-ride' on cultural engineering by other institutions and reduces the demands on the chief executive's leadership role. The second strategy allows the firm to recruit more widely and to tailor the moral system to the specific requirements. MNEs will tend to favor the latter strategy because they need to recruit a range of different nationalities and to combine the expertise of members of very different professional groups.

AN EXAMPLE

What does a scholar pursuing the new research agenda actually *do*? How does the formal specification of a dynamic model differ from that of a static one, and how exactly does a dynamic model differ from a 'framework' of the Porter type? A full answer can only be obtained from the literature cited above, but a simple example may clarify the position.

Consider the problem of modeling market entry from a dynamic, rather than a static, point of view (Chi and McGuire 1996). The most important new point to take into account is that the foreign market can decline as well as grow. Divestment or withdrawal must be considered as serious strategies. Clearly, these strategies do not apply until the market has been entered, but once it has been entered they may need to be used. Static models assume that the market will be constant, while very simple dynamic models, such as Buckley and Casson (1981), only suppose that the market will grow. In a volatile environment a market may grow to begin with, attracting investment, but then go into decline, requiring divestment instead. Such explicit recognition of adverse scenarios is a characteristic of the new research agenda.

Switching between strategies is costly, and the costs depend on both the strategy the firm is switching from, and the strategy the firm is switching to. In some cases, switching costs decompose neatly into a cost of exit from the old strategy and a cost of setting up the new strategy. Detailed modeling of such costs is a key element of the new research agenda.

To preserve flexibility, it is important for the firm to choose at the outset strategies whose exit costs are low. This tends to favor exporting over host-country production, and licensing over internalization. In other words, it reveals FDI as a high-risk strategy.

Switching decisions can be mistaken, however, because the information upon which they are based is poor. Expected switching costs are reduced by avoiding unnecessary switches. Different strategies afford different opportunities for capturing information from the host environment and feeding it back to inform subsequent switching decisions. The new agenda involves explicit modeling of how the strategy chosen at one stage affects the information available at subsequent stages.

Foreign direct investment offers better opportunities for information capture than either licensing or exporting, since ownership of assets confers ownership of information too. This means, for example, that if volatility caused the market to unexpectedly grow, the foreign investor would recognize this quickly. Since it is often cheaper to expand existing capacity than to build from scratch, the foreign investor also faces lower costs of capacity expansion than does an exporter who decides to switch to foreign production at this stage. While exporting continues to confer more flexibility in response to market decline, therefore, FDI investment confers more flexibility in respect of market growth.

Is it possible to find a strategy with a better combination of characteristics than either exporting, licensing or FDI? An IJV may provide the answer (Kogut 1991). Investing in a 50:50 partnership with a host-country producer lays off some of the risks associated with wholly owned FDI. At the same time, information capture remains reasonably good. There is an option to expand capacity if there is unexpected market growth, and a further option to increase commitment by buying the partner out. There is also an easy option to withdraw by selling out to the partner. The partner provides a ready market for divested assets that an ordinary direct investor lacks. There is a downside, of course – an obvious problem is that the partners may themselves become a source of volatility. This is why trust is such an important element in an IJV. In this way the emphasis on risk management within the new research agenda leads to the emergence of new 'compromise strategies', which would be dominated by more conventional strategies were it not for the 'option value' they possess within a volatile environment.

IJV options can only be exercised once, of course, unless the investor switches back to an IJV arrangement at a later date, when they can be exercised all over again. This explains IJV instability as a rational response to the role that IJVs fulfil. An IJV in which the options are never exercised is probably inferior to a wholly owned investment, while an IJV in which the options are exercised at the first available opportunity does not last for very long. When IJVs are chosen because of their option value, it is normally inefficient both to switch out right away, or never to switch at all. The optimal timing of a switch is one at which uncertainty about future market growth is dispelled for a reasonable period of time. This implies that the duration of IJVs is, on average, fairly short and relatively variable. The new research agenda provides a simple means of deriving such hypotheses about the period of time for which a given strategy will be pursued.

The globalization of markets has been a major factor in the growth of volatility, as explained above. A feature of many global markets is the use of regional production and distribution hubs, where several neighboring countries are serviced from the same location. The regional hub, like the IJV, can be understood as a strategy that offers superior flexibility. Just as an IJV offers a compromise ownership strategy, a regional hub offers a compromise location strategy. Because the hub is nearer to each market than is the home location, it reduces transport costs, and offers better information capture too. Yet, because it is close to several markets, it avoids exclusive commitment to any one. If one market declines, production can be switched to other markets instead. Provided the shocks affecting the national markets are independent (or less than perfectly correlated, at any rate) the hub provides gains from diversification. These are real gains that only the firm can achieve, as opposed to the financial gains from unrelated product diversification, which have proved disappointing in the past because they are best exploited through the diversification of individual share portfolios instead.

The two strategies of IJV and hub can be combined. Since one is an ownership strategy and the other a location strategy they can, if desired, be combined directly in an IJV production hub. Closer examination of the issues suggests that this is not normally the best approach, however. The model suggests that a combination of a wholly owned production hub supplying IJV distribution facilities in each national market is a better solution. A hub facility is too critical to global strategy to allow a partner to become involved because the damage they could do is far too great. Even with a wholly owned hub facility, the combination still affords considerable flexibility to divest or withdraw from any single market. The advantage of the combination is that when divesting, the distribution facility can be sold to the partner, while the production capacity can be diverted to markets elsewhere. These options for divestment are combined with useful options for expansion too.

This example illustrates the crucial role that the concepts of flexibility and volatility play in analysing foreign market entry in the modern global economy. Without these concepts it is impossible to fully understand the rationale for IJVs and production hubs. It is also impossible to understand why these strategies have emerged at this particular historical juncture and not before.

While some of the insights of this model can certainly be expressed in terms of a framework, a framework is too crude to analyse the interplay of the different factors in a rigorous way. The concepts of adjustment costs and exit costs can already be found in the strategy literature, for example, but even the simple example presented above is sufficient to show that the interplay of present entry and future exit cannot be properly understood without the aid of a fully specified model. This does not mean that the strategy literature is flawed. The new dynamic agenda is perfectly compatible with much of the existing strategy literature, but it goes beyond it by developing and refining the insights in a way that the strategy framework is unable to do.

CONCLUSION

There are many other subjects in international business to which the new agenda can be applied, and many other new techniques which can be used. Enough has been said to indicate the promise that the new agenda holds for future research. The key to success in international business theory is to avoid becoming overwhelmed by the complexity of the issues. New issues, centered on flexibility, call for theory to refocus on the new insights described above. The use of economic methodology means that these new issues can be addressed in a simple and elegant way. The traditional agenda has plenty of life in it yet. But it is not the only agenda. As Arpan (1997) has noted, international business research must change if it is to retain its relevance and its basic simplicity. The new agenda sets out the way in which this can be done.

REFERENCES

Allen, Linda, and Christos Pantzalis (1996), 'Valuation of the operating flexibility of multinational corporations', *Journal of International Business Studies*, **27** (4): 633–53.

Arpan, Jeffrey S. (1997), 'Palabras del Presidente', *AIB Newsletter*, **3** (3): 2.

Bartlett, Christopher A., and Sumantra Ghoshal (1987), 'Managing across borders: new strategic requirements', *Sloan Management Review* (Summer), 6–17.

Best, Michael H. (1990), *The New Competition: Institutions of Industrial Restructuring*, Oxford: Polity Press.

Buckley, Peter J. (1981), 'The optimal timing of a foreign direct investment', *Economic Journal*, **91**: 75–87.

Buckley, Peter J. (1983), 'New theories of international business: some unresolved issues', in Mark C. Casson (ed.), *The Growth of International Business*, London: Allen & Unwin, 34–50.

Buckley, Peter J. (1988), 'The limits of explanation: testing the internalization theory of the multinational enterprise', *Journal of International Business Studies*, **19** (2): 1–16.

Buckley, Peter J. (1988), 'A theory of co-operation in international business', in Farok J. Contractor and Peter Lorange (eds), *Co-operative Strategies in International Business*, Lexington, MA: Lexington Books, 31–53.

Buckley, Peter J. (1993), 'Economics as an imperialist social science', *Human Relations*, **46** (9): 1035–52.

Buckley, Peter J. (1996), 'An economic model of international joint venture strategy', *Journal of International Business Studies*, **27** (5): 849–76.

Buckley, Peter J., and Martin J. Carter (1996), 'The economics of business process design: Motivation, information and coordination within the firm', *International Journal of the Economics of Business*, **3** (1): 5–25.

Buckley, Peter J., and Mark C. Casson (1976), *The Future of the Multinational Enterprise*, London: Macmillan.

Buckley, Peter J., and Malcolm Chapman (1996), 'Economics and social anthropology – reconciling differences', *Human Relations*, **49** (9): 1123–50.

Buckley, Peter J., Christopher L. Pass and Kate Prescott (1988), 'Measures of international competitiveness: a critical survey', *Journal of Marketing Management*, **4** (2): 175–200.

Campa, Jose Manuel (1994), 'Multinational investment under uncertainty in the chemical processing industries', *Journal of International Business Studies*, **25** (3): 557–78.

Cantwell, John (1995), 'Multinational enterprises and innovatory activities: towards a new evolutionary approach', in J. Molero (ed.), *Technological Innovation, Multinational Corporations and the New International Competitiveness*, Chur: Harwood Academic Publishers, 21–57.

Capel, Jeanette (1992), 'How to service a foreign market under uncertainty: a real option approach', *European Journal of Political Economy*, **8**: 455–75.

Casson, Mark C. (1990), *Enterprise and Competitiveness*, Oxford: Clarendon Press.

Casson, Mark C. (1991), *Economics of Business Culture*, Oxford: Clarendon Press.

Casson, Mark C. (1994), 'Why are firms hierarchical?', *International Journal of the Economics of Business*, **1** (1): 3–40.

Casson, Mark C. (1995), *Organization of International Business*, Aldershot: Edward Elgar.

Casson, Mark, Robert D. Pearce and Satwinder Singh (1991), 'A review of recent trends', in Mark C. Casson (ed.) *Global Research Strategy and International Competitiveness*. Oxford: Blackwell, 250–71.

Caves, Richard E. (1996), *Multinational Enterprise and Economic Analysis*, second edition. Cambridge: Cambridge University Press.

Chi, Tailan, and Donald J. McGuire (1996), 'Collaborative ventures and value of learning: integrating the transaction cost and strategic option perspectives on the choice of market entry modes', *Journal of International Business Studies*, **27** (2): 285–307.

DeMeza, David, and Frederick van der Ploeg (1987), 'Production flexibility as a motive for multinationality', *Journal of Industrial Economics*, **35** (3): 343–51.

Dempster, Michael A.H., and Stanley R. Pliska (eds). (1997), *Mathematics of Derivative Securities*. Cambridge: Cambridge University Press.

Dixit, Avrinash, and Robert S. Pindyck (1994), *Investments Under Uncertainty*. Princeton, NJ: Princeton University Press.

Dunning, John H. (1977), 'Trade, location of economic activity and the multinational enterprise: the search for an eclectic approach', in B. Ohlin, P. O. Hessleborn and P. M. Wijkman (eds), *The International Location of Economic Activity*, London: Macmillan.

Dunning, John H. (1993), *Multinational Enterprises in the Global Economy*, Wokingham, Berks: Addison-Wesley.

Dunning, John H. (1997), *Alliance Capitalism and Global Business*, London: Routledge.

Ergas, Henry (1987), 'Does technology policy matter?', in B.R. Guile and H. Brooks (eds), *Technology and Global Industry*, Washington, DC: National Academy Press, 191–245.

Fransman, Martin (1995) *Japan's Computer and Communications Industry*, Oxford: Oxford University Press.

Fukuyama, Francis (1996), *Trust*, Harmondsworth: Penguin.

Geringer, J. Michael, and Louis Hébert (1989), 'Control and performance of international joint ventures', *Journal of International Business Studies*, **20** (2): 235–54.

Hedlund, Gunnar (1993), 'Assumptions of hierarchy and heterarchy: an application to the multinational corporation', in S. Ghoshal and E. Westney (eds), *Organization Theory and the Multinational Corporation*, London: Macmillan, 211–36.

Hirshleifer, Jack, and John G. Riley (1992), *The Analytics of Uncertainty and Information*, Cambridge: Cambridge University Press.

Hood, Neil, and Stephen Young (1994), 'The internationalization of business and the challenge of East European business', in P.J. Buckley and P.N. Ghauri (eds), *The Economics of Change in East and Central Europe*, London: Academic Press, 320–42.

Johanson, Jan, and Jan-Erik Vahlne (1977), 'The internationalization process of the firm – a model of knowledge development and increasing foreign market commitments', *Journal of International Business Studies*, **8** (1): 23–32.

Kogut, Bruce (1991), 'Joint ventures and the option to expand and acquire', *Management Science*, **37** (1): 19–33.

Kogut, Bruce, and Nalin Kulatilaka (1994), 'Operating flexibility, global manufacturing, and the option value of a multinational network', *Management Science*, **40** (1): 123–39.

Kogut, Bruce, and Udo Zander (1993), 'Knowledge of the firm and the evolutionary theory of the multinational corporation', *Journal of International Business Studies*, **24** (4): 625–45.

Kotter, John (1996), *Leading Change*, Cambridge, MA: Harvard Business School Press.

Kreps, David M. (1990), *Game Theory and Economic Modelling*, Oxford: Oxford University Press.

Krugman, Paul (1995), *Development, Geography and Economic Theory*, Cambridge, MA: MIT Press.

Krugman, Paul (1996), 'The myth of Asia's miracle', in Paul Krugman, *Pop Internationalism*, Cambridge, MA: MIT Press.

Lall, Sanjaya, and Paul Streeten (1977), *Foreign Investment, Transnationals and Developing Countries*, London: Macmillan

Loasby, Brian J. (1991), *Equilibrium and Evolution*, Manchester: Manchester University Press.

Marglin, Stephen A., and Juliet B. Schor (1990), *The Golden Age of Capitalism: Reinterpreting the Post-war Experience*, Oxford: Clarendon Press.

Marris, Robin L. (1979), *The Theory and Future of the Corporate Economy and Society*, Amsterdam: North-Holland.

Marschak, Jacob, and Roy Radner (1972), *Economic Theory of Teams*. New Haven, CT: Yale University Press.

Marshall, Alfred (1919), *Industry and Trade*, London: Macmillan.

Mello, Antonio S., John E. Parsons and Alexander J. Trianis (1995), 'An integrated model of multinational flexibility and hedging policies', *Journal of International Economics*, **39** (August): 27–51.

Mirza, Hafiz (1986), *Multinationals and the Growth of the Singapore Economy*, London: Croom-Helm.

Nelson, Richard, and Sidney G. Winter (1982), *An Evolutionary Theory of Economic Change*, Cambridge, MA: Harvard University Press.

Pearce, Robert D., and Satwinder Singh (1992), *Globalising Research and Development*, London: Macmillan.

Porter, Michael E. (1990), *The Competitive Advantage of Nations*, London: Macmillan.

Porter, Michael E. (1991), 'Towards a dynamic theory of strategy', *Strategic Management Journal*, **12** (Special Issue): 95–117.

Reich, Robert B. (1990), 'Who is us?', *Harvard Business Review*, **68** (1): 53–65.

Richardson, George. B. (1960), *Information and Investment*, Oxford: Oxford University Press.

Rivoli, Pietra, and Eugene Salorio (1996), 'Foreign direct investment under uncertainty', *Journal of International Business Studies*, **27** (2): 335–54.

Rugman, Alan M., Joseph R. D'Cruz and Alain Verbeke (1995), 'Internalisation and de-internalisation: will business networks replace multinationals?', in G. Boyd (ed.), *Competitive and Cooperative Macromanagement: The Challenge of Structural Interdependence*, Aldershot: Edward Elgar, 107–28.

Thurow, Lester C. (1992), *Head to Head: The Coming Economic Battle Among Japan, Europe and America*, New York: Morrow.

Trigeorgis, Lenos (1996), *Real Options*, Cambridge, MA: MIT Press.

Wu, Shih-yen (1988), *Production, Entrepreneurship and Profits*, Oxford: Blackwell.

3. Location and the multinational enterprise: a neglected factor?

John H. Dunning

INTRODUCTION

In 1986, the economist Wilfred J. Ethier, in seeking to explain the existence of multinational enterprises (MNEs), concluded that 'internalization appears to be emerging as the Caesar of the OLI triumvirate' (Ethier 1986, p. 803). I did not agree with this statement then; nor do I do so now. The OLI triad of variables (ownership, location and internalization, discussed below) determining foreign direct investment (FDI) and MNE activity may be likened to a three-legged stool; each leg is supportive of the other, and the stool is only functional if the three legs are evenly balanced. Insofar as the third leg completes this balancing it may be regarded as the most important, but there is no reason to suppose one leg performs this task better than another.

In the case of the eclectic paradigm, I would accept that the I component is the critical leg, if, given the O advantages of firms and the L advantages of countries, one is trying to explain why firms internalize the cross-border market for these advantages, rather than sell them or their rights to independent firms. But I would aver it is no less correct to argue that, given its O specific advantages, the critical choice of a multi-activity firm is whether it should internalize its intermediate product markets within its home country or in a foreign country; and that the outcome of this choice is primarily determined by the costs and benefits of adding value to these products in the two locations. I say 'primarily' because the geography of international business activity is not independent of its entry mode; nor, indeed, of the competitive advantages of the investing firms. This interdependence is particularly apparent when one examines the dynamics of knowledge-intensive MNE activity.

In the 1960s, scholars such as Raymond Vernon and his colleagues at Harvard (see especially Vernon 1966, 1974; and Wells 1972), working on the determinants of FDI gave pride of place to locational variables, and particularly those determining the siting of US market seeking FDI by US firms in advanced industrial countries (see also the work of some European scholars, such as Bandera and White 1968; and Scaperlanda and Mauer 1969). In the mid-1970s – apart from research on the internationalization process of firms (see, for example, Johanson and Vahlne 1977) – attention switched from the act of FDI per se to the institution making the investment. Here the main focus of interest was why firms should choose to set up or acquire foreign value-adding activities rather than export the intangible assets, or the right to use these assets, underpinning such activities, directly to foreign firms (see especially the writings of Peter Buckley and Mark Casson, J.C. McManus, Jean-François Hennart, Alan Rugman, and Birgitta Swedenborg, all of which are cited in Caves 1982 and 1996).

While I would be the first to acknowledge the value of this approach in advancing our understanding of MNE qua MNEs, I believe that the contribution of the internalization school has done more to explain the existence and growth of the multi-activity firm than that of the MNE per se. This is because, with relatively few exceptions,[1] the transaction and coordination costs identified with arm's-length intermediate product markets have not, in general, been specific to cross-border markets, or, indeed, to traversing space.

The emphasis on the firm-specific determinants of international economic activity, while still driving much academic research by scholars in business schools, is now being complemented by a renewed interest in the spatial aspects of FDI; and of how these affect both the competitive advantages of firms and their modes of entry into, and expansion in, foreign markets. We believe there are two main reasons for this. The first is that the changing extent, character and geography of MNE activity over the past two decades – itself a reflection of a series of path-breaking technological, economic and political events – is demanding an explanation by international business scholars. The second is that new research agendas, particularly those of economic geographers, trade theorists and international political economists, are not only paying more attention to the spatial aspects of value-added activity, but are also seeking to incorporate these aspects into the mainstream thinking about the growth and competitiveness of firms, the relationship between trade and FDI, and the economic structure and dynamic comparative advantage of regions and countries.

This paper seeks to review some of these happenings, most of which come into prominence between the two editions of the publication of Richard Caves, *Multinational Enterprise and Economic Analysis* (1982). To his credit, Richard Caves acknowledges many of these in his second (1996) edition. But, since much of his analysis relates to the work of scholars in the 1980s,[2] his chapter on the international allocation of economic activity (Chapter 2) does not fully embrace the events and academic research of the last decade or so. It is these which will be the main concern of this contribution. The paper will proceed in the following way. First it will briefly describe the changing global economic scenario in which MNE activity has been conducted since the mid-1970s, and also the various strands of thought which have sought to explain this. Secondly, it will examine how the micro-locational determinants of international production have changed; and how the location portfolio of MNEs may itself help promote their dynamic competitive advantages. Thirdly, it will consider how, from a more macroeconomic standpoint, the emergence of the MNE as a leading vehicle of cross-border transactions has affected our thinking about the determinants of trade and other non-MNE related transactions.

THE CHANGING WORLD SCENARIO FOR INTERNATIONAL BUSINESS ACTIVITY

The last two decades have witnessed a gradual movement towards a world economy characterized by three features. The first is the emergence of intellectual capital as the key wealth-creating asset in most industrial economies. In the 1990s, the market value of industrial corporations was variously calculated (for example, by Blair 1995, Handy 1989 and Edvinsson 1997) at between two-and-a-half and five times the value of their tangible assets, compared with one-and-a-half times in 1982. The annual capital expenditure on information technology by US corporations now exceeds that on production technology (Stewart 1997). The knowledge component of the output of manufacturing goods is estimated to have risen from 20 per cent in the 1950s to 70 per cent in 1995 (Stewart 1997); while those workers whose main task is to create new knowledge or disseminate information (that is, professional and technical workers, managers, sales and clerical workers – the so-called 'white collar' workers) increased their share of the American labor force from 42 per cent in 1960 to 58 per cent in 1990, and this share is expected to rise to more than 60 per cent by 2000.

A further indicator of the rising significance of non-material assets as creators or facilitators of wealth is the growth of services, and particularly those which are themselves knowledge or information intensive. In 1995, on average, services accounted for 63 per cent of the world's gross national product (GNP), compared with 53 per cent in 1980 and 45 per cent in 1965 (World Bank 1997). Insofar as knowledge intensive and knowledge supporting production has its unique spatial needs, and tends to require resources and capabilities which MNEs are particularly well suited to provide, it is not unreasonable to hypothesize that both these features will impinge on the geographical distribution of FDI and related activities.

Secondly, and even more transparent, is the increasing globalization of economic activity, made possible, *inter alia*, by advances in transport and communications technologies and the reduction in trade and investment barriers throughout the world (UNCTAD, various issues and World Bank, various issues). Over the last two decades, the growth of world trade has consistently outstripped that of world output, while in the mid-1990s the sales of the foreign affiliates of MNEs exceeded the value of world trade by 27 per cent (UNCTAD 1997). Moreover, between one-third and one-half of trade in non-agricultural products and between one-half and three-fifths of capital and knowledge flows are currently internalized within MNEs.[3]

At the same time, the ease with which MNEs can transfer intangible assets across national boundaries is being constrained by the fact that the location of the creation and use of these assets is becoming increasingly influenced by the presence of immobile clusters of complementary value-added activities. This is particularly the case with those activities in which the transaction costs of traversing space are high, or where the transactional benefits of spatial proximity are significant.[4] Thus while globalization suggests that the location and ownership of production is becoming geographically more dispersed, other economic forces are making for a more pronounced geographical concentration of such activity within both particular regions and countries.[5] In the words of Ann Markusen (1994) these events are presenting scholars and policy makers with a paradox of 'sticky places within slippery space'.

The third feature of the contemporary global economy is the emergence of what may be called 'alliance' capitalism (sometimes called relational, collective, stakeholder and collaborative capitalism – see Dunning 1995). While retaining many of the characteristics of hierarchical capitalism, the distinctive feature of alliance capitalism is the growing extent to which, in order to achieve their respective objectives, the main stakeholders in the wealth-seeking process are needing to collaborate more actively and purposefully with each other. Such collaboration includes the conclusion of closer, continuing, and more clearly delineated *intra*-firm relationships, for example, between functional departments and between management and labor; the growth of a variety of inter-firm cooperative agreements,[6] for example, between suppliers and customers and among competitors; and the recognition by governments and firms alike of the need to work as partners if the economic goals of society (for which the former are ultimately responsible) are to be best achieved.

Once again, the growing propensity of firms to engage in cross-border alliances has implications not just for the modality at which knowledge and other intangible assets are transferred across national boundaries, but for the location of value-added activities – especially high value asset-augmenting activities.

Underpinning and reinforcing each of the events just described are two other factors which also have had a profound effect on both the macro and micro-geography of MNEs. The first is the advent, in the 1980s, of a new generation of technological advances which, according to Alan Greenspan (in a speech given to New York bankers in April 1997) are only now, in the later

1990s, fully bearing fruit.[7] The second factor is the renaissance of the market economy, and the consequential changes in the macroeconomic policies and macro-organizational (micro-management) strategies of many national governments. This is most vividly demonstrated by the happenings in China and Central and Eastern Europe, but almost as far-reaching is the reappraisal of the role of the State and markets in economic development now being played out in India, and in several African and Latin American economies (World Bank 1997). Both factors have had a major impact on the economic and political risk assessment of FDI by MNEs.

THE CHANGING GEOGRAPHY OF MNE ACTIVITY

The developments just described have all impacted on the geography of FDI and MNE activity (as described in more detail in Dunning 1998). In the period 1991–6, 64 per cent of global FDI inflows were received by the developed countries, 33 per cent by developing countries and 3 per cent by Central and Eastern European countries. The corresponding percentages for the period 1975–80 were 77 per cent, 23 per cent and less than 0.1 per cent (UNCTAD 1997). No less noticeable have been the changes in the distribution of inbound FDI within these regions. While the shares of Western Europe and the United States, cf. all FDI in developed countries, have remained broadly the same,[8] those within developing countries have markedly changed. For example, in 1975–80 and 1991–6, South, East and South-East Asia (including China and India) increased their share of inbound investment to developing countries from 26 to 62 per cent, while that of Latin American and Caribbean fell from 53 to 34 per cent.

It is perhaps worth observing that although the share of inbound FDI to the gross fixed capital formation of the countries more than doubled between the second half of the 1970s and the first half of the 1990s (UNCTC 1988; UNCTAD, 1996a), the changing geography of FDI parallels reasonably well that of all investment, independently of its ownership. Between 1975 and 1980, and 1990 and 1995, for example, the share of world inbound FDI accounted for by developed countries fell from 78 to 70 per cent, while that of world gross fixed capital formation (including that part financed by foreign firms) fell from 84 to 73 per cent. The corresponding figures for all developing economies were 21 per cent and 30 per cent, and 15 per cent and 26 per cent; and for Asia 7 per cent and 19 per cent, and 7 per cent and 19 per cent. Although there are differences in the geography of FDI which can be specifically attributed to the political or economic conditions in the host country[9] – and it is most certainly the case that the geography of *outward* FDI is quite strongly country-specific[10] – the data suggest that many of the factors which explain the location of FDI may not be unique to its country of origin. We shall not elaborate on this point here; but it is, perhaps, worthy of more scholarly attention.

THE MICROECONOMICS OF THE LOCATION OF MNE ACTIVITY

With the caveat of the last paragraph, we now consider how scholarly thinking about the location of MNEs has evolved over the last two decades. Incidentally, we suspect that the fact that this subject has not been given much attention by international business scholars is partly because scholars have believed that the principles underlying the locational decisions of firms within national boundaries can be easily extended to explain their cross-border locational preferences;[11] and partly because economists were either generally satisfied with existing explanations, or just not interested in the subject. Certainly until the early 1990s, there was little in common between the methodologies of international trade economists and locational economists, excepting the work of Bertil Ohlin (1933) and his successors. This was primarily because the former were concerned with country-specific general equilibrium models or models under very restrictive conditions, whereas the latter were mainly interested in firm- or industry-specific partial equilibrium models with fewer constraints (Krugman 1993).

Earlier in this paper, we identified three major developments in the global economy which have impinged upon both the capabilities and the strategies of MNEs, or potential MNEs, and the locational attractions offered by particular countries to mobile investors. In particular, we emphasized first the growing significance of firm-specific knowledge-intensive assets in the wealth-creating process, and the kind of customized assets, for example, skilled labor and public infrastructure, which needed to be jointly used with these assets if they were to be effectively harnessed and deployed;[12] secondly, the reduction of many natural and artificial impediments to trade, but the rise of other spatially related transaction costs; and thirdly, the growing need and ease with which firms are able to coordinate their cross-border activities and form alliances with foreign firms.

Some of these factors have led firms to own and concentrate particular types of value-added activities within a limited number of locations; others have led them to disperse such activities across several locations. Some have favored a realignment of MNE activity towards advanced developed economies; others have favored a location in emerging market economies. All are symptomatic of a changing international division of labor which, because of their increasing role in the world economy, and their need to capture the economies of interdependent activities, MNEs have helped to fashion.

The literature on the locational preferences of foreign direct investors has long acknowledged that these will not depend on the types of activities in which they are engaged, but on the motives for the investment, and also on whether it is a new or a sequential one. Different kinds of investment incentives are needed to attract inbound MNE activity of a natural-resource-seeking, in contrast to that of a market- or efficiency-seeking, kind. Export-oriented FDI is likely to be less influenced by the size of local markets than is import-substituting FDI. Investment in R&D facilities requires a different kind of human and physical infrastructure than investment in assembling or marketing activities, and so on.

But perhaps the most significant change concerning the motives for FDI over the last two decades has been the growth of strategic asset-seeking FDI, which is geared less to exploiting an existing O-specific advantage of an investing firm, and more to protecting, or augmenting, that advantage by the acquisition of new assets, or by a partnering arrangement with a foreign firm. In some ways, such FDI is similar in intent to that of a natural resource-seeking investment in earlier times but its locational needs are likely to be quite different. Partly this is because it is frequently motivated by strategic considerations (especially in oligopolistic industries), and partly because the availability of the assets sought – that is, technical knowledge, learning experiences, management expertise and organizational competence – tend to be concentrated in advanced industrial countries or the larger developing countries. The growth of strategic-asset-seeking FDI in recent years is best demonstrated by the increasing role of mergers and acquisitions as modalities of FDI. According to UNCTAD (1997), between 55 and 60 per cent of FDI flows over the period 1985–95 were accounted for by mergers and acquisitions. Most of these were concentrated within North America, Europe and Japan, and in knowledge- and information-intensive sectors.

The locational preferences of firms making more traditional forms of FDI have also changed – as, indeed, have the attitudes of recipient countries to these investments. We might mention two of these. First, as foreign affiliates have become more embedded in host countries, this has led to a deepening of their value chains, and a propensity for them to engage in higher-order (for example, innovatory) activities. This fact has been documented in numerous studies both on the geographical distribution of R&D and on that of patents registered by MNEs (as recent examples of these, see Dalton and Serapio (1995), Almeida (1996), Dunning (1996), Kuemmerle (1996), Shan and Song (1997), and various studies of John Cantwell and colleagues, for example, Cantwell and Harding (1997), and Bob Pearce and Marina Papanastassiou, for example, Papanastassiou and Pearce (1997), of the University of Reading). *Inter alia*, the Cantwell and Harding study showed that between 1991 and 1995, 11 per cent of the US registered patents of the world's largest firms were attributable to research locations outside the home country of the parent company. Only in the case of Japan was there no rise in the proportion of patents registered by foreign affiliates since the early 1970s (for a more general discussion of asset-augmenting FDI, see an interesting dissertation by Wesson 1993). So far, however, this tendency of engaging in higher-order activities has been largely confined to developed countries. In 1994, for example, some 91 per cent of the foreign R&D undertaken by US MNEs was located in developed countries, compared with 79 per cent of their total foreign sales (Mataloni and Fahim-Nadar 1996).

Secondly, the location-specific assets which MNEs perceive they need to add value to the competitive advantages they are exporting (via FDI) are changing as their downstream activities are becoming more knowledge-intensive. Various surveys have demonstrated that, except for some labor or resource investments in developing countries, MNEs are increasingly seeking locations which offer the best economic and institutional facilities for their core competencies to be efficiently utilized. For example, in a field study by Fabrice Hatem (1997), apart from market access and market growth, economic and institutional facilities were not only valued much higher than traditional criteria of access to raw materials, cost of labor and fear of protectionism, but in all cases they were also thought to increase in significance over the five year period 1996–2001. There is a suggestion, too, that the presence of other foreign investors in a particular country is becoming more significant, both as an 'investment-stalk' or signaling effect to other foreign firms less familiar with that country (Srinivasan and Mody 1997; Liu 1998), and as an agglomerative magnet by which firms benefit from being part of a geographical network or cluster of related activities and specialized support services. In a study of the location patterns of US MNEs between 1982 and 1988, Wheeler and Mody (1992) identified three agglomeration benefits, namely infrastructure quality, degree of industrialization and existing level of FDI. They found that these exhibited a high degree of statistical significance and had large positive impacts on investment (p. 66). In a study of Swedish outbound FDI over the period 1975–90, Braunerhjelm and Svensson (1995) confirmed a positive and significant statistical relationship between that variable and the presence of pecuniary externalities associated with demand and supply linkages, including the diffusion of knowledge, for example, spillover effects resulting from a clustering of related firms.

A more formal examination of the changing nature and significance of external economies, and of how these are leading to a more concentrated pattern of certain kinds of FDI – particularly that of strategic asset-seeking investment in knowledge-intensive sectors – is set out in Krugman (1991). Indeed, it was his study which helped spark off the fruitful dialogue now taking place between industrial geographers, economists and business analysts. Though this dialogue is principally concerned with the role of subnational spatial units as repositories for mobile investment, it is also offering a number of valuable insights on the changing role of transportation and communication costs as location-specific variables, both by making easier the coordination and supply of end products from existing agglomerations, and by facilitating the decentralization of intermediate production;[13] and also on the changing competitive advantages of regions – particularly for minimizing spatial transaction costs and maximizing dynamic external economies, such as those to do with complex technologies, uncertain or unpredictable markets, interactive learning, face-to-face discussions and the exchange of uncodifiable knowledge (Florida 1995; Storper and Scott 1995).

Certainly the incentives offered by regional authorities within the European Union (EU) and of states within the United States, have been shown to be a decisive factor in influencing the intra-regional location of inbound MNE activity (for some interesting case studies, see, for example, Donahue 1996 and Ohmae 1995). There is also a good deal of casual evidence to suggest that the promotional campaigns and incentives – in the form of the speedy processing of planning applications, land grants, subsidized rents, tax holidays and generous investment allowances – offered by local or regional development agencies to attract FDI tend to resemble those of 'location tournaments'[14] (Taylor 1993; UNCTAD 1996b). Again, the experiences of the United States and the EU – or, indeed, of some of the larger countries in the EU, for example, the United Kingdom – are salutary in this respect.

In Table 3.1, we attempt to summarize some of the differences between the kinds of variables posited to influence the locational decisions of MNEs in the 1970s – most of which are well documented in Chapter 2 of *Multinational Enterprises and Economic Analysis* – and those which scholars are hypothesizing and field research is showing to influence these same decisions of MNEs in the 1990s. In doing so, we have separately classified the four main kinds of FDI identified earlier. However, we readily accept that other contextual variables, for example, size of firm, degree of multinationality, country or region of origin and destination and industry, insofar as these have different situational needs, may be no less significant.

The contents of the table are largely self-explanatory, but we would highlight just four main findings. The first is the changing role of *spatial transaction costs*, which reflect both the liberalization of cross-border markets and the changing characteristics of economic activity. While, in general, the reduction of these costs has led to more aggressive market-seeking FDI, and has promoted a welfare-enhancing international division of labor, it has also favored the spatial bunching of firms engaged in related activities, so that each may benefit from the presence of the other, and of having access to localized support facilities, shared service centers, distribution networks, customized

Table 3.1 Some variables influencing the location of value-added activities by MNEs in the 1970s and 1990s

Type of FDI		In the 1970s	In the 1990s
A. Resource Seeking	1.	Availability, price and quality of natural resources	1. As in the 1970s, but local opportunities for upgrading quality of resources and the processing and transportation of their output is a more important locational incentive.
	2.	Infrastructure to enable resources to be exploited, and products arising from them to be exported,	2. Availability of local partners to jointly promote knowledge and/or capital-intensive resource exploitation.
	3.	Government restrictions on FDI and/or on capital and dividend remissions.	
	4.	Investment incentives, e.g. tax holidays.	
B. Market Seeking	1.	Mainly domestic, and occasionally (e.g. in Europe) adjacent regional markets.	1. Mostly large and growing domestic markets, and adjacent regional markets (e.g. NAFTA, EU).
	2.	Real wage costs; material costs.	2. Availability and price of skilled and professional labor.
	3.	Transport costs; tariff and non-tariff trade barriers.	3. Presence and competitiveness of related firms, e.g. leading industrial suppliers.
	4.	As A3 above, but also (where relevant) privileged access to import licenses.	4. Quality of national and local infrastructure and institutions.
			5. Less spatially related market distortions, but increased role of agglomerative spatial economies and local service support facilities.
			6. Macroeconomic and macro-organizational policies are pursued by host governments.
			7. Increased need for presence close to users in knowledge-intensive sectors.

54

8. Growing importance of actions by regional or local development agencies.

C. Efficiency Seeking

1. Mainly production cost related (e.g. labor, materials, machinery).
2. Freedom to engage in trade in intermediate and final products.
3. Presence of agglomerative economies, e.g. export processing zones
4. Investment incentives, e.g. tax breaks, accelerated depreciation, grants, subsidized land.

1. As in the 1970s, but more emphasis placed on B2, 3, 4, 5 and 7 above, especially for knowledge-intensive and integrated MNE activities, e.g. R&D and some office functions.
2. Increased role of governments in removing obstacles to restructuring economic activity, and encouraging the upgrading of human resources by appropriate educational and training programs.
3. Availability of specialized spatial clusters, e.g. science and industrial parks, service support systems; and of specialized factor inputs. Opportunities for dynamic improvement of investing firms; an entrepreneurial environment and one which encourages competitiveness enhancing cooperation within and between firms.

D. Strategic Asset Seeking

1. Availability of knowledge-related assets and markets necessary to protect or enhance specific advantages of investing firms – and at the right price.
2. Institutional and other variables influencing ease or difficulty with which assets can be acquired by foreign firms.

1. As in the 1970s, but growing geographical dispersion of knowledge-based assets, and need of firms to harness such assets from foreign locations, makes this a more important motive for FDI.
2. The price and availability of 'synergistic' assets to foreign investors.
3. Opportunities offered (often by particular subnational spatial units) for exchange of localized tacit knowledge, ideas and interactive learning.
4. Access to different cultures, institutions and systems; and different consumer demands and preferences.

demand patterns and specialized factor inputs (Maskell 1996; Rees and McLean 1997).

The second finding is that the complementary foreign assets and capabilities sought by MNEs wishing to add value to their core competitive advantages are increasingly of a *knowledge-facilitating* kind, and that this is particularly the case as their affiliates become more firmly rooted in host economies (Grabher 1993). Examples include the deepening of value-added activities by Japanese manufacturing subsidiaries in Europe and North America. An exception to this finding is some low value-adding activities in the least developed areas of the world.

The third finding is that as strategic asset-acquiring investment has become more important, the locational needs of corporations have shifted from those to do with access to markets, or to natural resources, to those of *access to knowledge-intensive assets and learning experiences*, which augment their existing O-specific advantages.

The fourth finding is that much of the recent FDI in developing countries is prompted either by traditional market-seeking motives (for example, as in the case of China, Indonesia and India), or by the desire to take advantage of lower (real) labor costs, and/or the availability and price of natural resources. Yet, even there, where firms have a choice, the physical and human infrastructure, together with the macroeconomic environment and institutional framework of the host country, tend to play a more decisive role than they once did.

MACROECONOMIC ASPECTS OF THE CHANGING INTERNATIONAL ALLOCATION OF ECONOMIC ACTIVITY

In the previous section, we set out some of the reasons for the changing locational patterns of MNE activity over the past two decades. We concluded that developments in the global economy over these years had not only opened up or enlarged markets for products normally supplied by MNEs, but, by affecting the production and transaction costs of FDI, had markedly influenced its industrial structure and geography. In general, the 1990s witnessed a closer integration in the international value-added activities of MNEs. In the case of some kinds of FDI, falling material, transportation and communication costs, and rising transactional benefits arising from the common governance of interdependent activities have made for a more concentrated pattern of FDI, both between and within regions and/or countries. In other cases, however, the emergence of new – and often important – markets, and the lowering of tariff and non-tariff barriers have made for a more dispersed pattern of FDI.

We now turn to consider some macroeconomic, or country-specific, issues. In particular, we wish to address two questions. First, to what extent is the changing locational pattern of FDI affecting our understanding about the determinants of the optimal international allocation of economic activity; and second, how far, in light of the growing significance and integration of MNEs, does one need to reconsider the policy implications for both national and regional governments as they seek to advance their particular economic and social objectives?

Until the 1950s, most explanations of the allocation of economic activity were based on the distribution of natural resources – especially labor, land and finance capital. The principle of comparative advantage espoused that countries should specialize in the production of those products which required the resources and capabilities in which they were relatively the best endowed, and trade these for those which required resources and capabilities in which they were relatively poorly endowed. This was the basis for a general equilibrium model of trade. Its restrictive assumptions – namely perfect competition, the immobility of factors, homogeneity of traded products, constant returns to scale and zero transportation costs – as recently reiterated by Krugman (1993), are well known. In that model, there was little or no room for innovatory activities, or for the deployment of such created assets as intellectual capital, organizational expertise, entrepreneurship and interactive learning either by countries or firms; and even less for the distinctive characteristics of MNEs.

Over the last four decades, these restrictions have been gradually relaxed in three main ways. First, independently of the work of scholars on FDI and MNE activity, there has been a growing appreciation by trade economists of the need to incorporate such variables as economies of scale, fabricated assets, learning experiences and market structure into their models, and to recognize that the role of these varies with type of economic activity. It is, for example, now generally accepted that different parts of the value chain may be distributed between countries, or regions within countries, according to their knowledge, capital, natural resource and labor content, and to their geography of these inputs. Secondly, more attention is now being paid to the extent to which the external economies which arise from the clustering of related activities may lead to a concentration of economic activity in certain countries or regions. Thirdly, more recognition has been given to the differences in consumer tastes between countries, while, very gradually, institutional factors, such as those specific to the multi-activity or multi-firm, and to the role of governments, have begun to be acknowledged.

In incorporating these changes into their thinking, the proponents of the *positive* theory of trade are now able to offer a more realistic explanation of the international allocation of economic activity; while, from a *normative* viewpoint, though dented, the principle of comparative advantage still has much going for it as a guiding light as to how best to allocate scarce resources between countries (Wood 1993). This is particularly the case when it is widened to embrace created assets, including those which are institutional, policy and culture related (Lipsey 1997).

However, a second intellectual lacuna remains, which makes it difficult to reconcile the approaches of location theorists and international trade economists in explaining the international allocation of production. This is the presence – and the increasing presence – of the MNE, whose central feature is its common ownership of cross-border value-adding activities. Here we need to turn once again to the work of the internalization scholars. For to explain how MNEs, qua MNEs, affect the international location of economic activity, we need to consider how they differ from uni-national firms. Otherwise, one should be able to use the tenets of contemporary trade and/or location theory to explain such activity. It is here that research by international business scholars is particularly relevant.

An earlier section of this paper suggested that the changes in the geography of FDI over the last two decades have been broadly in line with that of the capital expenditures of all firms. This could mean that the ownership or multinationality of firms was not a significant variable in explaining such changes, and that trade in intermediate or final products internalized, and/or controlled, by MNEs is no differently determined than trade between independent firms, that is, arm's-length trade.

However, as copious research shows (as reviewed, for example, in Caves 1996 and Dunning 1993), the main impact of the foreignness, or multi-nationality, of firms has not been on the *level* of economic activity and/or trade of the countries in which they operate, but on the *structure* of these variables. From the very earliest of studies on FDI, scholars have shown that the foreign affiliates of MNEs tend to be concentrated in different industrial sectors from those of their indigenous counterparts. Since each sector is likely to have its distinctive locational and trading propensities, it follows that FDI will have a differential impact on the geography of economic activity. Sometimes, this impact will reflect the characteristics of the country of the investing firms, for example, Japanese FDI in the European auto and electronics industries in the 1980s; sometimes a very unique competitive advantage or set of advantages; and sometimes their pattern and degree of multinationality. For it is the particular attributes, both of the geographical diversity of an MNE's operations and of the costs and benefits associated with the common governance of these operations, which constitute one of the singular features of contemporary MNE activity, especially in developed countries.

Scholars such as Bruce Kogut recognized these specific attributes of MNEs many years ago (see, for example, Kogut 1983 and 1985), but as the degree, scope and intensity of the foreign operations of firms have increased over the last decade (as demonstrated, for example, in the annual *World Investment Reports* of UNCTAD), and as these are now used to harness new resources, capabilities and markets, as well as to exploit the existing O advantages of firms, so have these particular qualities of multinationality become more prominent.

Though such qualities can be readily embraced by location theory, they are less easily incorporated into general equilibrium trade models. Primarily, this is because, unlike industrial organization theory, trade theory has not come to grips with the multi-activity firm, or multi-plant production, or has included innovation in its thinking (one notable exception is Grossman and Helpman 1991). Recent papers by James Markusen (1995) and Markusen and Venables (1995) have made a brave attempt to integrate the OLI framework paradigm of international production and the newer models of trade (namely those embracing firm-specific economies of scale, product differentiation and imperfect competition), but they tend to concentrate on how the cross-border specialization of specific knowledge intensive activities may differ from that predicated by traditional trade theory. In a similar vein, research by Brainard (1993) and Horstman and Markusen (1992) has concluded that MNE-related production will be in equilibrium when firm-level fixed costs and spatial trans-action costs are large relative to plant level economies.[15] None of these approaches, however, fully takes into account the key properties of multina-tionality, as distinct from the foreign ownership of firms. While embracing some of the characteristics of internalized markets for O-specific assets, they ignore others – and especially those which elsewhere we have referred to as transaction cost-minimizing O advantages.[16]

Considering the normative implications of the work of Markusen and others, and using the language of traditional trade theory, we might say that it will be to the benefit of countries if their firms engage in outward FDI in two very different situations. The first is where the utilization of their O-specific advantages, the production of which is relatively well suited to the resources and capabilities of the home country, is best undertaken in a foreign country (or countries)[17] *and within the same firm* (that is, the benefits of 'first best' internalized intermediate product markets exceed those of 'first best' arm's-length transactions). The second is when, to protect or augment their global competitive advantages, firms engage in buying assets in a foreign country (or countries) more favorable to their creation, but not to their deployment. By contrast, a country will benefit from inward direct invest-ment when it has a comparative advantage in adding value to the services of the imported created assets – again within the investing entity – rather than producing these assets itself, or where a foreign firm chooses to buy assets created in the country (at the right price) and to utilize these assets in a foreign country (or countries).

In most cases, given the presence of MNEs, the recipe for an optimal allocation of economic activity between countries is quite similar to that in a world in which there is no FDI. But, the relative roles of markets, hierarchies and governments in this recipe are likely to be different. In conditions other than that of perfect competition, hierarchies, or heterarchies – in the guise of multi-activity and/or multinational firms – may be a more efficient coordinator of resources and capabilities than arm's-length markets (Caves 1996). This is particularly likely to be so in a dynamic knowledge-based economy in which some of the ingredients of endemic market failure, and particularly those of uncertainty, irregularity, complexity, externalities, scale economies, vertical integration and the interdependence of markets, are present, as it is these which tend to generate the kind of value-added activities which can be coordinated more efficiently under a single governance. In such cases, and providing that the final goods' markets served by MNEs are contestable, and national governments pursue positive and non-distorting market facilitating macro-organizational policies (Dunning 1997b), MNEs may act as surrogates for markets. By internalizing intermediate product markets, they may help protect or enhance, rather than inhibit, the efficiency of final goods' markets.

While not wishing to undervalue the role of governments in curtailing the anti-competitive behavior of firms, and in pursuing market friendly macro-organizational strategies, we believe that contemporary changes in the ways in which resources and capabilities are managed are facilitating a more appropriate balance between cross-border hierarchical (that is, internalized) and external market transactions. Perhaps the one area for potential concern is the widespread growth of international mergers and acquisitions and strategic alliances (UNCTAD 1997). Insofar as these may assist firms to be more innovatory, entrepreneurial and competitive in global markets, they are all to the good; but where they better enable companies to engage in structurally distorting business practices they need to be carefully monitored.

The unique impact of MNEs on the international allocation of production rests on the extent to which the internalization of cross-border intermediate product markets produces a different and more efficient structure of economic activity than would otherwise have occurred. Herein lies an interesting paradox. On the one hand, the liberalization of markets and the reduction of some kinds of spatial costs are easing the trans-border movement of goods, intangible assets and services. On the other, technological and organizational change, whenever it enhances the interdependence of value-added activity, is encouraging international production to be undertaken within plants and firms under the same ownership, and for at least some of this production to be spatially concentrated. It would seem that as fast as structural and distance-related market distortions are removed, others, making for internalized intermediate product markets and untraded spatial interdependencies, are becoming more important.

Hints of this 'new' international division of labor are shown not only by the growing participation of MNEs in global production – as described earlier in this paper – but also by their increasing share of world export markets, at least in the manufacturing sector (documented by, *inter alia*, Dunning 1993; UNCTAD 1996a; and Caves 1996). Other data also suggest that the export propensity of MNEs or their affiliates, in the sectors in which they are most active, exceeds that of indigenous competitors. Except in the case of a few countries, notably Japan, the payments for the services of knowledge-intensive assets received by US MNEs from their foreign affiliates, expressed as a proportion of their total exports, is considerably greater than the equivalent proportion between US and independently owned firms. For example, in 1996, royalties and fees received by US firms from their foreign affiliates amounted to 6 per cent of their exports to these affiliates. The corresponding proportion of non-affiliation royalties and fees received by all US firms as a proportion of total US exports was 3 per cent (US Department of Commerce 1997). Furthermore, of all royalties and fees received by US firms from foreign-based firms in the years 1993 to 1996, 79 per cent were internal to US MNEs.[18]

The extent to which MNEs promote, or gravitate to, spatial clusters within a country or region is an under-researched area. Clearly, some older clusters – for example, the Portuguese cork industry, the Swiss watch industry, the North Italian textile industry and the City of London financial district – developed without much MNE participation. But many of the newly established clusters, which are geared more to accessing the external economies of knowledge creation, interactive learning and the upgrading of the competitive advantage of the constituent firms, are influenced by a rather different set of costs and benefits; and a casual examination of the membership of science and technology parks, export processing zones, research and development consortia and service support centers would certainly suggest that MNEs are actively involved, often as flagship firms. Certainly among developed regions (for example, the European Union) and countries (for example, United States), knowledge-intensive and export-oriented activities tend to be more geographically concentrated than other kinds of activity (see, for example, illustrations given in Porter 1990; Dunning 1997b, Chapter 3; and Dunning 1997c).

Any modern theory of international economic activity must then take account of how the common ownership of cross-border production and transactions may result in a different structure, efficiency and spatial configuration than that which would arise if such functions were separately undertaken by uni-national firms. *Inter alia*, the extra attributes comprise the spreading of firm-specific overheads and risks; the intra-firm sharing and transference of knowledge, experience and markets; and the external economies arising from jointly organized innovatory, production and marketing activities. For many of these activities, there is no external market; the output of one part of the firm can be sold only as an input to another part of the same firm. However, these interdependent activities may not need to be undertaken in the same region or country. For other activities, internal markets may offer more coordinating benefits and/or less transactional costs than arm's-length markets. In both cases, however, it may be preferable to think of the MNE not as a second-best substitute for the market, but as a partner with the market to promote allocative efficiency throughout and across value chains.

The notion of efficiency-promoting internal markets needs to be more formally built into both positive and normative macro models of international economic activity. In addition to acknowledging the different geographical needs of asset-producing and asset-exploiting activities, models of trade need to incorporate the benefits of organizing the two sets of activity under common ownership vis-à-vis that of the external market. This, in principle, is not a difficult thing to do. Essentially, it comes down to an identification and evaluation of the country, activity and firm-specific variables which determine whether the different transactional and coordinating functions are best organized within market friendly hierarchies or by the market per se. We have already argued that markets for created assets, and the goods and services arising from them, are likely to be intrinsically more imperfect than those for natural assets and the goods and services arising from them. In some instances, too, it may be efficiency-enhancing for these markets to be internalized. We also contend, with Behrman and Grosse (1990) and Meyer (1998), that *most* cross-border markets are likely to be more imperfect than their domestic equivalents, and that, because of this, MNE activity *may* be more welfare-enhancing than multi-plant activity within an economy. We say 'most' cross-border markets, because some domestic markets, particularly in emerging developing economies, are likely to be more imperfect than those in developed countries. But issues such as foreign-exchange uncertainty, institutional and cultural differences, and the differential role of governments are obviously likely to play a more important role in affecting the workings of cross-border than domestic markets. And we say 'may' be more welfare-enhancing because as much will depend upon the conditions under which MNE investment takes place.

At the same time, the extent to which cross-border markets are internalized via FDI or trade between independent firms will itself depend on the characteristics of the trading partners and the countries involved, as well as on the types of assets, goods and services being exchanged. In their attempts to explain the alternative forms of trans-border trade, and to advance both the positive and the normative theories of trade, international economists need to delve deeper into the structure of country-specific advantages in organizing trade (particularly in knowledge-related products), through FDI and inter-firm alliances, as compared with arm's-length markets.

CONCLUSIONS

The previous two sections of this paper have examined how changes in the global economy over the past two decades are affecting scholarly thinking about both the microeconomic geography of FDI and MNE activity, and the more macroeconomic explanations of the international allocation of all value-added activity. In particular, we focused on three points. The first is the growing importance of intangible assets – and particularly intellectual capital – in the wealth-creating process, and of the need of companies to harness, as well as to exploit, these assets from a variety of locations. Secondly, we emphasized the changing role of location-bound assets which mobile investors look for as complements to their own core competencies. In doing so, we again underscored the increasing significance of created assets (and particularly those which governments, in their macro-organizational policies, can and do influence), and also the benefits which spatial clusters offer whenever distance-related transactions and coordination costs are high.

Thirdly, we argued that, to adequately incorporate the activities of MNEs within existing trade-type theories of the international allocation of economic activity, more attention should be given both to the specific motives, determinants and consequences of the common governance of related cross-border activities, and to the conditions in which internalizing intermediate product markets might make for a more efficient (in the sense of the 'next best' realistic alternative, assuming that all cross-border avoidable structural market imperfections have been removed) spatial configuration of economic activity in the contemporary global and innovatory economy. We have also suggested that any paradigm of the geography of FDI, in contrast to that of the investments of all firms, needs to be constructed on similar lines.

What are the implications of our analysis and findings for future international business research? First, to return to the starting point of this paper, and in line with the thinking of Michael Porter (1994, 1996), I believe more attention needs to be given to the importance of location per se as a variable affecting the global competitiveness of firms. That is to say the locational configuration of a firm's activities may itself be an O-specific advantage, as well as affect the modality by which it augments, or exploits, its existing O advantages. With the gradual geographical dispersion of created assets, and as firms become more multinational by deepening or widening their cross-border value chains, then, from the viewpoint of both harnessing new competitive advantages and more efficiently deploying their home-based assets, the structure and content of the location portfolio of firms becomes more critical to their global competitive positions.

Secondly, in seeking to make optimal use of the existing location-bound assets within this jurisdiction, and to promote the dynamic comparative advantage of their resource-capabilities, governments need to give more attention to ensuring that their actions help fashion, support and complement those of efficient hierarchies and markets. This involves a greater apprecia-tion both of the changing locational requirements of mobile investments, and of how, in the case of those markets where endemic failure is most wide-spread, governments may work in partnership with firms either to improve markets (that is, by a 'voice' strategy), or to replace these markets (by an exit strategy).[19] With the growing importance of knowledge-related infrastruc-ture, and accepting the idea of subnational spatial units as nexus of untraded interdependencies (Storper 1995),[20] this presents both new challenges and opportunities to both national and regional governments in their macro-orga-nization and competition-enhancing policies.

NOTES

1. Such international-specific transaction costs have recently been explicitly identified by Klaus Meyer in a volume (Meyer 1998) based upon his doctoral dissertation at the London Business School.
2. For example, of the 1 150 or so publications cited in his volume, only 13 per cent are mono-graphs or articles published after 1990.
3. Author's estimate, based on data on the royalties paid for managerial know-how, and on the relationship between foreign portfolio and foreign direct investment.
4. There have been only a few attempts to use transaction cost analysis to explain the spatial distribution of economic activity. One example is that of the industrial geographers Michael Storper and Allen Scott. See, for example, Storper (1995), Storper and Scott (1995) and Scott (1996). Yet, such analysis offers a powerful tool for explaining why firms requiring idiosyncratic inputs, for example, tacit knowledge of various kinds, and/or those supplying idiosyncratic and uncertain markets tend to value proximity with their suppliers and/or customers. Perhaps the best illustration of a spatial cluster, or agglomeration, of related activities to minimize distance-related transaction costs, and to exploit the external economies associated with the close presence of related firms is the Square Mile of the City of London.
5. Scott (1996) gives some examples, including the growing concentration and specialization of both manufacturing and service activities in large metropolitan areas within both devel-oped and developing countries. In an interesting recent paper, Davis and Weinstein (1997) conclude that intra-national concentration of value-added activity is likely to obey the dictates of economic geography more than that of the international concentration of such activity.
6. Estimates of such ventures vary enormously. A recent study by Booz, Allen and Hamilton (1997) has put the number of cross-border alliances (including mergers and acquisitions) formed in 1995 and 1996 to be as high as 15 000. Another assessment by Hagedoorn (1996) suggests that between 1980 and 1994 the number of newly established cross-border tech-nology-related inter-firm agreements rose by over three times. Finally, the value of interna-tional mergers and acquisitions over the same period was estimated to have accounted for between 50 and 60 per cent of all new FDI (UNCTAD 1997).
7. For a detailed exposition of the development of a new trajectory of technological advances, see Lipsey (1997) and Ruigrok and Van Tulder (1995).
8. Though there have been marked fluctuations in the shares within and between these periods, which reflect, *inter alia*, changes in exchange rates and the positioning of countries in their

cycles of economic development. For example, during 1975–80, the United States attracted 32 per cent of FDI received by developed countries; by 1985–90 that share had risen to 42 per cent. However, it fell again to 18 per cent in 1991 and 1992; but since then it has recovered, and in 1995–6 it stood at 35 per cent.

9. Japan is a classic case in point. In the period 1990–94 it accounted for 29 per cent of the world's gross fixed capital formation, but only 0.8 per cent of inbound FDI flows.

10. To give just one example, in the period 1990–94, 49 per cent of US direct investment flows were directed to Western Europe, 10 per cent to Asia and 25 per cent to Latin America. The corresponding percentages for Japanese direct investment flows were 20 per cent, 19 per cent and 10 per cent (UNCTAD 1997; Dunning 1998).

11. Unlike the theory of the firm; although if there had been a well developed theory of the multi-activity firm prior to the work of scholars such as Buckley, Casson and Hennart, one wonders if this aspect of international business activity would have attracted so much attention!

12. We use the word 'customized' deliberately, following the contention of Peck (1996) that host governments may sometimes need to individualize or customize the upgrading of their physical and human infrastructure both to meet the specific needs of mobile investors, and promote the competitive dynamic advantage of the location-bound resources within their jurisdiction.

13. I am indebted to the reviewer of this paper for making this point.

14. An expression first used in David (1984), and since taken up by Wheeler and Mody (1992) and Mytelka (1996).

15. In Markusen's words 'multinational enterprises in this framework are exporters of the services of firm-specific assets . . . subsidiaries import these assets' (Markusen 1995 p. 175).

16. Abbreviated, O_t transaction (or coordinating) cost-minimizing advantages, c.f. O_a = asset-specific advantages.

17. Which foreign country, or countries, is decided by the normal locational criteria.

18. Other data on royalties and management fees received by US firms from foreign firms are regularly published by the United States Department of Commerce in the *Survey of Current Business* and in the *Benchmark Surveys of US Direct Investment Abroad*. See also UNCTAD (1995, 1996a and 1997).

19. The concepts of 'voice' and 'exit' strategies as applied to MNE-related activity are explained in Dunning (1997a).

20. The idea of a region as a spatial unit which internalizes distance-related transaction costs which otherwise would fall upon its constituent firms is an interesting notion worth pursuing by international business scholars. For, like a firm, the strategies pursued by a region to provide a set of unique, non-mobile and non-imitable locational advantages for its firms may well determine its own competitive advantages relative to those of other regions. At the same time, regions, like firms, may decline as well as prosper; but our knowledge about the focus leading to the spatial dis-agglomeration of related activities is woefully inadequate.

REFERENCES

Almeida, P. (1996), 'Knowledge sourcing by foreign multinationals: patent citation analysis in the US semi-conductor industry', *Strategic Management Journal*, **17** (Winter): 155–65.

Bandera, V.N., and J.T. White (1968), 'US direct investments and domestic markets in Europe', *Economia Internazionale*, **21** (February): 117–33.

Behrman, J.N., and Robert Grosse (1990), *International Business and Governments*, Columbia, SC: University of South Carolina Press.

Blair, M.M. (1995), *Ownership and Control: Rethinking Corporate Governance for the 21st Century*, Washington DC: The Brookings Institution.

Booz, Allen and Hamilton (1997), *Cross Border Alliances in the Age of Collaboration*, Los Angeles, CA: Booz Allen and Hamilton.

Brainard, S.L. (1993), 'A simple theory of multinational corporations and trade with a trade-off between proximity and concentration', Working Paper No. 4269, Cambridge, MA: National Bureau of Economic Research.

Braunerhjelm, P., and R. Svensson (1995), 'Host country characteristics and agglomeration in foreign direct investment', mimeo, Stockholm: Industrial Institute for EC and Social Research (October).

Cantwell, J., and R. Harding (1997), 'The internationalization of German companies R&D', Discussion Paper in International Investment and Management No. 233, University of Reading.

Caves, R. (1996), *Multinational Firms and Economic Analysis*, Cambridge: Cambridge University Press. (First pub. 1982.)

Dalton D.H., and M.G. Serapio (1995), *Globalizing Industrial Research and Development*, US Department of Commerce, Office of Technology Policy, Washington, DC: US Department of Commerce.

David, P. (1984), 'High technology centers and the economics of locational tournaments', mimeo, Stanford, CA: Stanford University.

Davidson, W. (1970) 'The location of foreign direct investment activity: country characteristics and experience effects', *Journal of International Business Studies*, **11** (2): 9–22.

Davis, D.R., and D.E. Weinstein (1997), 'Economic geography and regional production structure: an empirical investigation', Working Paper Series No. 6093, Cambridge, MA: National Bureau of Economic Research.

Donahue, J.D. (1996), *Disunited States*, New York: Basic Books.

Dunning, J.H. (1993), *Multinational Enterprises and the Global Economy*, Wokingham, England and Reading, MA: Addison Wesley.

Dunning, J.H. (1995), 'What's wrong – and right – with trade theory', *International Trade Journal*, **9** (2): 153–202.

Dunning, J.H. (1996), 'The geographical sources of competitiveness of firms: some results of a new survey', *Transnational Corporations*, **5** (3): 1–30.

Dunning, J.H. (1997a), *Alliance Capitalism and Global Business*, London and New York: Routledge.

Dunning, J.H. (ed.) (1997b), *Governments, Globalization and International Business*, Oxford: Oxford University Press.

Dunning, J.H. (1997c), 'The European internal market program and inbound foreign direct investment', *Journal of Common Market Studies*, **35** (1 and 2): 1–30 and 189–223.

Dunning, J.H. (1998), 'The changing geography of foreign direct investment', in N. Kumar (ed.), *Internationalization, Foreign Direct Investment and Technology Transfer: Impact and Prospects for Developing Countries*, London and New York: Routledge.

Edvinson, L. (1997), *Intellectual Capital Development*, Stockholm: Skandia.

Ethier, W.J. (1986), 'The multinational firm', *Quarterly Journal of Economics*, **101**: 806–33.

Florida, R. (1995), 'Towards the learning region', *Futures*, **27** (5): 527–36.

Fujita, M. and J.R. Thisse (1996), 'Economics of agglomeration', Institute of Economic Research Discussion Paper No. 430, Kyoto: Kyoto University.

Grabher, G. (ed.) (1993), *The Embedded Firm*, London and New York: Routledge.

Grossman, G.M., and E. Helpman (1991), *Innovation and Growth in the Global Economy*, Cambridge, MA: MIT Press.

Hagedoorn, J. (1996), 'Trends and patterns in strategic technology partnering since the early seventies', *Review of Industrial Organization*, **11**: 601–16.

Handy, C. (1989), *The Age of Unreason*, London: Hutchinson.

Hatem, F. (1997), *International Investment: Towards the Year 2001*, Geneva: United Nations.

Helpman, E., and P.R. Krugman (1985), *Market Structure and Foreign Trade*, Cambridge, MA: MIT Press.

Horstman, I.J., and J.R. Markusen (1992), 'Endogenous market structures in international trade', *Journal of International Economics*, **32**: 109–29.

Johanson, J., and J.E. Vahlne (1977), 'The internationalization process of the firm – a model of knowledge development and increasing market commitments', *Journal of International Business Studies*, **8**: 23–32.

Kogut, B. (1983), 'Foreign direct investment as a sequential process', in C.P. Kindleberger and D. Audretsch (eds), *The Multinational Corporation in the 1980s*, Cambridge, MA: MIT Press.

Kogut, B. (1985), 'Designing global strategies: corporate and competitive value-added chains', *Sloan Management Review*, **25**: 15–28.

Krugman, P. (ed) (1986), *Strategic Trade Policy and the New International Economics*, Cambridge, MA: MIT Press.

Krugman, P.R. (1991) *Geography and Trade*, Cambridge, MA: MIT Press.

Krugman, P.R. (1993), 'On the relationship between trade theory and location theory', *Review of International Economics*, **1** (2): 110–22.

Kuemmerle, W. (1996), 'The drivers of foreign direct investment into research and development: An empirical investigation', Harvard Business School Working Paper No. 96:062.

Lipsey, R.G. (1997), 'Globalization and national government policies: An economist's view', in John H. Dunning (ed.), *Governments, Globalization and International Business*, Oxford: Oxford University Press.

Liu, S.X. (1998), *Foreign Direct Investment and the Multinational Enterprise. A Reexamination Using Signaling Theory*, Westport, CT: Greenwood Publishing.

Loree, D.W., and S.E. Guisinger (1995), 'Policy and nonpolicy determinants of US equity foreign direct investment', *Journal of International Business Studies*, **26** (2): 281–300.

Malmberg, A., O. Slovell and I. Zander (1996), 'Spatial clustering, local accumulation of knowledge and firm competitiveness', *Geografiska Annaler Series B, Human Geography*, **78** (2): 85–97.

Markusen, A. (1994), 'Sticky places in slippery spaces: the political economy of post-war fast growth regions', Rutgers University Working Paper No. 79, New Brunswick Center for Urban Policy Research.

Markusen, J.R. (1995), 'The boundaries of multinational enterprises and the theory of international trade', *Journal of Economic Perspectives*, **9** (2): 169–89.

Markusen, J.R., and A. Venables (1995), 'Multinational firms and the New Trade Theory', Working Paper No. 5036, Cambridge, MA: National Bureau of Economic Research.

Maskell, P. (1996), 'Local embeddedness and patterns of international specialization', mimeo, Copenhagen Business School.

Mataloni, R., and M. Fahim-Nader (1996), 'Operations of US multinational companies: preliminary results from the 1994 benchmark survey', *Survey of Current Business* (December): 11–37.

Meyer, K. (1998), *Direct Investment in Economies in Transition*, Cheltenham, UK, Lyme USA: Edward Elgar.

Mytelka, L.K. (1996), Locational tournaments, strategic partnerships and the state, mimeo, Ottawa: Carleton University.

Ohlin, B. (1933), *Inter-regional and International Trade*, Cambridge, MA: Harvard University Press, revised edition 1967.

Ohmae, K. (1995), *The End of the Nation State: The Rise of Regional Economies*, London: Harper.

Papanastassiou, M., and R. Pearce (1997), 'Technology sourcing and the strategic role of manufacturing subsidiaries in the UK: local competencies and global competitions', *Management International Review*, **37** (forthcoming).

Peck, F.W. (1996), 'Regional development and the production of space: the role of infrastructure in the attraction of new inward investment', *Environment and Planning*, **28**: 327–39.

Porter, M.E. (1990), *The Competitive Advantage of Nations*, New York: The Free Press.

Porter, M.E. (1994), 'The role of location in competition', *Journal of Economics of Business*, **1** (1): 35–39.

Porter, M.E. (1996), 'Competitive advantage, agglomerative economies and regional policy', *International Regional Science Review*, **19** (1 and 2): 85–94.

Rees, D., and T. McLean (1997), 'Trends in location choice', in A. Jolly (ed.), *European Business Handbook 1997*, London: Kogan Page (for CBI).

Ruigrok, W., and R. Van Tulder (1995), *The Logic of International Restructuring*, London and New York: Routledge.

Scaperlanda, A., and L.J. Mauer (1969), 'The determinants of US direct investment in the EEC', *American Economic Review*, **59** (September): 558–68.

Scott, A.J. (1996), 'Regional motors of the global economy', *Futures*, **28** (5): 391–411.

Shan, W, and J. Song (1997), 'Foreign direct investment and the sourcing of technological advantage: evidence from the biotechnology industry', *Journal of International Business Studies*, **28** (2): 267–84.

Srinivasan, K., and A. Mody (1997), 'Location determinants of foreign direct investment: an empirical analysis of US and Japanese investment', *Canadian Journal of Economics* (forthcoming).

Stewart, T.A. (1997), *Intellectual Capital*, London: Nicholas Bradley.

Storper, M. (1995), 'The resurgence of regional economies: ten years later: the region as a nexus of untraded interdependencies', *European Urban and Regional Studies*, **2** (3): 191–221.

Storper, M., and A.J. Scott. (1995), 'The wealth of regions', *Futures*, **27** (5): 505–26.

Taylor, J. (1993), 'An analysis of the factors determining the geographical distribution of Japanese manufacturing investment in the UK, 1984–91', *Urban Studies*, **30** (7): 1209–24.

UNCTC (1988), *Transnational Corporations and World Development*, New York: UN.

UNCTAD (1995), *World Investment Report 1995: Transnational Corporations and Competitiveness*, New York and Geneva: UN.

UNCTAD (1996a), *World Investment Report 1996: Transnational Corporations, Investment, Trade and International Policy Arrangements*, New York and Geneva: UN.

UNCTAD (1996b), *Incentives and Foreign Direct Investment*, Geneva and New York: UN.

UNCTAD (1997), *World Investment Report 1997: Transnational Corporations, Market Structure and Competition Policy*, Geneva and New York: UN.

US Department of Commerce (1997), 'US international sales and purchases of private services', *Survey of Current Business* (October): 95–138.

Vernon, R. (1966), 'International investment and international trade in the product cycle', *Quarterly Journal of Economics*, **80**: 190–207.

Vernon, R. (1974), 'The location of economic activity', in John H. Dunning (ed.), *Economic Analysis and the Multinational Enterprise*, London: Allen and Unwin.

Wells, L.T. (ed.) (1972), *The Product Life Cycle and International Trade*, Cambridge, MA: Harvard University Press.

Wesson, T.J. (1993), 'An alternative motivation for foreign direct investment', Ph.D. dissertation, Harvard University.

Wheeler, K., and A. Mody (1992), 'International investment and location decisions: the case of US firms', *Journal of International Economics*, **33**: 57–76.

Wood, A. (1993), 'Give Heckscher and Ohlin a chance', mimeo, University of Sussex, Institute of Development Studies.

World Bank (1997), *World Development Report: The State in a Changing World*, Oxford and New York: Oxford University Press.

4. Market structure and the multinational enterprise: a game-theoretic approach[1]

Edward M. Graham

INTRODUCTION

Chapter 4 of *Multinational Enterprise and Economic Analysis*, second edition (Caves 1996), is entitled 'Patterns of Market Competition'. The second edition serves as a useful survey of contributions to the literature on multinational enterprises that have appeared since the first edition (Caves 1982). Caves emphasizes, in his preface, the need to review 'significant new theoretical contributions' in a number of areas. Thus, what is perhaps surprising about Chapter 4 is that no reference is made to recent articles in the literature attempting to apply the 'new' theories of industrial organization to the behavior of multinational firms. These new theories are, in turn, largely driven by applications of game theory (see, for example, the introduction to Tirole 1988).

Admittedly, there is a rather small number of applications of the new industrial organization to multinational behavior.[2] But, although this literature might be, in terms of the number of articles published, small, it is important nonetheless. In fact, the 'new' theories of industrial organization largely underpin the 'new' theories of international trade (on this, see the introduction to Krugman 1990) which have led to substantial rethinking about this important subject.[3] Given both the importance of multinational firms and the historical relevance of concepts from industrial organization to explaining the existence and behavior of these firms (for example, the much-cited PhD dissertation of Stephen Hymer, written during the late 1950s but published as Hymer 1976), it is perhaps surprising – and even dismaying – that so little effort has been made to rethink multinational firm behavior in light of new theory. The present article, therefore, rethinks key issues about the behavior of multinational firms using concepts from the new theories of industrial organization based on cooperative game theory.

As stressed by Hymer (and by Caves himself in the opening paragraphs of Chapter 4), the multinational firm is prevalent in markets where sellers are concentrated, that is, where the necessary conditions for 'perfect competition' apparently do not exist. In such markets, sellers are not 'price takers'; rather, the actions of individual sellers can affect price and, importantly, because this applies in most cases to more than one seller, the actions of each seller can affect the outcome. An important implication is that the 'best response' of each seller is conditional upon the actions of other sellers. Hence, in determining what should be its actions, each seller will take into account the likely response of other sellers.

This strategic interdependence is of critical importance in understanding the dynamics of competition among multinational firms but it is almost wholly absent in the 'transaction costs' approach to explaining multinational firm behavior that has so dominated the literature of international business during the past two decades. This approach asserts, in the words of Caves in Chapter 1, 'that horizontal MNEs will exist only if the plants they own and operate attain lower costs or higher revenue productivity than the same plants under separate management'.[4] But, as will be explained in the next section of this article, under a 'new' industrial organization approach, this condition simply is *not* necessary for a firm to become multinational nor, indeed, is it sufficient.[5]

It is precisely such markets that industrial organization – whether the 'new' or the 'old' – addresses. As noted in the opening paragraph, what distinguishes the 'new' theories of industrial organization from the 'old' is mostly the use of concepts derived from game theory. Game theory attempts to explain the behavior of 'players' where the optimal moves of these players depend critically upon the moves taken by other players. Of particular relevance is 'noncooperative' game theory, wherein it is assumed that each player will maximize their own interests, as opposed to the collective interests of a group of players. It is not ruled out, however, that these interests might coincide: an individual player might in fact cooperate with other players. If, however, this happens, it is because the player chooses to cooperate out of self-interest, rather than because the player is bound by some sort of obligation that is enforced by an external agent.[6] Noncooperative game theory offers insights into the strategic behavior of firms selling in markets where there is seller concentration that are missing from the traditional theory of industrial organization; importantly, these insights can change traditional thinking.

This chapter is not meant as a thorough review of this theory and its applications, although some of the relevant literature is cited. Rather, it is meant as something of a primer, to show how certain concepts from noncooperative game theory can be used to illuminate issues of behavior of multinational enterprises. The main motive is, taking note of the paucity of work that has been done in this domain, to stimulate further work. The strand of thinking presented here remains in its infancy, and the best work is surely to come.

MULTINATIONAL ENTERPRISES AND THE FOLK THEOREM[7]

Let us begin by reviewing one of the most important results of noncooperative game theory (and one that is, arguably, greatly underappreciated). This is the 'folk theorem' for repeated noncooperative games.[8] What this theorem does is to establish formal conditions under which players in a game with the properties of a 'prisoner's dilemma' (see Box 4.1) might choose to cooperate with one another rather than narrowly maximize self-interest. The theorem is of great relevance to such issues as stability of cartels or tacit collusion among oligopolistic rivals. Where the underlying conditions of the cartel, or of the tacit collusion, have the structure of a prisoner's dilemma (as is, in fact, often the case), traditional thinking on industrial organization would predict a rapid disintegration of the collusion. The folk theorem says, in effect, 'not so fast, under certain conditions the collusion can be very stable'.

BOX 4.1   THE PRISONER'S DILEMMA

The classic prisoner's dilemma is depicted as follows: two persons cooperate in committing a crime, but both are caught. The police have enough evidence to convict both of the crime in the second degree, for which both will receive minor sentences, but not enough to convict in the first degree, which carries a severe sentence. Individually, each prisoner is offered by the prosecutor the following plea-bargain offer: if the prisoner will turn state's evidence, and the other prisoner does not, he or she will go scott-free while the other will receive the maximum sentence. If both prisoners turn state's evidence, both will receive a sentence less than the maximum but considerably more severe than if neither turns state's evidence.

The dilemma faced by each prisoner is that if he or she refuses to turn state's evidence and can trust the other to do likewise, a light sentence is assured. But if he or she does so and the other does so too, a heavy sentence will follow. Indeed, under the circumstances, there is a positive incentive for each to turn state's evidence no matter what the other does. If the other does not turn, the first goes scott-free, whereas if the other turns and the first does not, the result is a heavy sentence. Thus, the outcome (which is a Nash equilibrium, see footnote 3) is that both turn state's evidence and receive the moderate sentence,

---

whereas had each refused to turn, the outcome would have been a light sentence.

The cooperative outcome (neither turns state's evidence) is said to 'Pareto-dominate' the Nash equilibrium outcome: under the former outcome both are better off than under the latter. (Strictly speaking, Pareto-dominance requires only that at least one player be better off while all others are no worse off. 'Pareto' is after nineteenth-century Italian economist/mathematician Vilfredo Pareto.) The reader might want to confirm that, in spite of Pareto-dominance of the cooperative outcome, both prisoners actually have an incentive to turn state's evidence.

Sellers in an oligopolistic market, where entry by new sellers is blocked, might earn the highest profits by cooperating to set total output equal to that which would be offered by a profit-maximizing monopolist and then splitting the resulting monopoly rent. This implies that each firm would be subject to a production quota (that is, that a production quota cartel is established among all sellers). However, if it can do so without being observed, each firm might be able to earn slightly more than its share of the rent by offering some additional output to the market (say, by offering sub-rosa discounts to buyers to get them to switch suppliers and, by doing so, take market share away from rival firms). If all firms believe that they can do this, and simultaneously attempt to implement it, they will drive the market towards a Nash equilibrium that is Pareto-dominated by the cooperative outcome. Thus, a cartelized market can have the characteristics of a prisoner's dilemma.

A central feature of these conditions is that some mode of cooperation must Pareto-dominate a noncooperative Nash equilibrium. A Nash equilibrium is achieved if, for all players, the optimal response to the current move of each player is to continue with the same move.[9] In the classical prisoner's dilemma, the cooperative outcome indeed Pareto-dominates the noncooperative Nash equilibrium (see Box 4.1). But the cooperative outcome is not itself a Nash equilibrium, at least not if the game is only played once, as it is in the classical case. Cooperation breaks down in a classical prisoner's dilemma game because the best response of each player to any move by the other player is to choose not to cooperate, and hence noncooperation by both players is the only Nash equilibrium. The folk theorem demonstrates conditions, however, where cooperation by both players can become a Nash equilibrium. The key to these conditions is that the underlying game be repeated indefinitely so that, if any player deviates from the cooperative outcome now, assured future punishment of that player by the other players will offset any current gains from the deviation. The punishment must be assured and, for this to be the case, it must be in the interests of the nondeviant players actually to execute the punishment if deviation occurs (the formal term for such a punishment condition is 'subgame' (or ε) perfect).[10]

There are a number of variations of the folk theorem (see, for example, Fudenberg and Maskin 1983). The following version, attributable to Friedman (1971), serves the purposes of this chapter:

> If, in an n player game, players do not discount future payoffs and if there exist both a Nash equilibrium and an individually rational strategy (that is, one that Pareto-dominates the maximum 'assured payoff' of each player, for example, the Nash equilibrium), then the individually rational strategy will be a Nash equilibrium in an infinitely repeated game if, in the event of a deviation by j players, j < n, for each player not in the deviating group, the noncooperative Nash equilibrium yields a higher payoff than the deviation.

The 'punishment' is simply for each (nondeviating) player to move immediately to the noncooperative Nash equilibrium. This strategy is subgame perfect because the best response of remaining players to any move other than cooperation by any player will lead to the noncooperative Nash equilibrium anyway.

Let us turn to applying this theorem to multinational firm behavior. Some of the treatment that follows will be formal in nature, and hence some additional terminological conventions are introduced.

We shall, for the sake of simplicity (and with some admitted loss of reality) assume that the world consists of two nations, A and B, each of which is populated initially with only one firm (two firms in total). In this 2x2 world, variables will be subscripted according to the following convention: the first subscript refers to the national market and the second to the home country of the firm. Thus, for example, P_{AA} would refer to the price received by the firm based in country A in the market of this same country.[11] If only a single subscript appears, the variable pertains to the whole national market and not to the firm. Finally, let us assume that demand in each national market is linear (and hence, trivially, invertible). Thus, demand in each of the two markets can be written as

$$P_i = D_i - m_i Q_i \qquad i = A, B$$

where D_i and m_i are constants.

Initially, both firms are monopolists in their home markets. Assume that the marginal cost of production of Firm A is C_A and of Firm B is C_B, where each cost is a constant (but not necessarily equal to the others). Then, as is well known, if both firms maximize profits, they will choose to produce output

$$Q_i = \frac{(D_i - C_i)}{2m_i} \qquad i = A, B$$

and will earn profits

$$\pi_i = \frac{(D_i - C_i)^2}{4m_i} \qquad i = A, B$$

Suppose now that Firm A is not entirely happy with its monopoly in Market A and has its eye on Market B. It believes, in fact, that it can compete successfully in Market B because it has observed that it is more efficient than its rival, that is, that $C_A < C_B$.[12]

If Firm A were to enter market B, it would earn profits equal to:

$$\pi_{BA} = -m_B(Q_{BA}^2 + Q_{BB}Q_{BA}) + (D_B - C_A)Q_{BA}$$

the first order conditions for profit maximization are:

$$\frac{\partial \pi_{BA}}{\partial Q_{BA}} = 0$$

and these yield the so-called 'reaction function' for Firm A:

$$-m_B(Q_{BA}(2 + \frac{\partial Q_{BB}}{\partial Q_{BA}}) + Q_{BB}) + D_B - C_A = 0$$

or

$$Q_{BA} = \frac{\dfrac{1}{m_B}(D_B - C_A) - Q_{BB}}{(2 + \dfrac{\partial Q_{BB}}{\partial Q_{BA}})}$$

This reaction function poses a problem because it is a differential equation in Q_{BB}, where Q_{BB} is an unknown function of Q_{BA}. In terms of the underlying economics, Q_{BB} is in fact the *conjectured* reaction of Firm B to any change in quantity offered by Firm A. To determine an equilibrium solution, it is necessary to solve simultaneously the reaction function of Firm A with that of Firm B, which is given by

$$Q_{BB} = \frac{\dfrac{1}{m_B}(D_B - C_B) - Q_{BA}}{(2 + \dfrac{\partial Q_{BA}}{\partial Q_{BB}})}$$

where now Q_{BA} is a function of Q_{BB}. These equations cannot be solved simply as two simultaneous differential equations because, as noted, the derivative terms reflect each firm's conjecture about how the other firm will react to its quantity changes and this conjecture must be explicitly specified (or, in other words, this conjecture cannot be solved endogenously).

Solution of this pair of equations thus requires some specification of the conjectured response of each firm to the other's quantity adjustments, as reflected in the derivative term. One standard specification is that each firm conjectures that the other firm will in fact do nothing. While this conjecture (known as the Cournot conjecture) violates any reasonable sense of reality, it leads to the convenience that, for purposes of taking the derivative in the two reaction functions, the variables Q_{BA} and Q_{BB} can be treated as constants so that the derivative simply vanishes. Using this assumption, one calculates the equilibrium quantity offered by Firms A and B in Market B to be

$$Q_{BA} = \frac{D_B - 2C_A + C_B}{3m_B}$$

and

$$Q_{BB} = \frac{D_B - 2C_B + C_A}{3m_B}$$

These quantities prevail at the so-called 'Cournot equilibrium', the equilibrium that results if both firms' conjectures are 'Cournot conjectures'.[13] It is easily demonstrated that the Cournot equilibrium is a Nash equilibrium. At this equilibrium, Firm A earns profit in Market B equal to

$$\pi_{BA} = \frac{D_B^2 - 4C_A D_B + 2C_B D_B + 4C_A^2 + C_B^2 - 4C_A C_B}{9m_B}$$

The key questions that arise from a game-theoretic approach are as follows: given a move by Firm A to enter Market B, what is the likely reaction of Firm B, and, given this reaction, will Firm A continue to covet its share of market B? In other words, because the decision of Firm A to expand internationally, that is, to become multinational, depends (in part) on what its rival will do in response, the key issues for Firm A are, first, to assess what is the best response of Firm B to its expansion and, second, to decide whether to undertake this expansion in light of this response. *This point is missed entirely in the transaction cost theory of the firm.*

In fact, it is entirely possible that the strategy 'thou shalt not impinge upon thy rival's monopoly' might be, under the folk theorem, a repeated-game Nash equilibrium that Pareto-dominates the strategy 'Firm A enters Market B and takes part of the rent away from Firm B'. This could be the case if, in response to Firm A's entry into Market B, Firm B were to enter Market A and to force a Cournot equilibrium there. Were this to happen, Firm B's profits in Market A would be equal to:

$$\pi_{AB} = \frac{D_A^2 - 4C_B D_A + 2C_A D_A + 4C_B^2 + C_A^2 - 4C_B C_A}{9m_A}$$

Firm B would have an incentive to proceed with this entry as long as these profits were positive; as a result, subject to the condition of positive profits, entry into Market A is a best response by Firm B to entry into Market B by Firm A.[14] *Thus, counterentry by firm B is a subgame perfect 'punishment strategy' to Firm A's deviation from a cooperative strategy 'thou shalt not impinge upon thy rival's monopoly'.* The profit function is bounded by the constraint that both the price received by Firm B and the quantity sold by it be greater than zero. This implies that $C_B < \pi(D_A + C_A)$. Because

$$\frac{\partial \pi_{BA}}{\partial C_B} = 8C_B - 4(D_A + C_A)$$

for $C_B < \pi(D_A + C_A)$,

$$\frac{\partial \pi_{BA}}{\partial C_B} < 0$$

Thus, Firm B's profits are negatively related to C_B. The higher Firm B's costs, the less likely it is that it could successfully enter Market A, as one might expect.[15]

A major point thus is the following: if Firm B is in fact able to achieve a positive profit by entering Market A, then it has a positive incentive to do so if Firm A has previously entered its home market. *This is true even when, as in this example, $C_B > C_A$.* This in fact demonstrates the point made in the introduction that, for a firm to become international, it is not strictly necessary for that firm to have lower costs than its rivals.[16]

But also: if Firm B does enter Market A in response to Firm A entering Market B, then Firm A loses its monopoly profit in its home market, earning instead only its share of a Cournot profit. If Firm A's (Cournot equilibrium) profit in Market B does not exceed its lost profit in its home market, then, anticipating Firm B's counterattack, it would choose to stay out of Market B altogether. If the 'thou shalt not impinge' strategy (enabling each firm to earn monopoly profits in the home market) Pareto-dominates the 'each shall enter the other's home market and be satisfied with a Cournot profit in both markets', then the conditions of the folk theorem are met because counterentry into Market A by Firm B is, by the above reasoning, a subgame perfect 'punishment strategy' to be implemented in the event that Firm A should break from the 'thou shalt not impinge' strategy. Thus, the situation depicted in this example is, in fact, a special case of a prisoner's dilemma game.

This establishes a second point: just as it is true that it is not necessary that a firm, to become multinational, have lower costs than its rivals, it is also not true that, if a firm does have lower costs, this is a sufficient condition for it to become multinational. *Thus, transaction cost theory provides neither necessary nor sufficient conditions for a firm to become multinational* (although, as will be seen, costs do matter!).

When will Firm A break from this strategy? Letting a superscript m (^{m}) indicate monopoly profit and superscript c (^{c}) indicate profit in a Cournot equilibrium, it is clear that the condition is the following:

$$\pi^m_{AA} - \pi^c_{AA} < \pi^c_{BA}$$

or, equivalently,

$$\rho_A = \frac{\pi^m_{AA} - \pi^c_{AA}}{\pi^c_{BA}} < 1.$$

This expression, when written out, yields the following fairly daunting expression

$$\rho_A = \frac{m_B}{4m_A} - \frac{5D_A^2 - 2D_AC_A - 7C_A^2 - 4C_B^2 + 8C_B(2C_A - D_A)}{(D_B - 2C_A)^2 + C_B^2 - 4C_AC_B + 2C_BD_B} < 1$$

If this condition is met, then Firm A will enter Market B, accepting that Firm B will then enter Market A. Under these circumstances, the conditions for the folk theorem to hold break down. A cooperative solution no longer Pareto-dominates the case where both markets are driven to a Cournot equilibrium. Rather, this latter equilibrium will prevail as the only possible Nash equilibrium. At this equilibrium, Firm A is better off than *ex ante*, but Firm B is unequivocally worse off, even after it makes its best response by entering Market A. It should be noted that, although Firm B is worse off than *ex ante*, consumers in Market B are better off – competition has replaced monopoly. Indeed, the same situation prevails in Market A and, hence, global welfare is enhanced.

Two things immediately follow (and are intuitively obvious):

$$\frac{\partial \rho_A}{\partial D_A} = k_1(10D_A - 8C_B)$$

where k_1 is a constant (and, henceforth, subscripted k's are always constants). Thus, for $D_A > 8C_B$, increasing D_A, the reservation price of the good in Market A, and holding all else equal, will tend to drive the ratio ρ_A down and reduce the likelihood that Firm A will *not* choose to enter Market B. This makes complete intuitive sense because the larger this price, the more a firm has to lose if foreign rivals enter this market and thus the less likely it is that the firm will provoke such entry. Also,

$$\frac{\partial(\dfrac{1}{\rho_A})}{\partial D_B} = k_2(D_B - 2C_A + C_B)$$

This simply says that the higher the reservation price in Market B, the more likely that the ratio ρ_A will be less than one (subject to the constraint $C_A < 1/2$ $(D_B + C_B)$. Again, this is an intuitive result.

The total size of the markets in A and B are a function both of the reservation prices and of the slope of the inverse demand functions, m_A and m_B. A decrease in the value of either of these slopes indicates larger size of the relevant market (the larger the equilibrium of Q_i, $i = A,B$) at any given equilibrium price. Because all profits are constrained to be positive, it is clear that

$$\frac{\partial p_A}{\partial(\frac{m_A}{m_B})} < 0$$

This implies, as one would expect, that the smaller m_A is relative to m_B (and, hence, the larger the demand in Market A relative to demand in Market B at equal prices), the less likely that it will be profitable for Firm A to invest in Market B, if Firm A anticipates a counterinvestment in Market B from Firm B.[17]

How will relative costs affect A's entry strategy? The effects of a change in C_B are unambiguous. Differentiating separately the numerator and denominator of p_A, we get

$$\frac{\partial(\pi^m_{AA} - \pi^c_{AA})}{\partial C_B} = k_3(- C_B + 2C_A - D_A)$$

and

$$\frac{\partial \pi^c_{BA}}{\partial C_B} = k_4(C_B - 2C_A + D_B)$$

Thus, subject to the constraints that $C_A < 0.5(C_B + D_B)$ and $C_A < 0.5(C_B + D_A)$, the following hold:

$$\frac{\partial(\pi^m_{AA} - \pi^c_{AA})}{\partial C_B} < 0$$

and

$$\frac{\partial \pi^c_{BA}}{\partial C_B} > 0$$

and, because an increase in C_B decreases the numerator of p_A but increases the denominator, the result is a decrease in p_A. The constraints are, in fact, conditions that must be met if Firm A is to participate at all in the two markets; if the constraints are not met, firm A's profits would be negative and the exercise moot. Hence, as one would intuitively expect, the higher C_B, all else being equal, the more likely that Firm A will enter Market B. This result is, of course, consistent with transaction cost theory.

A problem arises, however, when one considers effects of changes in C_A. This is that the lower C_A, the higher will be Firm A's profits in Market B but also the greater will be its losses if it must abandon its monopoly position in Market A. To get the effects of a change of C_A on profits in Market B by differentiating the denominator of ρ_A with respect to C_A, we get

$$\frac{\partial \pi^c_{AB}}{\partial C_A} = k_5(-D_B - 2C_A - C_B)$$

and hence, subject to the same constraint as the first in the paragraph above, a decrease in C_A will cause this denominator to increase, raising the likelihood that Firm A will enter Market B. This result of course is expected.

However, differentiating the numerator of ρ_A yields

$$\frac{\partial(\pi^m_{AA} - \pi^c_{AA})}{\partial C_A} = k_6(8C_B - 7C_A - D_A)$$

If this expression were unambiguously positive, the net result would be that a decrease in Firm A's costs would always increase Firm A's total profits in the event that it invested in Market B relative to the profits of staying at home. As can be seen, however, the expression is positive only if $8C_B > (D_A + 7C_A)$. This is in fact a likely condition (if, as required, $C_B < 0.5(D_A + C_A)$, the former condition would imply that $C_A > 0.5D_A$, a condition under which Firm A is driven out of Market A if Firm B enters the market.

Thus, considering separately the effects of a change in C_A on the numerator and denominator of ρ_A yields an ambiguous result. One alternative, of course, is to examine the derivative of ρ_A as a whole with respect to C_A, but even a cursory inspection of ρ_A when written out reveals that this will result in many terms that will be difficult to evaluate. Proceeding nonetheless and designating as U the terms in the numerator of ρ_A to the right of the m_i's and as V the corresponding terms in the denominator v and noting the identity

$$d(\frac{U}{V}) = \frac{VdU - UdV}{V^2}$$

then, because we are only interested in the sign of $d\rho_A/dC_A$, the first thing to note is that we only need to consider the derivative terms in the identity, because the terms involving the m_i's and V^2 are unambiguously positive and so do not affect the sign. Alas, the derivative terms involve a plethora of cross-products, simplification of which is impossible:

$$V\frac{\partial U}{\partial C_A} - U\frac{\partial V}{\partial C_A} = 2C_A D_A D_B - 5D_A^2 D_B - 21C_A^2 D_B - 12C_B^2 D_B$$
$$+ 30C_A C_B D_B + 4C_A D_A D_B + 10C_A D + 15C_A C_B^2$$
$$- 21C_A^2 C_B - 18C_A C_B D_A - 5C_B D_A^2 - 4C_B^3 + 9C_B^2 D_A$$
$$- 8C_B D_B^2 + 7C_A D_B^2 + D_A D_B^2 + 2C_B D_A$$

So, all that can be said is that, if specific values of the four variables are known, Firm A can easily decide whether or not entry into Market B will raise or lower total profits by calculating ρ_A. But a simple rule for determining whether a reduction in C_A will raise or lower these total profits is not possible. One is left with evaluating specific situations.

Thus, several specific cases are illustrated in Tables 4.1 to 4.4.

Table 4.1 indicates values of ρ_A for $D_A = D_B = 100$, $m_A = m_B$, where C_A and C_B are both allowed to vary from 1 to 10. Firm A will enter Market B if and only if C_B is high and C_A is simultaneously low. The results here are completely consistent with transaction cost theory.

Tables 4.2 and 4.3 examine the effects of a change in relative sizes of the two markets under the same cost configurations as shown in Table 4.1. Thus, for example, $m_A = 0.25m_B$, so that at any price demand in A is four times greater than in B, all values of ρ_A are multiplied by four and at no cost combination is ρ_A less than unity – hence, at none of the cost configurations will Firm A enter Market B at all. In this situation, market-size effects completely swamp cost effects, and the results are not consistent with pure transaction

Table 4.1   *Effects on rhoA of changes in C_A and C_B ($D_A = D_B = 100$,*
               $m_A = m_B$)

C_A C_B	1	2	3	4	5	6	7	8	9	10
1	1.25	1.21	1.16	1.12	1.08	1.04	1.00	0.96	0.93	0.89
2	1.30	1.25	1.20	1.16	1.12	1.08	1.04	1.00	0.96	0.92
3	1.35	1.30	1.25	1.20	1.16	1.12	1.08	1.03	1.00	0.96
4	1.40	1.35	1.30	1.25	1.20	1.16	1.12	1.07	1.03	0.09
5	1.45	1.40	1.35	1.30	1.25	1.20	1.16	1.13	1.07	1.03
6	1.51	1.45	1.40	1.35	1.30	1.25	1.20	1.16	1.11	1.07
7	1.57	1.51	1.46	1.40	1.35	1.30	1.25	1.20	1.16	1.11
8	1.64	1.57	1.52	1.46	1.40	1.35	1.30	1.25	1.20	1.16
9	1.70	1.64	1.58	1.52	1.46	1.41	1.35	1.30	1.25	1.20
10	1.78	1.71	1.65	1.58	1.52	1.46	1.41	1.35	1.30	1.25

Source: Author's calculations.

Table 4.2 *Effects on rhoA of changes in C_A and C_B ($D_A = D_B = 100$, $m_A = 0.25m_B$)*

C_A C_B	1	2	3	4	5	6	7	8	9	10
1	5.00	4.82	4.65	4.48	4.31	4.16	4.00	3.85	3.70	3.56
2	5.19	5.00	4.82	4.64	4.47	4.31	4.15	3.99	3.84	3.69
3	5.38	5.19	5.00	4.82	4.64	4.47	4.30	4.14	3.98	3.83
4	5.59	5.39	5.19	5.00	4.82	4.64	4.46	4.29	4.13	3.97
5	5.81	5.60	5.39	5.19	5.00	4.81	4.63	4.46	4.29	4.12
6	6.04	5.82	5.60	5.40	5.19	5.00	4.81	4.63	4.45	4.28
7	6.28	6.05	5.83	5.61	5.40	5.20	5.00	4.81	4.63	4.48
8	6.54	6.30	6.06	5.84	5.62	5.40	5.20	5.00	4.81	4.62
9	6.82	6.50	6.32	6.08	5.85	5.62	5.41	5.20	5.00	4.81
10	7.11	6.84	6.58	6.33	6.09	5.86	5.63	5.41	5.20	5.00

Source: Author's calculations.

Table 4.3 *Effects on rhoA of changes in C_A and C_B ($D_A = D_B = 100$, $m_A = 4m_B$)*

C_A C_B	1	2	3	4	5	6	7	8	9	10
1	0.31	0.30	0.29	0.28	0.27	0.26	0.25	0.24	0.23	0.22
2	0.32	0.31	0.30	0.29	0.28	0.27	0.26	0.25	0.24	0.23
3	0.34	0.32	0.31	0.30	0.29	0.28	0.27	0.26	0.25	0.24
4	0.35	0.34	0.32	0.31	0.30	0.29	0.28	0.27	0.26	0.25
5	0.36	0.35	0.34	0.32	0.31	0.30	0.29	0.28	0.27	0.26
6	0.38	0.36	0.35	0.34	0.32	0.31	0.30	0.29	0.28	0.27
7	0.39	0.38	0.36	0.35	0.34	0.32	0.31	0.30	0.29	0.28
8	0.41	0.39	0.38	0.36	0.35	0.34	0.32	0.31	0.30	0.29
9	0.43	0.41	0.39	0.38	0.37	0.36	0.34	0.33	0.31	0.30
10	0.44	0.43	0.41	0.40	0.38	0.37	0.35	0.34	0.33	0.31

Source: Author's calculations.

cost theory.[18] If the reverse is true, $m_B = 0.25m_A$, then Market B is the bigger and all values of ρ_A are divided by 4. Then, at any cost combination, including ones where $C_A > C_B$, Firm A enters Market B (the results are shown in Table 4.3). Again, market-size effects dominate cost effects.

Table 4.4 indicates the result where there is a large divergence in reservation prices; here $D_A = 10D_B$. The result is again that Firm A would not at any cost combination invest in Market B. Interestingly, unlike in the previous three

Table 4.4   *Effects on rhoA of changes in C_A and C_B (D_A = 100, D_B = 1000, $m_A = m_B$)*

C_A C_B	1	2	3	4	5	6	7	8	9	10
1	0.0123	0.0121	0.0118	0.0116	0.0114	0.0111	0.0109	0.0107	0.0105	0.0102
2	0.0123	0.0121	0.0118	0.0116	0.0114	0.0112	0.0109	0.0107	0.0105	0.0102
3	0.0123	0.0121	0.0118	0.0116	0.0114	0.0112	0.0109	0.0107	0.0105	0.0103
4	0.0123	0.0120	0.0118	0.0116	0.0114	0.0112	0.0110	0.0107	0.0105	0.0103
5	0.0122	0.0120	0.0118	0.0116	0.0114	0.0112	0.0110	0.0107	0.0105	0.0103
6	0.0122	0.0120	0.0118	0.0116	0.0114	0.0112	0.0110	0.0108	0.0105	0.0103
7	0.0122	0.0120	0.0118	0.0116	0.0113	0.0112	0.0110	0.0108	0.0105	0.0103
8	0.0122	0.0120	0.0118	0.0116	0.0114	0.0112	0.0110	0.0108	0.0150	0.0103
9	0.0122	0.0120	0.0118	0.0116	0.0114	0.0112	0.0110	0.0107	0.0105	0.0103
10	0.0121	0.0119	0.0117	0.0115	0.0113	0.0111	0.0109	0.0107	0.0105	0.0103

Source: Author's calculations.

cases, in this case, for low values of C_B, the value of ρ_A rises with declining C_A, indicating the complex relationship between these two variables: although at all combinations of cost Firm A would invest in Market B, the additional profits from making this investment decline with decreasing cost rather than increase.

The model as presented is very basic and simple, and it of course does not capture reality fully. Thus, while the scenario depicted in Table 4.1 conforms to empirical evidence (and to transaction cost theory), the scenarios depicted in Tables 4.2 and 4.3 do not. Indeed, these scenarios do not seem to explain why, when ones examines the massive flows of foreign direct investment that have occurred in the past forty years or so, firms based in the United States were, with few exceptions, the first to invest on a global scale. The model in fact would seem to predict that US firms, because of the large size of the home market, should not be 'first movers' in this regard.

There are, however, a number of possible explanations that can reconcile this apparent discrepancy between empirical observation and reality.[19] One such explanation is that the sheer scale of the US domestic market has historically accorded to US firms cost advantages borne of experience from operating on such a scale, and that such advantages dominate market-size effects. Also, although the US market, when compared to any other single national market, was very large (especially during the relevant time period, about thirty to forty years ago), US firms might have considered 'Market B' not to be that of another single nation but in fact most of the non-US world. Hence, perhaps market-size effects worked as predicted by this model, in spite of the large size of the US home market. Yet another possibility derives from the fact that, prior to entry by foreign firms, US markets are not monopolistic, as assumed in the model. In fact, most US firms that have become multinational have originated as sellers in markets in the US home market that are oligopolistic (Knickerbocker 1973). In such markets, the amount of profit per firm to be lost in the event of entry by a foreign multinational (or multinationals) would be less than if one firm monopolized the whole market.

Furthermore, the model presented here assumes perfect information, but this might not hold; for example, Firm A might not know for certain Firm B's costs. The assumption of a Cournot conjecture is almost surely wrong and is made for ease of calculation and exposition, not because it captures reality. And other criticisms are easily leveled. Doubtlessly, for example, there would be sunk costs of entry into non-home markets (see next section) that this model does not account for.

Thus, it is easy to think of extensions of the model. One example has already been explored by this author, that is, the case where, when a firm makes a *de novo* entry into a market there are time lags required for both the building of market share and for rivals to react. If profits are discounted, the first will cause would-be entrants to be more hesitant while the second will cause them to be more bold. The folk theorem might still apply, but the equilibria might be different than envisaged in the model above. For example, one outcome that could Pareto-dominate the Cournot equilibrium under these circumstances would be for the two firms jointly to monopolize the market. If market share is built slowly, there will be a threshold market share below which a new entrant will compete aggressively, because at low market share the joint appropriation of monopoly rent does not Pareto-dominate the Cournot equilibrium. But, above this share, the joint appropriation does Pareto-dominate and hence the conditions for the folk theorem (Friedman variant) do hold.[20] This approach could help to explain why, in many instances, multinational firms when entering a new market quickly build market share to a point beyond which market share stabilizes.

PRECOMMITMENT COSTS AND THE PRISONER'S DILEMMA

Veugelers (1995) presents a variant of the two-market, two-firm model described above where, in order to become multinational, each firm must precommit to a sunk cost interpreted as an R&D cost 'to build advantages which can be capitalized in international markets' (p. 48). This precommitment thus is in the spirit of transaction cost theory; the idea is that to create ownership-specific advantages in the spirit of Dunning (1988), the firm must commit resources. 'Precommitment' means that the decision is made before each firm knows what its rival is going to do, the rival being faced with the same opportunity and decision. By committing to the R&D cost, the firm increases its profits in the home market; in the formal model, this is achieved via achievement of 'scope advantages' that causes (using notation consistent with that of the previous section) an enlargement of the D_i parameter ('reservation price') associated with demand in each market. The scope advantages can be captured in the home market as well as the foreign market; indeed, transaction costs reduce the realized gains from the scope advantages for both firms in the foreign market. Thus, one outcome is that either or both firms choose to sink resources into the R&D but nonetheless choose to stay at home.

Four outcomes then are possible in terms of market cross-penetration: both firms choose to stay at home, both firms enter each other's market (note that in this framework, the decision to enter is taken simultaneously and, unlike in the previous section, this decision is not taken as a best response to the other's previous entrance), Firm A enters Market B, while Firm B stays at home, and Firm B enters Market A, while Firm A stays at home. In the event that a market is not entered by the foreign firm, the outcome in this market is that the home firm has a monopoly, whereas if such entrance does occur, the outcome is the Cournot equilibrium.

Veugelers is able to show that, under certain conditions, a prisoner's dilemma can arise where both firms will enter each other's market but where this outcome is Pareto-dominated by both firms staying at home. However, the formal framework is essentially a two-period one, where in the first period each firm chooses to commit or not commit to the sunk cost and in the second period each firm either does or does not enter the other's market. Thus, there is no formal appeal to the folk theorem, arguably a fatal weakness in the approach. Veugelers nonetheless appeals implicitly to the folk theorem, arguing that 'through the threat of reciprocal entry, the local outcome can be established as the stable configuration, at least if firms are sufficiently patient' (p. 52).[21]

Veugelers discusses but does not analyse formally a possible extension of this model, one that arguably would make it significantly more interesting. This is the case where the precommitment can be made sequentially rather than simultaneously. This would be of most interest if one firm could, by precommitting, achieve some sort of 'first mover' advantage over the other that would foreclose options to the second firm. Such a model would be of most interest in a context of imperfect or incomplete information (otherwise, the incentive to both firms to precommit would be increased, leading to prisoner's dilemma outcomes once again). However, this extension, on a formal basis, is undone.

SUMMARY AND CONCLUSIONS

The formal analysis as presented here requires, as is often the case, simplification in order to keep the mathematics to a manageable level. Often, the cost of such simplification is that elements of reality are lost, and the analysis here is not an exception to this general rule. However, it is also true that, in spite of this loss, the formal analysis is capable of adding insights that are missed in a more descriptive type of analysis. And, when compared to the results of transaction cost theory, which largely is a descriptive analysis, the game-theoretic approach here does quite well by this last test. In particular, transaction cost theory, taken to its *reductio ad absurdum*, would seem to imply a world in which every major global market is dominated by a single monopolist or by, at most, a few very large sellers – those firms that had succeeded in achieving the lowest systemic costs of selling to the relevant market worldwide. This *reductio ad absurdum* does not exist. The United Nations' World Investment Report (UNCTAD 1997) suggests that worldwide, there exist thousands of firms that are multinational, far more than the number of meaningful markets. In most major markets (as measured by product or industry classification, admittedly a rather imprecise measure) there are at least ten, and often many more, multinational firms of significant size. Decreased seller concentration over time, rather than increased concentration, has been the dominant trend.

Although the theory as developed is far from complete, a game-theoretic approach does yield an important insight into why this is occurring. What is key to this insight is that a firm simply does not have to be a low-cost seller in order to have an incentive to become multinational, nor is being a low-cost seller a necessary precondition in order for a firm to become multinational. This is not, of course, to say that a low-cost seller has no advantages over its rivals. It clearly does and, as suggested in the analysis that is presented here, those advantages might indeed cause it to be a 'first-mover', that is, to be the pioneer that first ventures out of its home market. But what follows from this first step can be a reaction on the part of rivals that has much less to do with these firms' efforts to exploit their own proprietary advantages than their efforts to keep the pioneer from gaining even more advantage, and this reaction can entail foreign investment.

In the end, then, a game-theoretic approach is not an alternative to transaction cost theory. Rather, a game-theoretic approach is a very rich supplement, one that can provide theoretical underpinnings to phenomena that are actually observed in the real world but that are not well explained by transaction cost theory. As such, application of game theory to multinational firm behavior deserves more emphasis than it has so far received.

NOTES

1. Copyright © 1998 Institute for International Economics
2. Virtually all of these have appeared since 1989; the vast majority (over 90 per cent) of the references in Caves are to articles that appeared prior to 1989. Some of the recent items include Graham (1990) and Veugelers (1995). Incomplete reviews are contained in Onida (1995) and Graham (1996).
3. The word 'new' is contained in quotation marks because in fact these 'new' theories are now approaching adulthood; the relevant literature began appearing about twenty years ago.
4. This is not to say that transaction costs theory is wholly inappropriate to MNE behavior; indeed, as is argued later in this article, it is of some considerable validity. The point is that this theory leaves out some important considerations. Transaction cost theory, as applied to MNEs, was first prominently placed into the literature by Buckley and Casson (1976). See also Dunning (1988).
5. Indeed, empirical work by Knickerbocker (1973) would suggest that competing firms in major industries tend to make foreign direct investments in lock step. Not all competing firms can have costs lower than their rivals simultaneously, and hence Knickerbocker's empirical observations should cast doubt on the strict necessity of lower transaction costs as a prerequisite for multinational investment.
6. This latter situation is analysed by cooperative game theory.
7. Some of the results of this section have appeared in Graham (1990).
8. It is called the 'folk theorem' because the central result was well known among game theorists as long ago as the 1950s, and a significant literature had accumulated by the middle 1970s, but no one seems to know who was the first person to formulate this result. Thus, the theorem belongs to the 'folklore' of modern game theory but it is attributed to no single person. The term 'folk theorem' first appears in Auman (1981). An early version of the theorem is found, but not by this name, in Luce and Raiffa (1957).
9. 'Move' in this instance is used in the sense of a 'move' in a chess game but with one important difference: to do nothing is also a permissable 'move'. Thus, for example, in the context of a 'game' where individual players sell in a market, a 'move' by an individual player might consist of a change in the quantity of product offered by that player. In this context, a Nash equilibrium (after American mathematician John Nash, who invented the concept during the 1950s) is attained if, taking into account the likely response of each other player, every player decides not to change this quantity.
10. There is a small difference between subgame perfect and ε perfect. See Selten (1975).
11. This convention was introduced in Casson (1987), Chapter 3.
12. In what follows, sunk costs of entry are ignored, a safe assumption if neither firm discounts future profits. More realistically, of course, a necessary condition for entry would be that expected discounted future profits from entry exceed any sunk cost of entry. It should be noted that entry by Firm A into Market B is consistent with transaction cost theory.
13. A lot of time and energy have been devoted to showing that the Cournot equilibrium prevails under a variety of (generally implausible) circumstances, for example, the oft-cited result of Kreps and Scheinkman (1983) that if, in a two-period game, firms fix capacity in the first period and then maximize profits in the second period using a 'Bertrand' conjecture, the result is a Cournot equilibrium. At the end of the day, however, theorists probably should accept the fact that the Cournot conjecture is employed out of frustration with the mathematical difficulties that arise from use of any more realistic conjecture. The term 'Cournot equilibrium' is after early nineteenth-century French mathematician and economist Augustin Cournot.
14. Again, if there were sunk costs of entry and Firm B discounted future profits, there would be an incentive only if the present value of these profits exceeded the sunk costs.
15. And conversely, the lower C_B, the more likely it is it will earn a profit. For a very large D_A it is in fact conceivable that Firm B might wish to enter Market A even in the absence of Firm A's entry into Market B. We shall simply assume that D_A is not this large.
16. There is quite a lot of empirical evidence that cross-investment does occur and that it is in

response to earlier investment in a firm's home markets by rival firms from other nations. See Graham (1978) and Encarnation (1987).

17. One way of viewing this outcome is that, in this instance, FDI is driven by the 'L' component of Dunning's 'OLI' paradigm, indeed so much so that the 'O' and 'I' components become moot. See Dunning (1988).

18. But, again, in this case and in the next, it could be argued that the results are consistent with Dunning's 'OLI' framework, with 'L' effects dominating 'O' and 'I' effects.

19. Exactly why US firms were pioneers in this regard is explored by Vernon (1966 and 1974).

20. A formal analysis is presented in Graham (1990).

21. Veugelers seems to have missed that an earlier article by me (Graham 1990) makes exactly the same point but more formally!

REFERENCES

Auman, Robert J. (1981), 'Survey of repeated games', in R.J. Auman et al. (eds), *Essays in Game Theory*, Mannheim, Germany: Bibliographisches Institut.

Buckley, Peter J., and Mark C. Casson (1976), *The Future of the Multinational Enterprise*, London: Macmillan.

Casson, Mark C. (1987), *The Firm and the Market*, Cambridge, MA: The MIT Press.

Caves, Richard E. (1996), *Multinational Enterprise and Economic Analysis*, 2nd edition, Cambridge, UK: Cambridge University Press. First edition 1982.

Dunning, John H. (1988), 'The eclectic paradigm of international production: A restatement and some possible extensions', *Journal of International Business Studies*, **19**, pp. 1–31.

Encarnation, Dennis (1987), 'Cross-investment: A second front of economic rivalry', *California Management Review*, **29** (2), pp. 20–48.

Fudenberg, D., and E. Maskin (1983), 'The folk theorem in repeated games with discounting or with incomplete information', *Econometrica*, **54** (3), pp. 533–54.

Friedman, James W. (1971), 'A noncooperative equilibrium for supergames', *Review of Economic Studies*, **38** (1), pp. 1–12.

Graham, Edward M. (1978), 'Transatlantic investment by multinational firms: A rivalistic phenonemon?', *Journal of Post-Keynesian Economics*, **1**, pp. 82–99.

Graham, Edward M. (1990), 'Exchange of threat between multinational firms as an infinitely repeated noncooperative game', *International Trade Journal*, **4** (3), pp. 259–77.

Graham, Edward M. (1996), 'The not wholly satisfactory state of the theory of foreign direct investment and the multinational enterprise', *Economic Systems*, **20**, pp. 183–206.

Hymer, Stephen (1976), *The International Operations of National Firms*, Cambridge, MA: The MIT Press.

Jacquemin, Alexis (1989), 'International and multinational strategic behavior', *Kyklos*, **42**, pp. 495–514.

Knickerbocker, Frederick T. (1973), *Oligopolistic Reaction and Multinational Enterprise*, Boston: The Harvard Business School Press.

Luce, R.D., and H. Raiffa (1957), *Games and Decisions*, New York: John Wiley and Sons.

Kreps, D., and J. Scheinkman (1983), 'Quantity precommitment and Bertrand Competition yield Cournot outcomes', *Bell Journal of Economics*, **14**, pp. 326–37.

Krugman, Paul R. (1990), *Rethinking International Trade*, Cambridge, MA: The MIT Press.

Onida, Fabrizio (1989), 'Multinational firms, international competition, and oligopolistic rivalry: theoretical trends', *Revista di Politica Economica* (3rd series), **79**, pp. 79–138.

Selten, R. (1975), 'Reexamination of the perfectness concept for equilibrium points in extensive games', *International Journal of Game Theory*, **4**, pp. 25–55.

Tirole, Jean (1988), *The Theory of Industrial Organization*, Cambridge, MA: The MIT Press.

Vernon, Raymond (1966), 'International trade and investment in the product cycle', *Quarterly Journal of Economics*, **80**, pp. 190–207.

United Nations Conference on Trade and Development (UNCTAD) (1997), *World Investment Report*, Geneva: United Nations.

Vernon, Raymond (1966), 'International trade and investment in the product cycle', *Quarterly Journal of Economics*, **80**, pp. 190–207.

Vernon, Raymond (1974), 'The location of industry', in J.H. Dunning (ed.), *Economic Analysis and the Multinational Enterprise*. London: George Allen and Unwin.

Veugelers, Reinhilde (1995), 'Strategic incentives for multinational operations', *Managerial and Decision Economics*, **16**, pp. 47–57.

5. Multinational enterprise and economic analysis: technology and productivity

Sylvia Ostry

INTRODUCTION

The 1996 edition of Richard Caves' *Multinational Enterprise and Economic Analysis* provides an excellent summary of both the theoretical and the empirical literature stemming from the transaction costs model. This template is particularly relevant to the technology issue since at the heart of the firm-versus-market concept is knowledge, and the raison d'être of the multiplant and multinational enterprise is rooted in the fundamental flaws in markets for intangible assets. But, of course, adherence to any template – which, by definition, is restricted to 'key' variables – will exclude both issues and literature that do not fit into the master design. As these issues proliferate the question naturally arises as to whether the basic theory can or should be adapted. This paper will not attempt to grapple with the theoretical questions but rather try to summarize some of the analytical and empirical work related to knowledge production and dissemination which highlights the inadequacy of the transaction costs approach. Research in this area is severely hampered by data gaps, not a novel complaint, of course, but arguably more acute here than in other fields, so some suggestions will be made with respect to data and research proposals. Better data, more empirical analysis and more analysis of the inadequacies of the basic model could, of course, lead to adaptive improvements (incremental innovation) or even a dramatic breakthrough in the form of a new model. But there is a long way to go and whether by 2020 there will be a new or significantly improved version of the firm-versus-markets concept is – like all innovation – beset by uncertainty.

Finally, because the traditional approach virtually ignores the interaction between multinationals and governments in the policy process this chapter will also briefly review some of the key policy issues, which will arise in the trade–investment–technology nexus. The future role of the multinational enterprises (MNEs) in policy is likely to be even greater and more pervasive than it was in the past two decades, in part because of the significant changes in international markets which began in the second half of the 1980s.

GLOBALIZATION

Almost precisely at the time the Uruguay Round, the eighth round of multi-lateral trade negotiations since the GATT was established nearly half a century earlier, was launched in September 1986 to develop new rules for the international economy, the international economy was beginning a process of dramatic transformation. The term 'globalization' was first used in 1986 and was spawned by the investment surge of the second half of the decade which involved all the leading countries of the OECD and not, as in the earlier postwar period, just the USA. Most of it was in capital- and technology-intensive sectors. Hence technology flows (as captured from the very inadequate measure of royalties and fees) also exploded, increasing from an annual negative growth rate of 0.1 to 22 per cent between the first and the second half of the decade. After a slowdown in the early 1990s (because of recession in the OECD countries) investment flows started to pick up again, but this time with a difference. No longer overwhelmingly dominated by the OECD countries of the triad of Europe, Japan and the USA, non-OECD countries, especially in East Asia, are now increasingly important host and home countries. Further, a 'new form' of investment, strategic technology alliances (STAs), also proliferated during the 1980s and 1990s (see below).

The growing importance of foreign investment is highlighted by a few facts. In 1995 worldwide sales of foreign affiliates were over $6 trillion, 30 per cent higher than world exports. Between 1985 and 1995, investment outflows increased by nearly 20 per cent, twice the growth rate of exports or output. The total global stock almost quadrupled: from $679 billion in 1985 it rose to $2.7 trillion in 1995. Further increases, albeit at more moderate rates, were evident in 1996 (UNCTAD 1997, p. 4).

Trade and investment are increasingly being linked. For the MNE, entry by trade and investment is becoming essential to 'effective' market access as corporations seek to capture economies of scale and scope, customize products to satisfy consumer tastes, generate sophisticated, high-quality inter- and intra-corporate networks and strive to gain access to knowledge, both technology and tacit, which may be accessible only on-site.

This linkage between trade and investment is illustrated by data on intra-firm trade. An estimated one-quarter of exports are intra-firm but that global average is far higher for capital and technology-intensive industries. Thus for the USA, nearly half of manufacturing exports and over 60 per cent of imports flow within the firm. Once licensing and royalty payments, as well as franchising fees are taken into account, a recent estimate for the USA suggests that 80 per cent of earnings for goods and services sold abroad are linked to the activities of American multinationals (UNCTAD 1995, p. 38).

Most of the intra-firm trade is in intermediate goods and, as suggested above, reflects the creation of vertical intra- or inter-firm global networks which link different parts of the value-added chain. Even within service industries, rapid developments in information and communication technologies (ICT) have increased tradability and enabled firms to allocate portions of the production process to foreign affiliates. With international rivalry intensifying, global integration of production will grow as firms seek to capture the economies of geographic diversification. Their ability to do so is enhanced by the ongoing revolution in ICT, which is both an enabling factor and a driver (about which more below) and by the significant reduction of border barriers resulting from successive rounds of trade negotiations. Moreover, in industrial sectors where product customization is essential for market penetration, horizontal integration, which involves geographic differentiation of products, is now of growing importance, especially in the rich industrialized countries of the OECD.

Thus if we think of linkages between countries in terms of successive stages of global integration, first, the postwar linkages have been strengthened by successive rounds of trade liberalization which have reduced the border barriers of interwar protectionism and, in the case of the Uruguay Round, launched a shift of policy focus from border barriers to domestic regulatory policies and institutions. The second stage was the linkage by vastly increased financial flows spurred by the recycling of the OPEC surpluses of the 1970s and the wave of deregulation of the 1980s. The third is investment-led globalization which is leading to global production networks and far deeper integration of the global economy.

Arguably, a fourth stage is now visible with the emergence of electronic commerce on the Internet, strengthening the argument that the ICT revolution is 'the biggest technological juggernaut that ever rolled' (Freeman and Soete p. 44).[1] At each successive stage of integration the ubiquity and influence of MNEs has increased. However, given the low barriers to entry for information-related services the advent of electronic commerce could change this structure in these business sectors.

Just as these investment patterns suggest the emergence of new locational strategies, the rapid growth of technology alliances since the mid-1980s points to changes in knowledge production strategies. While data are scarce and patchy, one source documents an increase in technology alliances in the fields of information, biotechnology and new materials from a mere handful in the 1970s to an average annual increase of over 200 since the mid-1980s (Hagedoorn 1996, pp. 173–98). These partnerships have a variety of contractual or equity arrangements and different organizational structures. A number of studies beginning at the end of the 1980s[2] suggest that the most important background factors explaining the emergence of these 'new forms' of knowledge investment have been the increased range of scientific and technological knowledge required in high-tech innovation; the global spread of knowledge; the consequent need for global monitoring of both knowledge and new product markets; and the acceleration of product life cycles: in other words, factors which span the full range of the innovation trajectory from basic science to product development. Given the inherent uncertainty of the innovation process, as well as the rising costs and risks of increasingly complex R&D investment, a more flexible mode of knowledge production and appropriation was clearly preferable to the traditional merger and acquisition mode: hence the inter-firm alliance. While the vast majority of alliances are among firms from developed countries, by the early 1990s the participation of developing-country firms has become evident (UNCTAD 1997, p. 14).

In addition to these strategic technology alliances, which are private sector partnerships, government-sponsored research consortia also proliferated during the 1980s and 1990s.[3] Favored by the Japanese as a form of industrial policy in the postwar period, consortia were later adopted by the USA and Europeans in large part as a response to the Japanese. The theoretical rationale for the consortia was to increase private sector incentives to investment in R&D by 'internalizing' the externalities within the consortium and thus increasing the rate of return to the individual firm. A recent (first) large-sample econometric study of Japanese firm-level data lends some support to the theory (Branstetter and Sukakibara 1997). But a wide range of other studies have been inconclusive or have demonstrated the key importance for international partnering of factors such as firm-specific complementary capabilities, arguing for a resource-based model as more appropriate for understanding these management strategies (Mowery, Oxley and Silverman 1996). Clearly much more research – and much better data – is required since consortia are likely to remain a favored policy not only in OECD countries but also in East Asia and other regions. Some key questions remain unanswered, including the impact of program design (for example, vertical or horizontal linkage); the extent and nature of variation by country, technology and industry category; and the nature of knowledge diffusion among firms. These issues, of course, will determine the motivation of the firm which must weigh the costs and benefits of joining or not joining. In some countries the decision to opt out could be costly in terms of market access for example, or, as in China, where the key knowledge in many alliances will not be science or technology but *guanxi* or the right connections with the political powers. This will often require significant investment in 'foreign policy' and a new intangible asset we could call 'corporate diplomacy'. Consortia also raise a number of contentious policy issues of which the most significant for MNE competitiveness is the status of foreign subsidiaries as candidates for inclusion (Ostry 1996, p. 141–75).

An account of these developments in the international economy since the

1980s would not be complete without noting a broader aspect of networking (as it is sometimes called) which goes beyond technology. Technology partnering reflects a response to increased international competition based not on price but on innovation. The spread of a wide variety of (non-R&D) cross-border agreements among firms based in different countries as either substitutes for or complements to traditional FDI increased fourfold between 1990 and 1995 (UNCTAD 1997, p. 12). There is, again, a serious paucity of data but longer-term series suggest an acceleration of growth in what have been termed international corporate alliances (ICAs) since the mid-1980s. Some smaller firms in low- and medium-tech sectors are using sophisticated information technology to coordinate regional production networks which permit more flexible and rapid response to demand. These new types of network seem to be growing most rapidly in the overseas Chinese firms of East Asia (Fung 1997). Serious data inadequacies have precluded any rigorous empirical analysis and an unresolved debate about the significance of these developments is likely to continue. Some have argued that ICAs represent a new generic form of 'network firm' which combines elements of markets and hierarchies while others defend the traditional transaction costs model which provides for licensing or joint ventures under specified circumstances (Buckley and Casson 1996). The debate (which has implications for both firm strategies and government policies) is unlikely to be resolved in the absence of a better information base.

INSIDE THE BLACK BOX?

As the preceding section demonstrates, there is growing evidence from various sources that MNEs from both OECD and non-OECD countries are in the course of developing new locational and capabilities strategies. These strategies are presumably linked to enhancement of the innovation capabilities of the MNE but precisely how is by no means clear. For example, MNE strategies seem to be differentiated at least by: home country origin (Japanese firms in electronics have strategies in East Asia different from those of American or Overseas Chinese firms (Ostry Chapter 5); many Asian firms follow tactics and strategies that 'turn textbook management thinking on its head' (Williamson 1997); by generic technology category (pharmaceutical firms do not choose location or strategic alliances in the same way as information technology firms) (Hagedoorn 1996); host country location (Supapol 1995 Siddarthan and Safarian 1997); and by broad industry category, for example, manufacturing versus services (Grosse 1996). But mostly these differences are demonstrated *ex post*, as it were, by macro data of varying reliability and inadequate coverage and a small number of case studies. Are these differences compatible with the standard model? The answer should be 'don't know'. Case studies are extremely useful in providing insights – for example, the impact of host country policies on technology transfer modalities of foreign subsidiaries[4] – but the problem of integrating these studies in order to assess the current model or any of the current alternate contenders hardly needs underlining. The black box remains basically black except when a replicate interior is designed by economists. Nonetheless, research on a number of the 'don't knows' cited here is worth a brief review to demonstrate that better links between micro and macro aspects of technological change are being explored in both empirical and theoretical work.

The impact of the home country environment on a firm's competitive advantages ('core competencies' in some management literature) has been attributed to the so-called Porter diamond (Porter 1990), that is, access to resources and assets; consumer demand; inter-firm competition; linkages with foreign or domestic firms and institutions. The Porter approach ignores the impact on the capabilities of the MNE derived from global scope and has been augmented by a 'double-diamond' concept (Rugman 1993; Rugman, Van der Broeke and Verbeke 1995) which embraces the host country environment as well. In a recent survey of MNE executives, John Dunning provides new empirical information on the home/host country links (Dunning 1996). An important finding of the survey is that foreign-based activities are a source of competitive advantage of the leading MNEs and likely to increase in significance in this regard. Since most studies of MNEs have concentrated on technology diffusion, this study is important in underlining that with the ongoing spread of knowledge – technoglobalism – the MNE is a two-way funnel for technology, and global strategies will increasingly reflect this linkage between location and capabilities.

While transnationality was significant (by way of either FDI or strategic alliances), the survey results supported the 'home link' view that the primary source of innovation capabilities stemmed from home country features such as high-quality human capital and innovation-related infrastructure (the categorizations used were highly generalized) and it is not possible to know in a survey of this type how they were interpreted by the respondents.[5] In addition, while the findings more or less accord with the transaction-costs approach, one result was intriguingly out of line. Firms in high technology sectors, which would be expected to prefer FDI to either non-equity or arm's-length transactions (because transaction costs are highest as asset specificity increases) ranked cooperative alliances highest. But when the data were disaggregated by country of origin this turns out to be a Japanese view, in rather marked contrast to US firms. There are other home country differences which are also revealed in the findings and provide suggested routes for more micro data gathering. Thus these and a number of other interesting results presented in the article demonstrate the importance of more micro data and provide insights for improved questionnaire design.

The advantage of the 'double-diamond' approach for analysis of MNEs and innovation is that it combines both the home and host country impact. The disadvantage, inevitable and not surprising, is that it requires rigor and parsimony to pare down each component of the model to synthesize the firm's experience. It extends somewhat the transaction-costs model by including some additional institutional variables. Of course the transaction model itself modifies the neo-classical concept of the firm by introducing an institutional element. But the modification is minimal and, as William Baumol has put it, the firm is still basically a 'calculating robot' (Baumol 1993, p. 14).

A radically different approach to the home country impact is the concept of a national innovation system (NIS) (Freeman 1987; Nelson 1993; Ostry and Nelson 1995). This vastly extends the institutional approach by embedding the firm in a 'system' (no precise boundaries are defined) or set of institutions which interact in the production, diffusion and use of new technologies and thus determine the firm's innovative capability and performance. The approach stems from a range of different sources but is essentially evolutionary (unplanned, uncertain) and interactive (firms, people, organizations, and institutions interact and the NIS evolves). Historical research on technological change; a growing number of case studies focused on the innovation process and the nature of technological progress; and analyses of the postwar convergence of the OECD countries all fed into the concept of the national innovation system and the production of a volume of comparative studies (Nelson 1993) covering a wide range of countries. A central element in this systemic approach to technological change is the rejection of the linear model (science; technology; innovation) and the emphasis on complex feedback loops within the system, with the firm as the focal point. The firm is thus the organizing mechanism for absorbing knowledge and generating market output or innovation.

While the diffuse and descriptive nature of the first set of country analyses makes synthesis very difficult, there has been further development of the concept by the OECD. A Working Group on Innovation and Technology Policy was established in June 1994 to develop a conceptual framework of the NIS with the purpose of identifying measurable indicators and testing this new information on different analytical models. So far no new data have been produced but the intent is to concentrate on a set of innovation indicators which extend the conventional data on knowledge investment and embodied knowledge (R&D expenditure; patents; high-tech production and trade) by flow measures (human resource mobility; cross-country publication citations, and so on) which are comparable across the OECD countries. These data should thus provide useful two-way diffusion measures to supplement the present crop of indicators. Mapping knowledge codified in publications and other sources is now facilitated by improved information technology. Capturing uncodified knowledge embedded in the 'wetware' of the brain requires information on human capital mobility and interaction. Identifying the main diffusion flows at the national level and the links among the main institutions – industry, government, academia – will begin the mapping of the NIS.

The longer-term objective of the OECD project on the NIS is to feed into government technology and innovation policy by enhancing the channels of knowledge diffusion at the national level; identify the impediments; and thus highlight policies which could enhance fluidity. Seen in this light, the purpose is not to capture the 'Holy Grail' (innovation) but to map enough of the environment to improve understanding of the incentives which foster and the impediments which deter a firm's innovation capability. This is essentially the view of Baumol (and Keynes, who never tried to define 'animal spirits' but underlined their quintessential contribution to economic growth). Baumol argues that neoclassical theory excludes the entrepreneur from the firm. The firm is conceived as a manager who performs mathematical calculations involving highly specific variables. The entrepreneur innovates 'new ideas, new strategies' and therefore catalyzes continuing change. Like Keynes' animal spirits, the entrepreneur must be exogenous and the origins of entrepreneurship remain too complex to reduce to a few measurable variables (just think about all the articles on Silicon Valley). Socrates said measure what is measurable and make measurable what is not. But he presumably was not concerned with the sources of innovation in ancient Greece!

So Baumol's policy approach to this fundamental aspect of the role of the firm in the innovation process is not unlike the OECD's NIS project: identify the market variables and institutional arrangements that improve the payoff to entrepreneurial activity so that policy is geared in this direction and, equally or more important, strengthen the policy focus on improving and speeding up the diffusion of innovation. Both require more and better information which is quantifiable.

This same issue is also highlighted in some aspects of the new endogenous growth theory. Neoclassical models recognized technology as the key driver of growth but it was exogenous to the market (manna from heaven). The new endogenous growth theory incorporates technological advance into the firm's calculations. The growth of knowledge (which depends on a variety of economic decisions such as investment in R&D, human capital, or new capital goods, or is accumulated in learning by doing, and so on) is central to the new model, but knowledge is captured by minimalist 'proxy' variables and the anatomy of the complex knowledge generation and diffusion process at the micro level is absent. The firm is still a calculating robot but more sophisticated and complex calculations are involved. In other words, the major change in the new theory is a technical modification of the neoclassical model (especially incorporating increasing returns) and the main improvement has been in extending the macro dimensions of the growth process.

However, included among the macro dimensions of the new theory is an increased focus on knowledge diffusion channels, especially trade. For example, recent analyses of the impact of trade on growth (Coe and Helpman 1995) quantifies the impact via trade flows of R&D expenditures in developed countries on total factor productivity in developing countries. Another (Hejazi and Safarian 1996) used the same approach to show that some of these spillovers funnel through FDI. Other diffusion channels – people, migration, education and training abroad, training contracts by specialist firms, and so on – have not yet been incorporated into the new models, in part because of a paucity of data. Yet in services the intangible assets are embodied in people and innovation is rooted in knowledge and experience and managerial skills, as well as technical knowledge. The OECD diffusion indicators, which will include 'people', could become an important input to improving growth models. Similarly, improved data on human capital (more sophisticated measurement of education and training outcomes rather than output) would strengthen both the technical aspects and the policy relevance of the model.

NEW NEW ISSUES

The term 'new issues' refers to the items on the Uruguay Round agenda, which had never been considered in any previous negotiations – services, intellectual property and investment. These are now key in all ongoing or future negotiations, whether multilateral or regional. All three are of fundamental importance to the MNEs' locational and innovation strategies, which is why they were included in the Round despite powerful and prolonged opposition from many developing countries. Rising protectionism in the USA, spawned by the overvalued dollar in the early 1980s, had seriously diminished American business support for a new multilateral round of negotiations so it would have been impossible to launch the Uruguay Round without the 'new issues', clearly signalling their relevance to corporate strategy – a relevance which is now far greater than it was in 1986, as our earlier discussion on globalization demonstrated.

Although many problems remain in the services negotiations and in intellectual property protection (especially in terms of effective enforcement), and the Uruguay Round failed to achieve much in investment (which prompted a launch of negotiations in the OECD, still ongoing), a number of other items high on the corporate agenda will also require policy input by governments and policy interaction between firms, governments and international institutions. This last section will briefly note two of these issues.

Electronic Commerce

Perhaps the most obvious of the 'new new issues' – certainly the one which has received the most attention in the popular media – is electronic commerce. This is hardly the place to write about the borderless economy or the global information society or whatever metaphor is the flavor of the week. There is little question that commercial transactions over the Internet are now growing rapidly and will continue to grow significantly, with major implications for the organization and behavior of the firm. Some firms will benefit from the supply side of the technology, both hardware and, especially, software. Some will have to adapt or go under – especially those involved in information activities which mediate between the consumer and the producer (travel agents, retailers, music and entertainment products, retailers of real estate, insurance agents, and so on). And start-ups will abound in information-type niche activities since monetary barriers to entry are close to zero. One interesting question that arises is whether the reduced cost and enhanced speed of communication will so reduce transaction costs that, at least in some industries, a process of deverticalization will be catalyzed. This would, of course, have important implications for the locational strategies of the MNEs described earlier.

A wide range of policy issues arise in the electronic commerce domain, ranging from intellectual property, privacy, culture, regulatory principles, consumer protection, fraud and crime prevention to liability, auditing, the definition of identity and of residence, taxation, and so on. None of these can be considered 'domestic' – the term is obsolete by definition in a global information society. Yet the current international institutional architecture established after World War II is clearly inadequate in both mandate and scope to deal with this list – which no doubt will keep growing. The 1997 G-7 Summit proposed that the OECD undertake an initiative to explore the policy dimension of electronic commerce in cooperation with member governments and business representatives. The OECD project will no doubt contribute to the international policy debate. But it will not be alone in that regard. One can expect a vast proliferation of meetings, conferences, studies and other initiatives. Since the stakes in what kind of rules will govern this new game are very high, corporations will be devoting more and more time and resources to policy-related activities. Indeed, there is a growing view among many experts that the main form of regulation in this new domain should be self-regulation and that governments should just get out of the way.[6] When combined with a growing need for corporate foreign policy, especially in Asian markets, the governance structure of the MNE may come to resemble that of government – a little-noted irony as governments are trying to reinvent themselves to resemble corporations!

Standards Competition and Innovation Markets

The economics of systems markets – markets composed of two or more components together with an interface that allows them to work together, ranging from nuts and bolts to automatic teller machines and ATM cards – were spelled out in an important article by Michael Katz and Carl Shapiro several years ago (Katz and Shapiro 1994). The article (and others presented at a symposium on the subject) focused on three important issues in systems competition: how expectations are formed by consumers; how coordination among firms and among consumers is achieved; and compatibility issues, that is, the 'interface' or standards questions. While all three issues are highly relevant to technological change and innovation, I want to concentrate on one aspect of the compatibility issue, more specifically, standards competition in network markets, because of the important implications for corporate strategy and new policy developments.

In network markets – for example, the communications network of the public telephone system – the value to one user is enhanced by adding other users, thus generating 'network externalities'. In such markets competition among incompatible systems obviously reduces the benefits to consumers, so there is a strong tendency towards *de facto* standardization (a proprietary standard). The competitive battle to establish a proprietary standard as a *de facto* standard can be very intense because the gains are so great: winner takes all.

A range of corporate strategies can be deployed to parlay a small initial advantage into a dominant, lasting single system. This tendency of systems markets has been termed 'tipping' and is well documented in a number of markets, such as AM radio, black-and-white television, video cassette recorders and typewriter keyboards.[7] Strategies range from penetration pricing, massive advertising to establish consumer acceptance of the inevitability of one system, and buying actual or potential competitors, to heavy investment in R&D to foreclose future new markets. A firm with a strong brandname, an established, widely-known and aggressive reputation, and deep pockets would be unlikely to favor open systems because it would have the most to gain from standards incompatibility. A proprietary standard would entrench market dominance because of the incumbent's long-run declining costs and the high barriers to entry stemming not only from sunk costs, but also R&D and advertising costs.

While standards competition clearly has enormous significance for the analysis of corporate innovation strategy, there have been remarkably few theoretical or empirical studies on the subject. The view of most experts in the field of standards is that the capture of private standards will create only a transitory monopoly; that examples of such 'market failure' are rare; and that the policy implications are clear, that is, the complexity and uncertainty of the innovation process would mitigate against any policy intervention. The costs of 'government failure' would likely outweigh any possible (but improbable) benefit of redressing of 'market failure' (Sykes 1995, pp. 34–36).

This view, based largely on goods markets, is becoming rapidly outdated in the policy realm with the recent launch of new directions in antitrust policies targeting future markets (the anticompetitive effects of products not yet in existence) and the related but not identical concept of innovation markets.[8] Both developments are responses to the growing importance of high-tech industries in the USA and to the changes in the economics discipline noted earlier (academic scribblers do matter). The concept of future markets was incorporated into the 1995 merger guidelines for the pharmaceutical industry and was the basis for the consent order in the merger of Ciba-Geigy Chiron and Sandoz (Kobak Jr. and McGuire 1997). The more controversial (and arguably more complex) notion of innovation markets is less relevant to the drugs industry and 'killer patent portfolio' strategies than to systems markets and, to be specific, to standards competition in these markets. The question which will be hotly debated is the impact on future innovation of market control of a standard in a rapidly changing systems market. The outcome of this debate, or indeed the debate itself, will (has, in the case of Microsoft?) become factored into corporate strategy. The need for more research in this area is well summarized by Katz and Shapiro (1994, p. 106):

> We suspect that in the long run the greatest difference between systems markets and other markets arises because firms' innovation incentives are altered by network considerations . . . there is little to believe that, in the presence of network externalities, the marginal private and social returns to keeping one more technology in the portfolio of those under development are likely to be well-aligned.

CONCLUSIONS

This discussion has sought to deal with two aspects of the multinational firm and technology. The first concerns the utility of the transaction-costs model. For example, the term innovation rather than technology has been used in order to underline the changing focus of much of the new research which has modified the more traditional linear approach to knowledge generation. This is but one example of several questions which are arising from a growing number of empirical and historical studies. While there are at present no answers to these questions, a number of potentially encouraging developments have been noted. Nonetheless, the accelerating pace of technological change and the growing importance of non-OECD countries, especially in Asia, present a formidable challenge to analysts in this field.

Thus, over the next 25 years (the time horizon selected for this volume) I would suggest there are two subjects that will dominate research in the field of multinationals and technology. The first will reflect the shift in economic gravity outside the OECD. The notion that there is one 'universal' model of the firm, 'transaction costs plus', may well not survive as we learn more about firms in these regions. This concept of the firm is implicitly rooted in Western models of transparency of domestic rules and governance structures and the development of strategies to constrain opportunistic behavior. But it is rather obvious that different strategies are required where transparency is the exception rather than the rule. A predatory animal operates best in a jungle, after all.

The other subject concerns standards competition in network markets, especially the emerging multi-media global market. As noted above there has been remarkably little analysis in this rapidly changing field. If there is now growing evidence of a new technological trajectory driven by software and one of the key drivers is entertainment (after all, knowledge of the English language is now a key feature of network externalities) then Hollywood, not Silicon Valley, could become the central focus of future research. A recent article entitled 'From Science to Fiction' provides an intriguing insight, namely the flow of NASA engineers to the entertainment industry. There is growing similarity in the expertise required to fight the next war and to design the next action film. As the article noted, 'a few movies now cost almost as much to make as spacecraft like the $250 million Pathfinder-102 (*Wall Street Journal* 1997). The post-war spin-off of military R&D to the civilian sector, which was a major engine of growth for both American and other MNEs, has been eroding since the 1980s. A new spin-on to the military from films about dinosaurs, aliens from outer space, and exploding planes, seems not only possible but increasingly probable. It will be essential to rethink the role of Dr Strangelove in the sequel.

The second theme highlighted in the discussion concerns the changing nature of the policy agenda in the trade, technology and investment domain. The growing role of MNEs in the policy process has received scant attention. Yet the interaction of government and corporate strategy, especially in the field of high tech, is likely to be increasingly important. Will MNEs be the key actors in the global governance structure of the twenty-first century? What will this mean for the nation-state, and for the immobile 'factors of production' within its borders, especially less skilled human capital? How will the growing concern about the erosion of social cohesion stemming from rising structural unemployment in Europe and growing income inequality in the United States be factored into corporate strategy? I suspect that this too will become an important field of research which does not fit easily into the standard model.

NOTES

1. The term is adapted from George Gilder, as quoted in Freeman and Soete (1994). The analysis of the new information revolution is comprehensively documented by the authors.
2. For a literature review see Hagedoorn (1996). See also Safarian (1997), pp. 30–40.
3. See Ostry and Nelson (1995). See also Waverman et al. (1997), Part III, R&D Consortia, pp. 197–306.
4. See Basant and Fikkert (1996); Supapol (1995); Siddharthan and Safarian (1997).
5. For example 'innovatory capacity'; 'organizational capacity'; and 'relational skills' are classified as resources and assets. Universities and other research institutions are not so classified but are included in Group 4 or Linkages with foreign or domestic firms and institutions (p. 11).
6. A recent example of the move to self-regulation is the development of guidelines for ensuring security of Internet transactions by the International Chamber of Commerce. See 'ICC to unveil rules for Internet Trade', *Financial Times* (6 November 1997), p. 4.
7. Katz and Shapiro (1994) cite relevant references (p. 106). See also Symposium on Network Externalities, *Journal of Economic Perspectives*, **8** (Spring 1984).
8. The Federal Trade Commission Hearings in 1995 and 1996 on global and innovation-based competition and related intellectual property issues included papers by many academic experts, as well as government officials, which cover theoretical, empirical and policy aspects of future markets and innovation markets. See also Symposium: A Critical Appraisal of the 'Innovation Market' Approach, *Antitrust Law Journal*, **1** (1995).

REFERENCES

Basant, Rakesh, and Bria Fikkert (1996), 'The effects of R&D, foreign technology purchase, and domestic and international spillovers on productivity in Indian firms', *The Review of Economics and Statistics*, **78**(2).

Baumol, William J. (1993), *Entrepreneurship, Management and the Structure of Payoffs*, Cambridge, MA: The MIT Press.

Branstetter, Lee, and Mariko Sukakibara (1997), 'Japanese research consortia: a microeconomic analysis of industrial policy', Working Paper No. 6066, Cambridge, MA: National Bureau of Economic Research.

Buckley, Peter J., and Mark Casson (1996), 'An economic model of international joint venture strategy', *Journal of International Business Studies Special Issue 1996*, 849–75.

Coe, D., and E. Helpman (1995), 'International R&D spillovers', *European Economic Review*, **39**: 859–87.

Dunning, John H. (1996), 'The geographical sources of the competitiveness of firms: some results of a new survey', *Transnational Corporations*, **5**, (3) (December): 1–29.

Freeman, Chris, and Luc Soete (1994), *Work for All or Mass Unemployment?* London.

Freeman, Chris (1987), *Technology and Economic Performance: Lessons from Japan*, London: Pinter.

Fung, Victor (1997), 'A multinational trading group with Chinese characteristics', *Financial Times* (7 November), p. 12.

Grosse, Robert (1996), 'International technology transfer in services', *Journal of International Business Studies*, **27**, (4): 781–99.

Hagedoorn, John (1996), 'The economics of co-operation among high-tech firms – trends and patterns in strategic partnering since the early seventies, in Georg Koopmans and Hans-Eckart Scharrer (eds), *The Economics of High-Technology Competition and Cooperation in Global Markets*, Hamburg: HWWA.

Hejazi, W., and A. Edward Safarian (1996), 'Trade, investment and US R&D spillovers', Working Paper 65, Canadian Institute for Advanced Research.

Katz, Michael L., and Carl Shapiro (1994), 'Systems competition and network effects', *Journal of Economic Perspectives*, **8** (2) (spring): 93–115.

Kobak, Jr., James B., and Richard P. McGuire (1997), 'FTC looks at merger's antitrust effects on R&D', *The National Law Journal* (31 March), p. C03.

Mowery, David C., Joanne E. Oxley and Brian S. Silverman (1996), 'Technological overlap and interfirm cooperation: implications for the resource-based view of the firm', Working Paper No. 70, Toronto: Canadian Institute for Advanced Research Program in Economic Growth and Policy.

Nelson, Richard R. (ed.) (1993), *National Innovation Systems: A Comparative Analysis*, New York and Oxford: Oxford University Press.

Ostry, Sylvia (1996), 'Technology issues in the international trading system', in *Market Access After the Uruguay Round: Investment, Competition and Technology Perspectives*, Paris: OECD.

Ostry, Sylvia (1997), *The Post-Cold War Trading System: Who's on First?* Chicago: University of Chicago Press.

Ostry, Sylvia, and Richard Nelson (1995), *Techno-Nationalism and Techno-Globalism: Conflict and Cooperation*, Washington, DC: Brookings Institution.

Porter, M.E. (1990), *The Competitive Advantage of Nations*, New York: The Free Press.

Rugman, A.M. (ed.) (1993), *Management International Review*, **33**, 2 (Spring) (special edition on Michael Porter's Diamond of Competitive Advantage).

Rugman, A.M., J. Van den Broeck and A. Verbeke (eds) (1995), *Beyond the Diamond: Research in Global Management*, vol. 5, Greenwich, CT: JAI Press.

Safarian, A. Edward (1997), 'Trends in the forms of international business organization', in Leonard Waverman, William S. Comanor and Akira Goto (eds), *Competition Policy in the Global Economy*. London: Routledge.

Siddharthan, N.S., and A.E. Safarian (1997), 'Transnational corporations, technology transfer and imports of capital goods: The recent Indian experience', *Transnational Corporations*, **6**(1): (April): 31–50.

Supapol, Atipol Bhanick (ed.) (1995), *Transnational Corporations and Backward Linkages in Asian Electronics Industries*, New York: United Nations.

Sykes, Alan O. (1995), *Product Standards for Internationally Integrated Goods Markets*, Washington, DC: Brookings Institution.

United Nations Conference on Trade and Development (1995), *World Investment Report 1995*, Geneva: United Nations.

United Nations Conference on Trade and Development (1997), *World Investment Report 1997*, Geneva: United Nations.

Wall Street Journal (10 October 1997), p. B1.

Waverman, Leonard, William S. Comanor and Akira Goto (eds) (1997), *Competition Policy in the Global Economy*, London: Routledge.

Williamson, Peter J. (1997), 'Asia's new competitive game', *Harvard Business Review* (September–October): 55–67.

6. Multinationals and the developing countries

Louis T. Wells, Jr

The second edition of *Multinational Enterprise and Economic Analysis* attempts to capture within 260 pages the economic research on multinational enterprises (MNEs) to date. Yet, in spite of the comprehensiveness of the book, as well as its simultaneous brevity, I was struck by its shortcomings in addressing the issues that face managers – public and private – who are concerned with foreign direct investment (FDI) and the developing countries. The gaps are not the fault of Caves; he accomplishes as much or more than what he promises in the title of his book. But many of the issues that are important to policymakers and managers either have not attracted sufficient attention from economists, or are such that economic analysis is insufficient to shed adequate light on them. In the case of some recent problems, the gap between research and its publication may explain a few of the lacunae. The gaps for researchers to fill are manifold, especially if investigators do not constrain themselves to economic analysis alone.

First, a warning. Although Caves' Chapter 9 is entitled 'Multinationals in Developing Countries', it is inevitable that the contents of other chapters are relevant to this subject. A few examples: other parts of the book deal with the joint venture decision (Chapter 3), market behavior of multinationals (Chapter 4), employment and wages (Chapter 5), and the effects of taxation on multinationals' behavior (Chapter 8 and 10, as well as Chapter 9). These are important concerns of policymakers in developing countries.

From the point of view of the host country, two broad questions face policymakers:

- Is FDI good for the country? Appropriate to the task he undertakes, Caves puts the question in economic terms only: 'Does the MNE's presence mean more capital formation or productivity growth than otherwise?'
- How can government policy make the impact of FDI more favorable? Caves again puts it somewhat differently: 'Can sticks and carrots be applied to the MNE to produce more desirable allocations?'

Unfortunately, these simple questions are deceptive; they seem not to have simple answers. Some FDI is good; almost certainly some is harmful. But exactly what kind of investment falls into each category is frightfully difficult to determine, even if the effects are measured against only economic criteria. But, most governments would go beyond purely economic criteria in judging the impact of FDI. The implications of MNE activities for security and political independence matter in almost every country. Some countries also evaluate investment in terms of its impact on income distribution, including distribution among regions and ethnic groups. Moreover, where FDI can affect the ability of the regime to remain in power, this impact is likely to be as important as economic criteria. As a result, few governments are willing to judge FDI solely on its effects on capital formation and productivity growth, much to the chagrin of researchers who would like to work with econometric models, which are weak in handling multiple and non-quantifiable goals.

On the second question, economic research presents some evidence that the policies of host governments can increase the benefits of FDI, but again many unanswered questions remain. It is particularly important to note that research on the effectiveness of government policies has focused on the benefit side, with little attention to the cost side. Studies of tax incentives illustrate this. There has been considerable work to determine whether tax incentives have an impact on the decisions of investors as to which country they choose (but little on their impact on the total volume of investment). On the other hand, there has been practically no work on the costs of incentives, in terms of lost revenue, increased corruption, erosion of the tax system and difficulties of administration. Although one can, nevertheless, tease some policy implications out of the research reported in Caves' book, the many gaps in our knowledge mean that a great deal is still judgment and guesswork. Informed policy awaits more research.

Of course, host governments are not the only parties interested in multinationals and developing countries. Among other parties with an intense interest are the managers of the multinationals themselves. Yet, the chapter does not try to draw implications from economic research for managers of private enterprises. Some important concerns of managers of multinationals are:

- What special risks exist for foreign investors in developing countries: how can they be evaluated, and how can they be hedged or reduced?
- How should the environments – institutional, political, behavioral – of developing countries affect business decisions in the functional areas of business (finance, marketing, production, organization, and so on)?
- How should investments in developing countries fit into the strategies of MNEs, and how should those strategies change with evolution in those nations?

The kind of economic research reported by Caves helps in understanding these issues; but the help is limited.

Finally, host countries, business managers and home country governments all have an interest in the international regime that governs international direct investment flows. Caves devotes two and a half pages in his last chapter to this topic, which so often reflects the tension over FDI in the developing world. Yet, that treatment ignores the network of agreements that has grown up since the failure of the Havana Charter in the immediate post-World War II period. In fact, hundreds of bilateral investment treaties (BITs) have been signed; bilateral treaties for the prevention of double taxation have proliferated; bilateral efforts to deal with transfer pricing issues have recently widened; and regional integration agreements, such as the NAFTA, have included extensive provisions to govern FDI. Moreover, the Uruguay Round led to commitments on trade-related investment measures that will have a major impact on multinational–host government relations as they are phased in. With the current OECD discussions of an agreement that will be open for non-OECD countries to join, renewed efforts to extend the mandate of the GATT/WTO to cover investment, and progress on industry-specific agreements, such as in telecommunications, the security and freedom of MNEs and their host and home governments may be increasingly subject to international regimes. As Caves argues, there are fundamental economic issues that underlie the difficulties in reaching agreements on FDI, especially the lack of symmetry among parties to an agreement because of the division of countries into host and home. Further, MNEs themselves have not seen fit to support many of the proposals for an international regime. Equally important, the economics profession has not been a source of consensus on the economic benefits and costs of FDI. Direct investment stands in sharp contrast to trade, where symmetry is the rule and economists have been close to united on the benefits of open trade, if not always on the optimal timing of openness. Yet, consensus on benefits from international investment flows seems closer now than ever before, and symmetry has increased with growing FDI from the richer developing countries.

For discussion purposes, I want to group the gaps in knowledge into four research categories that contribute to answering the fundamental questions about multinationals and the developing countries:

1. There is virtually no work reported concerning the impact on multinationals of the profound changes in development strategy that have taken place in the developing world, even though those changes began more than a decade ago.
2. Although there are several pieces of research that contribute to understanding the impact of FDI on developing countries, they still do not

answer the question of net impact, even if criteria are solely economic; and they almost completely fail to address the issue of net impact using the broader criteria that prevail in practice. One would expect that the new development strategies that are so widespread in the developing world should lead to FDI that has a more favorable economic impact than did the investment associated with the old import-substitution strategies. Facts, however, are scarce.

3. There has clearly been a reduction in the tension between foreign investors and their host developing countries, but the research reported in Caves' book does not explain the sources and changes in tensions sufficiently for the analyst to decide whether the changes are lasting, or whether new threats to the multinational are on the horizon. Nor, as has been pointed out, does it deal adequately with recent efforts and prospects for proposals to manage tensions at the supra-national level.

4. Finally, since the work reported is largely economic, major gaps exist in applying this research to the tasks of managers, whether those managers are government officials or business executives. There is little work reported on the institutions involved and the behavioral and organizational matters that have to be taken into account by managers in developing countries – whether those managers are government officials or business executives.

MULTINATIONALS AND DEVELOPMENT STRATEGY

In the past decade or two, conventional wisdom about development strategy has undergone a sea change. Although practice has lagged behind the apparent new consensus, especially since the mid-1980s many developing countries have instituted reforms that reflect the new beliefs. Incomes have grown sharply – although not everywhere and not for everyone. Yet, the impacts on the multinational of the dramatic change in development strategy, and the presumably linked growth in incomes, seem to have been the object of little economic research. Indeed, the research reported by Caves does suggest that the decisions and much of the impact of MNEs in the developing world is a function of development strategies in those countries. Thus, it would be a major surprise if the kinds of changes that have been made in those strategies have not affected the behavior and economic impact of MNEs.

Some of the underlying factors that influence investment decisions have been studied and reported. In the 1950s and 1960s, prevailing wisdom was on the side of import substitution as a route to development. To encourage investment to manufacture at home what would otherwise be imported, the bulk of the developing countries maintained high tariffs and restrictive quantitative controls on imports. Multinationals responded with investment in facilities designed to serve markets that were smaller than optimal, and for products for which comparative advantage lay elsewhere. The impact of those tariffs and other import restrictions on the amount of foreign direct investment has been examined by a number of researchers, and the results are reported in Caves' Chapter 9, in the section 'Tariff Protection, Import-Competing Foreign Investment, and Welfare'. Moreover, some economic research has looked at the impact of protection on the benefits that a host country obtains from FDI (again reported in the section mentioned above). From the narrow perspective of economic efficiency, higher effective rates of protection are likely to lead to a higher percentage of investments that are bad for the host country.

The new consensus has concluded that proper development strategy calls for lowered restrictions on imports. Presumably, the mix and maybe quantity of FDI that new development strategies have produced have been different from that of the past. Whatever their impact on total investment flows, changes would suggest a higher proportion of economically beneficial FDI. Yet, there is no research reported in this edition of Caves' book that examines how multinationals' strategies have responded to the new policies.

In fact, in the previous edition of his book, Caves himself contributed to the analysis of the link between trade policy and types of investment. He was one of the first authors to point out the general and important point that progress in understanding multinationals in developing countries jumped ahead when researchers started breaking investment into some useful categories. On a number of dimensions, the foreign firm that comes in search of raw materials is a different animal from the firm that would manufacture in a developing country. Moreover, the manufacturing firm that invests for the local market is likely to be quite different from the firm that manufactures for export. The impacts of these different types of firm on developing countries are likely to differ. Moreover, there would be good reason to believe that different development strategies would affect these categories of investors quite differently. Yet, economic research seems not yet to have drawn the almost obvious hypotheses and put them to empirical test.

Changes in import restrictions have not been the only shifts in policy that have affected multinationals' investment in the developing world. In the spirit of the new belief in competition and private sector development, and perhaps in response to other reasons that include the decline in other sources of foreign funds, governments in the developing world began to dismantle their restrictions on FDI along with their tariffs and quantitative restrictions on imports.

In earlier days, domestic enterprises were often protected from competition

with foreign investors by a number of barriers. Elaborate government procedures were required to approve the entry of foreign firms. The power to grant
permission to invest might be centralized in a board of investment, or investors
might require the approval of numerous agencies or departments. Sometimes
transparent rules simply closed certain sectors to FDI. Closed sectors often
included infrastructure, but also other industries in which state firms were
involved, or where domestic enterprises seemed competent. Where transparent rules were absent, certain sectors were in practice closed. Elsewhere
foreign investors sometimes still had to invest jointly with local firms; otherwise approvals for investment were simply not forthcoming.

Over the past decade, under the new development strategies, the rules and
the screening organizations have been disappearing. This kind of change has
been documented elsewhere, and the reasons underlying that change have
perhaps been quite adequately explored. But the results – foreign investment
in activities that were not open to multinationals in the past – have not been
researched. New areas – or at least areas where FDI has long been excluded –
include power generation, telephones, and management of industrial estates
and export processing zones. We know little about what kinds of firm seize
these opportunities, their behavior, and their impacts. The fact that they were
excluded from the domains of the foreign investor in the past suggests that
governments were suspicious of the economic or political outcomes of FDI in
these activities. Moreover, investments in previously prohibited sectors challenge the adequacy of the three categories into which Caves divides investors;
maybe more are needed. In any event, there are many questions to be
addressed about the new investments.

New development strategies have not only involved the dismantling of
controls on imports and FDI, but they have also led to changes in currency
regimes. More realistic exchange rates have probably affected FDI. Moreover,
reductions in capital controls presumably encourage investment by guarantee-
ing that earnings, if they materialize, can be remitted. On the other hand, the
widespread reduction of restrictions on portfolio investment seems to have led
to instability in exchange rates. The recent instability – first in Mexico and
then in Southeast Asia – may shake the commitments of developing countries
to their openness. An understanding of the differences between the behavior of
foreign capital flows associated with multinationals and portfolio flows may
turn out to be important in determining the future role of multinationals in
developing countries. Moreover, as far as I know, no work has been undertaken on the impact of unstable exchange rates on the decisions of foreign
direct investors.

In fact, the very success of new development strategies may increase, or at
least change, the risks that foreign investors face. Successful local firms
impose new risks for foreign investors, as I will suggest later.

NET EFFECT OF FOREIGN DIRECT INVESTMENT ON DEVELOPMENT

Especially in the 1960s, analysis of the role of MNEs and development tended to examine whether foreign investors behaved in certain ways, the goal of this research being to determine eventually whether such investment was 'good' or 'bad' for the host country. Increasingly in the 1970s, empirical studies abandoned the effort to draw conclusions about the behavior of foreign investors, or the impact of FDI, and concentrated on categories of investment. As stated earlier, projects to exploit natural resources seemed to be quite different from investments in manufacturing, and projects which were primarily for the domestic market seemed different from projects that served principally export markets. Further, empirical work began to suggest that the behavior of MNEs might differ by their national origins. The answer to the basic question of whether FDI was good or bad for the host country was unlikely to be an unambiguous one. Any analysis of impact would have to take into account categories of investment.

Even granting the need to look at different categories of investor, it has also become clear that FDI affects many different goals – even if one limits the analysis to economic impact. As the early literature recognized, adequate understanding of overall impact was likely to be built from detailed studies of the effects that foreign investors had on much more narrow measures. Thus, Caves reports a range of research that provides a partial analysis of economic effects.

In looking at impact, researchers have dealt with multinationals and concentration, displacement of domestic entrepreneurs, location of R&D, productivity and profitability, training, choice of technology, propensity to import or buy locally, and balance of payments. Faced with dozens of studies of very specific kinds of impact, Caves points out: 'MNEs' effects on the LDC's rate of economic growth might seem to provide the ultimate relationship to be investigated'. He concludes, after a critical review of efforts to deal with the big question, that 'the relationship between an LDC's stock of foreign investment and its subsequent economic growth is a matter on which we totally lack trustworthy conclusions.' He leaves little room for optimism that efforts to study the overall impact directly, as opposed to the analyses of behavior across a wide range of fields, will yield useful results. Given the heterogeneous nature of FDI, he is likely right.

Even at the more micro level, many of the pieces of the puzzle remain unresearched. Some of the widest gaps involve externalities. Very little is known, for example, about the spillover effects of FDI. How many employees are trained by MNEs and then leave foreign subsidiaries to use their skills in other activities? How do training and transfer differ according to the nationality – or other characteristics – of the investor? (For an example of this kind of research, see Allen 1994, which compares the transfer of management skills from Japanese and US direct investors in Indonesia; there are other bits and pieces of research to draw on in this area.) Does host (or even home) government policy matter in training and transfer? To what extent do foreign investors serve as models for local firms – for exporting, or for other activities (for an example of this kind of work, see Rhee and Belot 1989).

The economic impacts of FDI remain rather uncertain. Still less is known about the political and social effects of the multinational enterprise in developing countries. Unfortunately, there appears to be no update or broader sequel to the under-cited study by Goodsell (1974). Wisely, Caves did not attempt to draw grand conclusions about whether foreign investment is good or bad for a country. In fact, given his own observation about the importance of differentiating investors by type, one can only conclude 'it depends'; it depends almost certainly on the type of FDI, but also probably on host government policy. It would be nice, however, to have clearer statements about the contingent relationships. One could, I believe, conclude with some degree of confidence that the bulk of FDI contributes to net economic output, at international prices, if protection against imports is low; and that high import protection leads to a high percentage of FDI projects that do not make a net contribution to economic output. Although the general conclusion is probably true for domestic investment as well, for foreign investment the remissions abroad of monopoly profits from protection increase the likelihood of harmful projects. One might qualify the conclusion a bit if it seems highly likely that FDI decreases domestic investment, or if there are really significant externalities. Even if they agree with the overall conclusion, however, few governments would be willing to allow completely unrestricted access for FDI. Non-economic goals remain important.

In the absence of answers to many questions, especially concerning non-economic impacts, the government policymaker is left with having to reject or take on faith the new consensus that they should open their economies to FDI.

SOURCES OF TENSION

As important as economic analysis is, it also captures relatively little of the tension concerning MNEs and development. There can be little doubt that tensions between foreign firms and host governments have declined in the past decade, in spite of the occasional examples of conflict. One of the measures of tension – expropriation, for example – has declined sharply. Yet, the lack of sufficient research on why tensions have declined in the developing countries makes it difficult to forecast the future environment for MNEs in the developing world.

Perhaps the changes in attitude on the part of host governments are simply the result of the shift toward favoring markets and competition. In that case, economic analysis may be sufficient. Yet, there may be more complicated factors behind the new attitudes. They may have emerged from the virtual disappearance of some alternative sources of foreign funds for development. The commercial bank loans of the 1970s, for example, dried up just before the new welcome was extended to FDI. The new attitudes may reflect new-found confidence on the part of host government officials who are increasingly well educated, and often in the home countries of the investors. Confident of their ability to understand the behavior and language of business managers, government officials may now believe that they can deal with the kinds of problem that frustrated them in the past. Some possible explanations suggest that the environment might last; others might lead to the conclusion that anti-foreign attitudes will again emerge and restrict the activities of the multinational. Whatever they are, the reasons for the new attitudes are worthwhile – if difficult – subjects for research.

In spite of the virtual disappearance of expropriation and the growing welcome to foreign investment, evidence of tension remains. In Chapter 10, Caves reports some of the work done earlier to examine tension, including 'the obsolescing bargain' model (see, in particular, the section on public policy in that chapter). But this work predates the shift in development strategies and attitudes toward foreign investors. There has been little research on the current usefulness of the old model and on new risks that might have appeared. In fact, anecdotal evidence suggests that risks facing the multinational in developing countries may have changed quite sharply, not simply declined. Some new risks may be the result of clashes between foreign firms and domestic firms, rather than between foreign firms and government. Although local state-owned, local privately owned, and foreign-owned firms used to have rather clear domains in the developing world, growth in the competencies and wealth of local firms has weakened the boundaries between these domains (for a useful contribution by a non-economist and an especially clear analysis of the 'domains', see Evans 1979). As local firms and MNEs conflict over profitable investment opportunities, powerful local firms use their political influence to gain advantages over multinationals. Political influence leads to actions on the part of government – more subtle than in the past – that discriminate against the foreign investor in favor of the local firm (for examples, see Wells, forthcoming). Although the results of this kind of conflict may on the surface look similar to those of the past, the motivations and prospects are quite different. It is also possible that, in the new environment, actions against the MNE are likely to occur in different kinds of industry than in the past: rather than being limited to 'strategic' sectors – that is, those that are highly visible and politically sensitive – conflicts may occur wherever local firms have the resources (money and access to technology) to compete and to attract governmental support. In sum, actions against the foreign investor may be less frequent and less 'abrupt' (like expropriation), but more widespread across sectors.

Conflicts over FDI have historically led to efforts to manage relations at the international level. The prospects for agreement may have improved, as attitudes of host governments have changed. The suspicions on the part of the developing countries have, in the past, contrasted with the attitudes of the industrialized countries, which sought agreements largely to protect their multinationals. Efforts such as those proposed in the immediate post-World War II period to build an International Trade Organization and those of the United Nations throughout the 1970s failed, as industrialized and developing countries clashed over their conflicting views about protection of the multinational and limits on its behavior, and managers of multinationals saw little gain for them in supporting the efforts. But changes in development strategy, and the accompanying new policies toward FDI, have made developing countries more eager to attract foreign investment. Thus, it appears that they are less eager to constrain the multinational and more willing to constrain their own actions. One wonders whether their new views might affect their willingness to consider agreements to govern flows of FDI. Further, there is some evidence that managers of multinationals are increasingly willing to support international accords. But that evidence remains anecdotal; it would be useful to know the degree to which managers have reduced their opposition to regional or global agreements.

Some observers are more optimistic, as reflected in renewed efforts to negotiate a global agreement. Yet no research is reported on how the existing bilateral and regional agreements are working. In fact, we do not even know whether bilateral and regional, or possible global agreements really matter in the decisions of MNEs.

The gaps in research on tensions are at least partly a result of the fact that economics is not adequate as a discipline to examine the subject. Tensions between host government and foreign investors arise partly from economic issues, but their importance and outcome are largely the result of politics. How the tensions work out in policy terms is probably a function of changes in the worldwide economy, but also, in some cases, a function of increased power in regional governments or decentralized functional agencies. Note, for example, that the contracts governing foreign power for Dabhol in India and for Paiton in Indonesia were strikingly similar; but so far only Dabhol has led to instability. The reasons may well lie in the different political systems of India and Indonesia, and in the differing responses at the regional level that arise from different structures of local government in the two countries. Similar differences appear in the behavior of regional investment boards in different kinds of country. In Vietnam, for example, some regional boards try hard to attract investment to their regions; in Indonesia, regional boards serve primarily as another barrier to investment, it seems. The differences can probably be explained by political scientists who examine the structure of local government. Economists may have little to offer on this kind of subject, but work is important for addressing the basic policy questions about FDI in developing countries that are posed by managers.

SPECIFIC MANAGEMENT ISSUES

One of the critical issues for managers of MNEs that invest in developing countries is the assessment of risk. Some of the possible changes in risk have been discussed above, but the management of those risks is a task hardly dealt with by economists or political scientists. Again, anecdotal evidence suggests that multinational firms are having a great deal of difficulty managing the evaluation of risks and designing appropriate policies for dealing with them. Part of the problem is organizational. Reward systems have been constructed to induce managers to make profitable decisions; but many of the reward systems do not build in adjustments for political risks. Some firms, for example, give managers bonuses based on the net present value of the projected cash flow from the deals they strike. Most ignore non-commercial risks in making such assessments; and efforts to introduce risk analysts into the decision and evaluation processes meet tremendous resistance from managers whose deals might be challenged. In the 1970s a number of firms – especially petroleum and banking – established internal units to analyse political risks; most such units have disappeared. In the eyes of managers, they seem not to have served the goals for which they were designed. However, little is known about best practice in multinationals that must deal with the risks of investment in developing countries – how do the best managed firms carry out risk analysis, attract managers' attention to important issues in the business environment, transfer within the organization learning from experience, and coordinate government relations? (For an example of a study of how MNEs coordinate government relations, see Mahini 1988.)

Like the study of tensions between foreign firm and host government, the study of other management issues is limited if the hypotheses and methodology are constrained to those offered by economics. Some management problems are, of course, partially addressed by analyses of the kinds discussed by Caves. For example, the decision about whether to establish a wholly owned subsidiary or a joint venture may well be the result of analysis of the strategy of the MNE – including the role the subsidiary is to play – and an analysis of the tensions over FDI in the host country. But, the implementation of the decision to form a joint venture requires the choice of partner. This raises management issues of a very different kind. The manager in the multinational must, for example, decide exactly what advantages or threats particular kinds of partner bring to the venture. An appropriate decision is likely to involve an analysis of ethnic conflicts, political roles of various parties, and protection offered by the legal system, as well as the more conventional business concerns of a partner's access to distribution channels or financial assets. Further, the establishment of a joint venture will require thinking about the role of contracts versus trust, conflicts of interest between the venture and the other interests of the parties, provisions for expansion, and so on. All these are likely to be influenced by the institutional and political environment of the host country, and the analysis is likely to require some cultural sensitivity, a great deal of institutional knowledge and political analysis, as well as an understanding of the economic resources needed and available.

It is similar with virtually every other management decision by the multinational. Decisions with regard to financing an affiliate in a developing country require the manager to consider currency instability, exchange controls, the development of local capital markets, rules on collateral, and the peculiar tax institutions and administrative capabilities of the host country. Production decisions require an analysis of political tensions – the degree of local vertical integration has, for example, often been a function of the vulnerability of various production stages to nationalization, and the willingness to concentrate production in particular countries turns partly on projections of political stability. Production decisions also involve understanding the skills of the local work force and how they are likely to evolve, availability of local and imported inputs, including the impact of likely government policies, as well as conventional analysis of comparative factor costs. Similarly, marketing and organizational decisions involve political, cultural and institutional analysis, as well as economic analysis.

One might not be surprised that a book which reports on economic analysis and multinationals has little to say about many issues that affect managers of multinational firms. The greater surprise may be the gaps in what such a review contains when it comes to government managers. Yet, the gaps are almost as broad. Economists have tended to limit their interests to broad policy issues; they have shown relatively little interest in implementation. The result, whatever the reason, is the absence of analysis on some of the tough issues that government managers face in dealing with the multinational.

One example is how best to select projects and reject others. Economists have been interested in the criteria and analytical methodologies underlying such a decision, and have developed tools such as economic cost/benefit analysis. But they have usually avoided the difficult management issues associated with an investment screening process. It turns out that almost no investment agency has actually used on a regular basis the tools that economists have provided for them. There has to be something to be learned from an examination of why the tools were so widely ignored.

Governments face organizational choices with respect to screening investment, as well as choices concerning how to analyse proposed projects. Many governments try to analyse proposals project-by-project through what might be called *ad hoc* approaches. But, there is a great deal of anecdotal evidence to support the belief that these approaches have led to corruption, and that the tediousness of the processes may discourage good as well as bad investors. On the other hand, automatic processes, guided by transparent laws and regulations, may have done a poor job of eliminating harmful projects. But no research seems to have been conducted to look systematically at the results of various kinds of screening process that have been designed to judge MNEs' proposed projects.

Economists have tried to determine the effects of incentives on the decisions of multinationals, but they have not explored the difficult management choices with regard to awarding those investment incentives. As in the case of screening processes, *ad hoc* systems to award incentives may, in theory, do a better job of reducing costs, by enabling government managers to award them only when they are essential to attract a particular investor. On the other hand, like *ad hoc* screening systems, they appear often to end up riddled with corruption, especially in the developing countries. Similar management choices face government officials charged with monitoring FDI to determine whether it has met the conditions attached to licenses or incentives.

In sum, too few studies have been undertaken to help government managers with the difficult tradeoffs that they must make in managing their foreign investment policies. Analytical tools have been developed; how and whether to use them remains a matter of judgment, with little research on which the manager can draw.

OUT-OF-FASHION SUBJECTS

I have focused on gaps in research, but it is also useful to look at some topics that have gone out of fashion. Chapter 7, for example, devotes almost three pages to research on choice of technology. However, only two of the references are dated after 1983, and none dates after 1990. This is not from laziness on the part of Caves in updating the book. Rather, choice of technology was a hot topic in the 1970s; it became unfashionable soon after.

An exploration of why this topic lost its appeal would have been interesting in a summary of research on multinationals. My own tendency is to reject the explanation that earlier research answered all the questions. Have economists lost interest in the subject because policymakers have decided that they cannot influence the outcome? Or, have development goals shifted such that the subject is of little interest? Or, have economists simply avoided such micro-studies that once attracted them, as the focus of the profession has shifted away from firm-level work and industrial organization? The reasons for the declining interest remain something of a puzzle.

To a lesser extent, government policymakers' interest in joint ventures appears to have declined. It is not clear whether this is because the economic advantages expected from requirements that foreigners have local partners failed to materialize, because the eagerness of governments not to frighten away investors has led to caution, or because the political process has some-how resulted in different pressures on governments. The answer is especially elusive because so little research has addressed the relative importance of economic considerations and political concerns in the earlier requirements of joint ownership.

In sum, there may be a great deal to learn from examinations of why inter-est on the part of researchers and decision makers in particular topics declines.

A NEW SUBJECT

The second edition of Caves' book has added only one new section in the chapter on multinationals in developing countries: 'third-world multination-als'. Although a few scattered articles on foreign investment from firms based in developing countries had appeared earlier, the bulk of the literature appeared in the period after 1976, when the first edition was put together.

All the literature suffers from the fact that the rapid growth (and probably rapid change) in investment from third-world multinationals was occurring as the research was being carried out. As a result, there is no sense of which types of investors 'survive'. Thus, there may well have been firms caught up in the investment frenzy who had no competitive advantage with which they could support distant operations; there have not been follow-up studies of the early third-world multinationals to see which did not survive competition abroad. A new look at the subject might, for example, suggest that many of the upstream – to richer countries – investments failed, or at least did not grow. To the extent that they were not based on some kind of competitive advantage, their purposes – often diversification of risk for the business or the owners – could be better served by portfolio investment. Many of the survivors that thrived probably had advantages or reasons that were similar to those that have moti-vated the more traditional multinationals from, say, Japan, that invested in richer countries: the need for internalizing a facility to support exports (distri-bution, service, assembly), for example.

Given how recent the phenomenon is, research has not yet captured a sense of change in types of investor from developing countries. The relative weight of different kinds of downstream investment has probably changed with shifts in development strategies and with growth in certain home countries. The advantages associated with skills in small-scale production that were important early on have declined in value with more open economies; third-world MNEs whose advantage rested in these skills have probably become less important. On the other hand, rapid growth in downstream investment by firms from the upper tier of developing countries seems to have occurred as their traditional exports were constrained by quotas (garments and textiles), rising real exchange rates (Republic of Korea and Taiwan [China] in the second half of the 1980s), and increased wages and shortages of labor for unattractive jobs. Although these and other changes have probably occurred, they seem to remain largely undocumented. One is left with the catalog of motivations for third-world MNEs without a good sense of their relative importance; and without a sense of how motivations for investment have changed in importance over the past two decades.

It may be that third-world MNEs have been one of the important mechanisms that make being in a 'good neighborhood' such an important factor in growth. Within East Asia, for example, Japanese firms carried know-how – production and market access – to the Republic of Korea and, to a certain extent, to Taiwan (China). Then, Korean and Taiwanese, and to some extent Hong Kong and Malaysian MNEs, carried the skills and access to others in the neighborhood. If this is accurate, there are probably profound lessons for the Sub-Saharan African countries, which are struggling at least partly because of the lack of successful 'neighbors'. The hypotheses of lessons seem not to have been examined in serious research (for some hypotheses, see Wells 1994).

CONCLUSION

My purpose in pointing out gaps in Chapter 9 has not been to criticize the book. On the contrary, this chapter, along with other relevant chapters, have done an outstanding job of summarizing economic analysis of multinational firms in developing countries. It seems that the gaps are largely the result of a shortage of some very difficult empirical research and the limits of economic analysis as a tool to deal with certain issues. It is up to other researchers – whether economists or not – to fill in some of the major gaps in knowledge.

REFERENCES

Allen, Nancy J. (1994), 'The cross-national transfer and transformation of managerial and organizational knowledge: American and Japanese direct investment in

Indonesia', unpublished Ph.D. organizational behavior dissertation, Harvard University, Cambridge, MA.

Caves, Richard E. (1996), *Multinational Enterprise and Economic Analysis*, second edition, Cambridge: Cambridge University Press.

Evans, Peter (1979), *Dependent Development: The Alliance of Multinational, State, and Local Capital in Brazil*, Princeton, NJ: Princeton University Press.

Goodsell, Charles E. (1974), *American Corporations and Peruvian Politics*, Cambridge, MA: Harvard University Press.

Mahini, Amir (1988), *Making Decisions in Multinational Corporations: Managing Relations with Sovereign Governments*, New York, NY: Wiley.

Rhee, Yung W., and Therese Belot (1989), 'Export catalysts in low-income countries: preliminary findings from a review of export success stories in eleven countries', Washington, DC: World Bank Industry and Energy Department.

Wells, Louis T. (1994), 'Foreign investment', in David D. Lindauer and Michael Roemer (eds), *Asia and Africa: Legacies and Opportunities in Development*, San Francisco, CA: ICS Press.

Wells, Louis T. (forthcoming), 'God and fair competition: do foreign direct investors face still other risks in emerging markets?' in Theodore Moran (ed.), [title unannounced], Davenport, Iowa: Blackmun Press.

7. Multinational enterprises and public policy

Alan M. Rugman and Alain Verbeke

INTRODUCTION

In this chapter we attempt to review and integrate representative literature on the exceptionally broad topic of multinational enterprises (MNEs) and public policy towards them. To help us in this difficult task we build upon the insights offered by Richard Caves (1996) in Chapter 10 on 'public policy' in his critically acclaimed advanced textbook *Multinational Enterprise and Economic Analysis*. This book was first published in 1982 and substantially revised for the second edition in 1996. Our specific task is to consider the literature on MNEs and public policy as it has emerged since 1970, and make projections concerning the relevance of this literature for the year 2020, which is the target date for the 18 members of the Asia-Pacific Economic Cooperation Forum (APECF) to realize full trade and foreign direct investment (FDI) liberalization. Such liberalization has already been implemented in the European Union (15 member states), and it will further expand as new countries are accepted as members in the twenty-first century.

In the first half of Chapter 10, Caves adopts a 'normative' approach, using neoclassical welfare economics to review the benefits and costs of national government policies. In the second half of that chapter, Caves considers some 'behavioral' approaches to public policy, based on the assumption that there are self-interested actors in the political domain who can influence the formation of public policy. While retaining these insights we introduce a third approach in this chapter. Using the resource-based theory of the firm, we develop an explicitly 'strategic' perspective for MNEs interacting with governments. This provides insight into the managerial aspects of the firm-level strategy process, dealing with core competencies and dynamic capabilities that need to be integrated into the MNE–government literature. Furthermore, we carefully differentiate the policies of home and host governments, and show how the institutional structures of both public policy and the MNE are relevant in the current international business literature.

The organization of this chapter is as follows. First, we review the analytical and policy contributions of Caves in Chapter 10 on public policy and MNEs (and in the rest of his book where public policy issues are discussed.) Next, we develop an original analytical framework of our own to synthesize the literature on MNEs and public policy. Finally, we relate some of the key references in the literature on MNEs and public policy by Caves and others to our new analytical framework.

EFFICIENCY ASPECTS OF MNEs AND PUBLIC POLICY

The analytical approach adopted by Caves in Chapter 10 is that of a traditional economist, essentially concentrating on the efficiency aspects of MNE activities in a world where government regulations on MNEs are imposed for equity/distributional reasons. This distinction between efficiency and equity is extremely useful from the viewpoint of an economist, and it has been used by many writers on MNEs, for example Safarian (1966, 1993), Rugman (1980), Casson (1987), and Dunning (1993a).

Analysis of the efficiency aspects of MNEs builds upon the normative foundation of neoclassical welfare economics (in which distributional issues are assumed away). In Chapter 10 Caves carefully lays out all the assumptions required for neoclassical welfare economics to work, namely that:

- each state attempts to maximize real national income;
- distributional issues are entirely separate from efficiency ones;
- each enterprise has a single 'home base' country to act as a numeraire;
- each MNE and nation-state operates in a competitive environment, with a downward-sloping demand curve for the proprietary assets of the MNE and an upward-sloping supply curve of MNE resource commitments for each nation;
- policymaking by governments can discriminate between foreign and home-based MNEs.

Using this welfare economics framework, Caves is able in Chapter 10 to summarize the normative conclusions of earlier chapters as they apply to key issues, such as:

- taxation;
- natural resource rents;
- competition policy;
- technology creation and transfer.

A flavor of the implications stemming from the welfare economics approach is given by the last issue of technology transfer. Many writers sympathetic to developing countries bemoan the perceived lack of technology transfer from the branch plant subsidiaries of foreign MNEs, and allege lower ratios of R&D to sales by subsidiaries as evidence of this. Caves, however, makes the brilliant point that technology transfer takes place when the consumers in developing countries have access to the goods and services that embody the technology. Thus, the focus is not upon the domestic production of technology-intensive goods and services in developing countries, but upon the end result of FDI, namely the consumption of technologically-intensive goods and services. Whether they are provided by foreign-owned or domestic firms is relatively unimportant.

In the second half of Chapter 10 Caves presents a behavioral approach to supplement the normative approach of the first half. In the behavioral approach, Caves allows for the self-interest of agents in government policymaking. He briefly reviews government policies which are aimed at regulating inward FDI, and then home government policy directed towards the promotion of FDI for reasons of market access. A first version of Caves' behavioral approach explains the actual focus of many governments on distributional issues and away from income maximization. Utility-maximizing electoral behaviour leads to redistribution at the expense of foreign MNEs because foreign equity holders cannot vote, and discrimination against foreigners may provide perceived utility to domestic citizens. In a second version, government policy is assumed to be the work of a coalition of government officials, who resent foreign MNEs mainly because of their ability to circumvent or avoid various types of regulation. In both versions of the behavioral approach, discriminatory measures are imposed on foreign MNEs. These behavioral models, however, do not appear very useful in explaining government support for domestic MNEs engaged in outward FDI. Finally, Caves discusses the role of multilateral agencies that attempt to regulate or facilitate FDI and MNE activity.

Caves' focus on the efficiency aspects of MNEs is fully consistent with the use of internalization theory (explained earlier in his book) as the key theoretical explanation for the existence of MNEs. The early work on such a transaction-cost approach to the MNE was pioneered by Buckley and Casson (1976), Rugman (1981), Hennart (1982) and others. All of these writers considered the public policy implications of the MNE in a similar manner to that in Caves (1996). This body of work is, of course, a significant departure from the seminal work of Hymer (1976), based on his 1960 doctoral dissertation. Hymer and many political science-based writers on the MNE, such as Gilpin (1975, 1987) and Grieco (1982), are not really interested in the efficiency aspects of MNEs; rather they wish to discuss such issues as the relative power of MNEs versus the nation-state.

There is a rich tradition of work looking into the relative power of the MNE versus the nation-state, with some of the more sensible observations being in Vernon (1971), Bergsten, Horst and Moran (1978), Behrman and Grosse

(1990), and so on. In this chapter we do not have space to review these arguments in detail, nor can we consider the relationship of this work on MNEs to
the relevant literature in international political economy (IPE) generated by
Susan Strange (1988, 1997) and Lorraine Eden (1991). In IPE, the focus is
upon the interaction between MNEs and nation-states, with emphasis upon the
ability of MNEs to transcend the traditional authority of the nation-state.
Susan Strange alleges that the MNE has increased its power relative to the
state in the areas of natural resources, finance and technology. In particular,
US-based MNEs have developed control in these three 'market' areas, leading
to an overall decline in the power of the 'state', but also, paradoxically, to the
reinforcement of US economic hegemony for most of the postwar period.
Another relevant consideration is that non-governmental organizations
(NGOs) and other subnational groups are exercising an increasing amount of
power in the Western democracies (Ostry 1997). The role of NGOs is especially important in analysis of trade and environment issues (Vogel 1995;
Vogel and Rugman 1997; Rugman and Verbeke 1998).

In another advance on Caves' 'efficiency-first' perspective on MNEs,
Stopford and Strange (1991) have addressed the relationships between MNEs
and states in an IPE triangular diplomacy framework in which there is a triad
of bargaining relationships: state/state; state/firm; firm/firm. As another example of IPE work, Milner (1988) and Goldstein (1993) built on Krasner (1978),
Keohane (1984), and Keohane and Nye (1977) to describe the role of institutional factors in the administration of US trade policy. Goldstein finds that the
US Congress protects the US domestic market by a variety of protectionist
trade laws, such as anti-dumping (AD) and countervailing duty (CVD)
measures (Rugman and Anderson 1987; Bhagwati 1988; Rugman 1996).

We shall not devote any more attention to IPE, hegemonic stability theory,
and related theories of MNE-government conflict because today governments
need to deal with both inward and outward FDI. We shall develop a framework
which considers the symmetry between these two types of FDI. Our approach
is consistent with that of Dunning (1993a, 1997) who traces the changing
nature of interaction between MNEs and governments over the last thirty
years. In particular, governments have switched attention from questions of
the distribution of rents and structural issues of technology transfer and regulation towards policies aimed at attracting the knowledge-based mobile FDI
taking place in a global system of alliance capitalism.

THE SIMPLE ANALYTICS OF MNEs AND PUBLIC POLICY

In this section we shall develop an analytical framework to incorporate the
work synthesized by Caves with other, more recent, literature in the field of

international business. To do so we need to build a framework consisting of three sequential components, which we now describe. In this section we will position Caves' perspective within this new conceptual analytical framework. In the following sections we shall place the wider literature in this framework. The first component of the framework reflects the issue of consistency between MNE goals and government goals, in both home and host countries. Most of the models of international economics on MNE–government relations build upon specific assumptions regarding this goal consistency, or lack thereof. Such assumptions determine both the substantive focus and the normative implications of these models. The four main possibilities in this area are shown in Figure 7.1.

In quadrant 1 of Figure 7.1, interactions between MNEs and both home and host governments are assumed to be driven by goal conflict. This reflects the tensions between the micro-efficiency-driven behavior of MNEs and the macro-efficiency or distributional objectives of governments. The opposite situation arises in quadrant 4 of Figure 7.1; here the goals of MNEs and both home and host governments are complementary. In quadrant 2 there is consistency between MNE and home country goals, but conflicts with host country

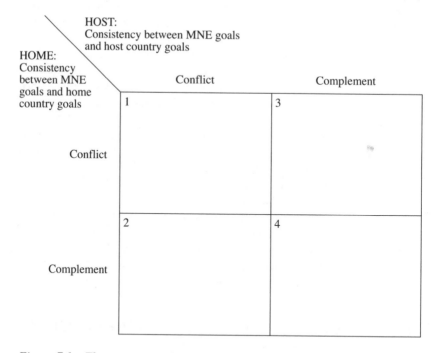

Figure 7.1   The consistency between MNE and home and host government goals

goals. The reverse applies in quadrant 3. In the next section, we shall use this matrix to position a large part of the existing literature in international business and public policy.

The Caves perspective on the literature requires that each MNE has a clearly defined nationality, usually with a strong home base in which its Firm Specific Advantages (FSAs) are developed. The MNE has a centralized, hierarchical organizational structure to control the global production of each line of business. In terms of government regulation, Caves makes a clear distinction between home and host country interests. Given that the Caves perspective is primarily one of synthesis, it is hardly surprising that literature covering the various quadrants of Figure 7.1 is discussed in his book, albeit with a focus largely situated in quadrant 1. Caves concentrates his focus on research dealing with conflict issues between MNEs and governments, for example, taxation and competition policy, bargaining over natural-resource rents, and technology transfer issues.

The second component of the framework builds upon more recent insights in the international business field. There, it is recognized that the institutional characteristics of specific MNEs and specific countries largely determine MNE–government interactions. In contrast to the macro-analysis provided by the first component of our conceptual framework, which assumed a particular level of inherent goal congruence between firms and public agencies (largely based on ideological elements), this second component attempts to highlight the most important institutional elements determining MNE and government behavior. These institutional elements are shown in Figure 7.2.

On the MNE axis, the key institutional issue is the dispersion of its FSAs across geographic borders. The FSAs of an MNE reflect its core competencies and dynamic capabilities (in terms of the resource-based theory of the firm). Incidentally, the FSA terminology precedes that of core competencies and dynamic capabilities (Rugman 1980, 1981). A conventional ethnocentric MNE will be characterized by a concentration of FSAs in the home country with a replication of home country production and managerial approaches in host nations. The product line manager in the home base controls the FSAs of the MNE. In contrast, a polycentric MNE is one with its FSAs dispersed into its various host nation subsidiaries. The country managers of the polycentric MNE develop and control the FSAs across whatever product markets they choose. Finally, a geocentric MNE attempts to develop a balance between the interests of product line and country managers. Here, some FSAs remain concentrated in the home base, whereas other FSAs are developed autonomously in the various host country subsidiaries. The Caves perspective on the literature, with a focus on adversarial interactions, especially between the MNE and host nations, is justified only in the first case of an ethnocentric

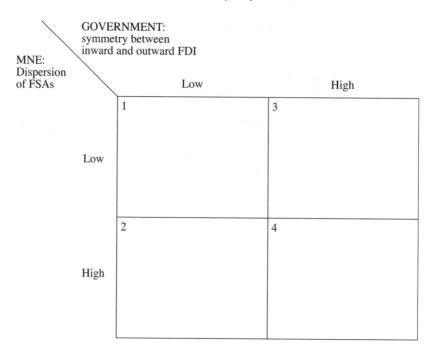

Figure 7.2   Institutional determinants of MNE–government interactions

MNE. In both the latter two cases (of polycentric and geocentric MNEs), when FSAs are developed and controlled in several nations simultaneously, we need to build upon a richer framework that would allow us to explain the interaction between MNEs and governments.

On the government axis, the key parameter determining MNE–government relations is the symmetry between inward and outward FDI. This parameter is viewed as an institutional element in this chapter because a high symmetry represents an *ex post* reflection of the willingness of government to allow inward and outward FDI. A nation's policies towards MNEs will depend on whether it is (i) a net exporter of FDI (with MNEs using a strong home base); (ii) a net recipient of FDI (a typical host nation); or (iii) a 'dual' player with both outward and inward FDI. In each of these cases, the incentive structure facing governments in terms of regulating MNE behavior is fundamentally different, Dunning (1993b). In Figure 7.2, we relate these two determinants of MNE–government interactions. On the vertical axis for the MNE, we represent the dispersion of the MNE's FSAs as either low or high. On the horizontal axis for government, we place the symmetry between inward and outward FDI as either low or high. As regards this latter parameter, we assume a high absolute volume of FDI. If the FDI volume were low, the symmetry issue would obviously not be critical.

The Caves perspective mainly describes one of the four cases in Figure 7.2; it is in quadrant 1. Here, there is no recognition of the dispersion of FSAs by the firm, and a low degree of symmetry between inward and outward FDI prevails. The view of MNEs as only demonstrating centralized structures (that is, they only develop FSAs in their single home country base), and the view of governments as acting narrowly in accordance with either home or host nation perspectives allows for elegant, albeit often over-simplified, modeling by economists. In reality, three more complex cases may occur that do not lend themselves to simple modeling. In quadrant 2, firm-driven national responsiveness may induce governments to provide national treatment. This requires that governments understand the economic and strategic significance of MNEs operating a network with dispersed FSAs. Governments also need to be interested in the creation of sustainable value-added domestically, whether by domestic or foreign MNEs. In contrast, in quadrant 3, the symmetry between a country's inward FDI and outward FDI positions provides incentives for the non-discriminatory regulation of foreign MNEs, irrespective of their ethnocentric, polycentric or geocentric strategies. National treatment of foreign MNEs may then induce foreign MNEs to become more nationally responsive themselves. Finally, in quadrant 4, there is a government preference for global regulation and a firm preference for a 'supranational' approach to government policy. This is the opposite of Caves' view. The reason for such preferences is that a symmetrical position of inward and outward FDI at the public policy level, and a dispersed FDI configuration at the firm level, leads to complexities in terms of optimal business–government interactions that cannot be solved at the national level.

To summarize, in Caves' analysis the MNE is a centralized, hierarchical organization that closely monitors and meters the use of its home-based FSAs. Government policy is systematically analysed from the viewpoint of either a host country (recipient of FDI), or a home country (exporter of FDI). Thus, Caves' perspective has a single (and simple) MNE–government context in quadrant 1 of Figure 7.2. However, the institutional determinants of MNE–government interaction are now recognized to be more complex than this, and so the other three quadrants of Figure 7.2 are necessary to properly explore the process of interactions between MNEs and home and host governments.

The third component of our new framework analyses the MNE's strategic approach to government policy in terms of strategic perspectives and desired outcomes. This is shown in Figure 7.3.

The strategic perspective on government policy reflects the extent to which it is viewed as either exogenous or endogenous by the managers of the MNE.

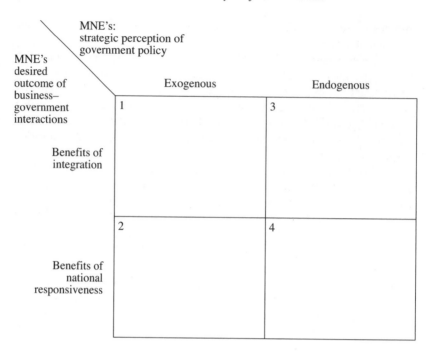

Figure 7.3   MNE's strategic approach to government policy

If it is endogenous, this means that the MNE will attempt to alter the content and/or process of government policy in its favor. If it is exogenous, the MNE will work within the rules set by public agencies. Given this choice of inter-action with governments, the MNE must design an appropriate strategy and structure to obtain either the benefits of integration or of national responsive-ness when interacting with home and host governments. This leads to several complex situations in Figure 7.3, only one of which is discussed in depth by Caves. This is quadrant 1, where the MNE views government policy as exoge-nous and its objective is to achieve the benefits of integration, that is conven-tional efficiency benefits in the area of scale economies, economies of scope and economies of exploiting national differences.

The other quadrants of Figure 7.3 represent the newer stream of interna-tional business literature. The four quadrants as a whole represent a 'transna-tional' approach to government policy. There the MNE has to make a strategic choice for each type of government regulation (or intervention) relevant to the firm. It does this within each region, for each SBU, and for each function and task. Each MNE has to decide two things. First, whether government policy will be viewed as an endogenous or exogenous variable; and secondly, whether benefits of national responsiveness versus integration will be pursued in its business–government interaction. The latter decision depends on the relative importance of the MNE's location-bound versus non-location-bound FSAs. The location-bound FSAs reflect proprietary competencies and capabilities which can be exploited in only a limited geographic region, for example, an excellent local reputation, a well positioned retail network, privileged relationships with domestic economic actors, and so on. If location-bound FSAs represent the key to competitive success, the MNE will focus on those areas of government regulation that constitute an opportunity or threat to developing and exploiting such FSAs. In contrast, if the MNE builds primarily on non-location-bound FSAs, such as global brandnames and technologies that can easily be transferred internationally, either as an intermediate good or embodied in a final product, then its focus in government relations will be on protecting and exploiting such FSAs.

There are four cases in Figure 7.3. In quadrant 1 government policy is used as a lever for global competitiveness. In quadrant 2 there is the good corporate citizen approach building upon a strategy of national responsiveness. In quadrant 4 the strategy of national responsiveness is extended to one of nation-bound bargaining, whereas in quadrant 3 the firm's interest will be in developing global bargaining strategies to be used when dealing with subnational, national and supranational public agencies. In fact, it could be argued that in quadrant 4 the MNE will develop location-bound FSAs in government relations in each country in which it operates, whereas in quadrant 3 the focus will be on non-location-bound FSAs. This is a strategy of developing systemic advantages in dealing with public agencies across borders.

A NEW SYNTHESIS OF THE LITERATURE

Using Figure 7.1 we can appreciate the penetrating insights that Caves brings to our understanding of the relationship between MNEs and governments. At the time of the first edition (1982), Caves offered a state-of-the-art approach which covered the great bulk of literature to that date. It is understandable, if unfortunate, that Caves chose not to update his approach in the 1996 second edition of his book. Later in this section we shall explore some of the limitations of Caves' approach, and how these can be overcome using our new analytical framework. At this stage, however, we explore the rich foundations provided by Caves.

In Figure 7.1A, where most of the conventional economics literature can be positioned, all of which is covered by Caves, quadrants 1 and 4 are the polar extremes of the MNE–state debate. In quadrant 1 we have the Hymer (1976) quasi-Marxist view of the conflicts between MNEs and home and host governments. The focus is upon distributional issues and the power of the MNE

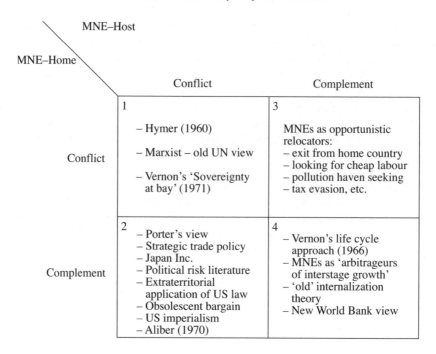

Figure 7.1A   Examples of Figure 7.1

versus the host nation-state (Dunning and Rugman 1985). We can also position the *Sovereignty at Bay* of Raymond Vernon (1971) in this quadrant. As Vernon (1991) himself states, the title of his book has been misinterpreted. He did not argue that the MNE would dominate the host nation-state, but rather that there would be antagonistic relations between them, as we show in quadrant 1. Also in this quadrant can be placed the Kojima (1973, 1975, 1978, 1985) hypothesis to the effect that trade and FDI are substitutes in the US experience but complements in the Japanese case, that is that there are MNE–host and home government conflicts.

In contrast, in quadrant 4 of Figure 7.1A we position the complementary nature of MNE–home and host state relations. This is more consistent with Vernon (1966) and Knickerbocker (1973) according to whom the MNE grows through a product life cycle of technology-intensive FSAs developed initially in a strong home base, then produced by wholly-owned subsidiaries in host economies and finally (when the product is mature) anywhere in the world with the lowest factor input costs. This is an efficiency-based view of the MNE–state relationship. This quadrant is also consistent with early views of internalization theory in Buckley and Casson (1976), Rugman (1980, 1981), Dunning (1981) and Hennart (1982). The internalization of technological and managerial know-how within the internal market of the MNE is a positive externality that overcomes the Coase (1937) problem of knowledge as a public good. Johnson (1970) and Magee (1977) explored how the MNE could 'appropriate', or own, firm-specific assets in know-how and in technology and thereby overcome the transaction cost of knowledge as a public good. The process of internalization is efficiency based since the MNEs help both home and host nations to develop; indeed the MNE is the engine of economic development in quadrant 4 of Figure 7.1A. To the extent that national governments understand the value to their country of access to the MNE's FSAs, goal conflict can be largely avoided. Dunning (1994) has described why most governments are now 'acclaiming FDI as good news' after a period of hostility in the 1970s and early 1980s. In fact, this change in attitude reflects the understanding that the FSAs of MNEs cannot be simply unbundled or purchased as intermediate goods. This view has also been echoed in recent World Bank reports and it represents a welcome shift in the public policy perspective.

There are then two more complex cases in Figure 7.1A. In quadrant 2 we place the Porter (1990) view of MNEs with a strong home base. There is a complementary relationship between the home government and its MNEs. In fact, appropriate government policy for each of the determinants of Porter's national diamond of competitiveness (that is factor conditions, demand conditions, related and supporting industries, firms' strategy, structure and rivalry in a specific industry) will strengthen the domestic firms' home base and allow them to become successful internationally. However, Porter also argues that foreign-owned firms are not sources of competitive advantage for host nations, that is that the MNE is in conflict with the host nation. This quadrant 2 viewpoint of Porter is also representative of a large literature on strategic trade policy starting with Krugman (1986) and Brander and Spencer (1985) and then misapplied to public policy by Tyson (1993) and Yoffie (1993), amongst others. Basically, all of these writers develop cases in which the home government can subsidize its MNEs to develop first-mover advantages in a zero-sum game. Strategic trade policy has home states giving discriminatory subsidies to home-based MNEs, who then act as national champions to take global market shares away from MNEs based in host nations. In reality, such policies have mostly failed, as few governments have the necessary knowledge and the required implementing apparatus to catapult domestic firms into becoming globally competitive MNEs (Rugman and Verbeke 1990). The earlier literature on Japan Inc. is also positioned in quadrant 2. Here the argument is that the Japanese *keiretsu*s have developed in a strong and rivalrous home base and, helped by the Japanese government, have succeeded in global markets at the expense of host country firms (Ohmae 1985; Gerlach 1992; Nonaka and Takeuchi 1995; Fruin 1997). Aliber's (1970) theory of FDI is also in quadrant

2. He argues that a strong currency allows home-based MNEs to capitalize expected earnings at a higher rate than can host country firms.

Finally, the more conventional literature on political risk management by Kobrin (1982), Brewer (1983, 1985), Ghadar (1982), Nigh (1985) and others, is also in quadrant 2. The literature assumes that host governments should be able to regulate foreign MNEs, or otherwise change the political environmental parameters facing MNEs in the host nations. In this work, MNEs are often seen as a modern instrument of colonization, bringing with them unwanted approaches (including managerial and labor practices) prevailing in their home nations. An extreme version of political risk is the 'obsolescing bargain' hypothesis by Encarnation and Wells (1985), Kobrin (1984, 1987). This argues that the manufacturing or resource-based MNEs in host economies have sunk costs in the form of factories, mines and plantations, all of which could be nationalized by the host government and result in losses for the MNE. Here, the main point is that host government goals can only prevail at the expense of foreign MNE goals once the MNE has engaged in irreversible resource commitments and its bargaining position has weakened substantially. To help overcome this, there is still a US legal viewpoint that argues for extraterritorial application of its laws. The Helms-Burton Act on Cuba is the latest manifestation of this old-fashioned view that US MNEs can be used as complementary instruments of US foreign policy against the interests of the host governments.

In quadrant 3 we have the opposite situation. Here there is a conflict between MNEs and their home governments, but a complementary relationship with host governments. An example is the 'pollution haven' argument, whereby MNEs are alleged to flee tight home market regulations to go to lax host nation regimes. The 'cheap labor offshore assembly platform' argument also fits here, as does the naive viewpoint that MNEs engage in transfer pricing and seek out tax havens at the expense of their governments. There has been less research on this quadrant than on quadrant 2. What literature there is tends to refute the political science-led rationale for quadrant 3. For example, Eden (1985, 1997), building on earlier work, for example, Copithorne (1971), Lall (1973), Nieckels (1976), Lessard (1979), Rugman and Eden (1985), finds no evidence for systematic transfer pricing by MNEs other than as a response to effective tax rate differentials and other exogenous market imperfections. The rationale for offshore assembly has been weakening as most manufacturing sectors are reducing the labor content of their processes; there are some exceptions such as the offshore assembly of disk drives and other high-technology commodity products. In NAFTA, the role of Mexico as a cheap labor and pollution haven for Asian and European MNEs was offset by rules of origin for autos and textiles which protect 'insider' North American MNEs (Rugman 1994; Gestrin and Rugman 1994; Eden and Molot 1993; Hufbauer and Schott 1992; Lustig, Bosworth and Lawrence 1992). In more general terms, it would be incorrect to assume that MNEs, faced with excessive goal conflicts in their home countries, seek cooperation with mostly poorer host nations, where goal complementarity prevails. However, institutional competition among potential host countries to attract FDI can lead to generous investment promotion programs, even in the most developed economies, sometimes creating a situation of reverse discrimination.

Turning to Figure 7.2A we can see that, while the Caves material covers the four quadrants of Figure 7.1A, it only fits into quadrant 1 here. The older literature in international business failed to address the ability of the MNE to disperse its FSAs globally, using its organizational structure and systems as a managerially-based core competence. Indeed, the literature up to Caves (1982), including early internalization theory, plus the Vernon (1966, 1971) and Porter (1990) work, all assume the creation of non-location-bound FSAs in the home country of the MNE that would lead to profits abroad through exports, licensing or FDI. Strategies for MNEs in quadrant 1 consist of replicating home country practices and are entirely dependent on decisions made in the home country concerning value chain configurations and coordination (Porter 1990). There is no recognition of

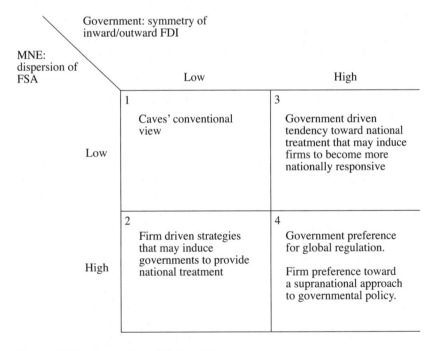

Figure 7.2A   Examples of Figure 7.2

the need to develop location-bound FSAs in host countries that would lead to benefits of national responsiveness.

The turning point in recognizing the ability of the MNE to be nationally responsive can be traced to the neglected work of Doz (1986) and to the more influential book by Bartlett and Ghoshal (1989). These authors have added rigorous strategic modeling methods to the original insight by Perlmutter (1969) into the decentralized role of polycentric managers. In Bartlett's and Ghoshal's work, it is also demonstrated that when MNEs feel sufficiently confident about the economic and strategic potential of a specific foreign subsidiary or business unit abroad, then non-location-bound FSAs may actually be developed there. This gives the host nation a characteristic conventionally reserved to home nations, namely to become a source country for new innovations. This leads to a quadrant 2 in Figure 7.2A situation with firm driven strategies that may induce governments to provide national treatment.

The conventional literature covered by Caves also assumes a low symmetry between inward and outward FDI, which is a key parameter determining government regulation of MNEs. The 'old' politics of international institutions, such as the GATT, concerned themselves with tariff cuts and the negotiation of the removal of trade barriers. This was a focus on 'shallow integration' (Ostry 1997; Brewer and Young 1998). This shallow integration of successive GATT rounds assumed that little could be achieved on trade in services and in the FDI area because governments would be either a net exporter or a net recipient of FDI. The new agenda of the WTO and of the OECD's Multinational Agreement on Investment (MAI) is to negotiate 'deep integration' and the removal of barriers to FDI. The objective of the MAI is to make domestic markets internationally contestable through the principle of national treatment, that is all MNEs are to be treated in the same manner as domestic firms by host governments. Thus, in quadrant 3 of Figure 7.2A, there is a new agenda for international relations which recognizes the reality of a high symmetry by governments between inward and outward FDI characterizing many countries, including the United States, Canada, the EU, and Japan. This symmetry has led to the widespread adoption of the national treatment principle, that is, it ends the discriminatory treatment of home and foreign firms by governments. This is consistent with Dunning (1994) who has suggested that inbound FDI may inject more market-oriented beliefs and practices in a domestic economic system and may alter the international competitiveness agenda of government.

The view that diverges most sharply from Caves is found in quadrant 4 of Figure 7.2A. Here, there is a mutual preference on the part of both MNEs and governments for a 'supranational' approach to public policy. This will take into account the dispersion of MNE FSAs and the high degree of symmetry of inward and outward FDI at the national level. Given the general institutional

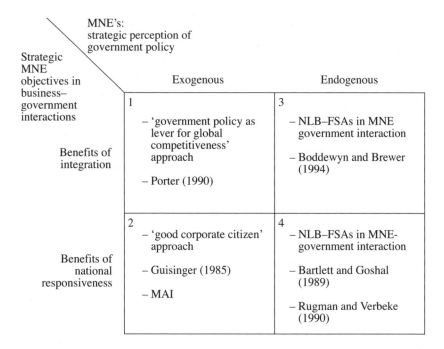

Figure 7.3A   Examples of Figure 7.3

trend towards quadrant 4 in Figure 7.2A, some possible MNE strategies towards MNE-government relations are analysed in Figure 7.3A.

In Figure 7.3A we can incorporate the resource-based view of literature on MNE strategy and public policy developed in Rugman and Verbeke (1991). In this work, a vital distinction is drawn between location-bound FSAs and non-location-bound FSAs. Location-bound FSAs include those that lead to benefits of national responsiveness, whereas non-location-bound FSAs are those that lead to integration benefits of scale, scope and exploiting national differences. Application of this model to issues of strategic trade policy and shelter theory, competitiveness and NAFTA, can be found in Rugman and Verbeke (1990) and Rugman (1996).

The prevailing view on the impact of MNE–public policy linkages on international competitiveness is that of Porter (1990), which can be positioned in quadrant 1 of Figure 7.3A. His use of the home base/cluster concept requires that the MNE adopts an integration strategy and regards the government policy as exogenous. The MNEs in the triad respond to, for example, home government subsidies and other policies strengthening the domestic 'diamond' (Porter 1990) and use their large home base to become globally competitive. This is partly consistent with the resource-based view, but it limits the public policy induced development of managerially-based FSAs to those generated by home government stimulus. There is no room in this work for subsidiary managers or foreign governments to contribute to the FSAs, except in the implementation stage of integration-based strategies. Applications of this thinking have been made to trade and environment issues by Porter and van der Linde (1995).

In quadrant 2 of Figure 7.3A, government policy is still viewed as exogenous, but here MNEs develop strategies (building upon such policies) whose aim is to achieve benefits of national responsiveness in the various countries where the firm operates. Government policy is not viewed as a major determinant of international competitiveness. This view is consistent with the proposition that public policy should focus on providing a level playing field rather than creating an international competitive advantage. Issues of public policy that are relevant in quadrant 2 of Figure 7.3A include work on negotiation of a subsidies code at the GATT and WTO. Here the research of Guisinger et al. (1985), Hufbauer and Erb (1984), and Gladwin and Walter (1980), is relevant. The OECD's work on the MAI would occur in this quadrant.

In contrast, quadrant 4 reflects a pro-active strategy of national responsiveness. The MNEs here have a decentralized or matrix organizational structure and they outperform average competitors through national responsiveness, as argued by Doz (1986), Prahalad and Doz (1987), and by Bartlett and Ghoshal (1989). An application of this has been made to corporate strategies and environmental regulations by Rugman and Verbeke (1998). In this work, government policy is viewed as a parameter that can be influenced (endogenized) through lobbying and negotiation. This is consistent with the conclusions of a body of political risk literature which argues that such risk is largely determined by micro-environmental factors.

In quadrant 3 of Figure 7.3A it is also argued that government policy is endogenous, but this time the MNE aims to achieve the benefits of integration-based FSAs. These are non-location-bound. The danger associated with active MNE strategies in this area is that they often represent a 'Trojan horse' approach. Firms themselves use strategic trade policy arguments to obtain government favors. First-mover advantages at the international level, strategic entry deterrence, technological spillovers, learning curve effects, credible retaliation to foreign support programs, and so on may be among the effects lobbied for by firms. The end result should be domestic MNEs with stronger non-location-bound FSAs. Unfortunately, such lobbying often disguises shelter-seeking strategies. These firms are unable to compete without artificial government support. Such behaviour has been variously defined as a political strategy by Boddewyn (1988) and by Boddewyn and Brewer (1994) or as a fourth generic strategy by Rugman and Verbeke (1990).

Perhaps the most interesting feature of the above analysis is that some firms are now actually adopting a 'transnational' strategy, in the Bartlett and Ghoshal (1989) spirit, that may cover each of Figure 7.3A's four quadrants, depending upon the area of regulation, the relevant country or the affected business unit.

CONCLUSIONS AND FUTURE RESEARCH

The conceptual framework described in this chapter suggests that there is more to the analysis of MNE–government relations than is described in Caves' synthesis of the conventional literature. Caves is useful when performing a general analysis of goal conflict between MNEs and governments in both home and host countries. The specific reasons for goal complementarity and conflict with particular governments can also be analysed using Caves' work.

However, the institutional reality driving much of today's business–government interactions is one whereby governments increasingly do not unambiguously represent either a home or a host country. The symmetrical status of countries both as source nations and as recipients of FDI makes it more difficult for governments to design specific incentives programs and regulatory policies. At the country level, national treatment of FDI is often the appropriate policy. In addition, many large MNEs now have a dispersed structure of FSAs, which reduces their legal and strategic commitment to a single home base. Thus, national responsiveness has developed as the key strategy for many firms.

When the symmetry in FDI positions at the government level and the dispersion of FSAs at the firm level are taken into account simultaneously, both sets of actors have a keen interest in international and multilateral trade and investment liberalization. Generally accepted rules need to guide MNE–government interactions. Finally, it is important to realize that the MNE's strategic approach to government policy is increasingly one in which choices tend to be made regarding the nature of the benefits sought (benefits of integration versus benefits of national responsiveness) and the extent to which actions will be undertaken to change or set the rules. This is the old issue of the extent to which government policy should be viewed as endogenous rather than exogenous to the firm. What is certain is that some MNEs have taken on board a broader spectrum of strategic alternatives in developing and exploiting their FSAs than was considered by Caves.

The next twenty years will see an international business literature develop which is based much more on this new thinking than on the literature reviewed by Caves. The next round of the WTO will probably focus on further liberalization of trade in services, issues of trade and the environment and issues of investment and competition policy. New work on the MAI at the OECD appears in Gestrin and Rugman (1995), Brewer and Young (1998) and this is consistent with earlier analyses of codes of conduct at the OECD by Safarian (1993) and Grosse (1980). The nature of networks and of R&D policy is also an area where our new framework provides guidance for future research. While the Japanese access Silicon Valley in the United States, US firms also draw R&D from Japan (Westney 1993). Work on alliance capitalism, as discussed in papers in Dunning (1997) and on strategic alliances and cooperative strategies, as discussed in Contractor and Lorange (1988), D'Cruz and Rugman (1997), and Beamish and Killing (1997) will grow in relevance. The alliance capitalism framework may well supplement the development and exploitation of FSAs by home country-based MNEs as the focus of public policy.

The field of international business is expanding rapidly across these, and related, dimensions. Yet in terms of analysis of the MNE and public policy, the analytical insights of Caves provide a solid foundation for present and future research. The 'multiple perspectives' approach now being used to bring disciplinary insights into the activities, operations and structures of MNEs is congruent with both the conventional, static Caves economic efficiency analysis and also the current dynamic resource-based theory of the firm viewpoint incorporated into the new framework developed here. The interaction between MNEs and governments has been, and will remain in the future, a lively area of research activity for scholarship in the field of international business.

REFERENCES

Aliber, Robert Z. (1970), 'A theory of direct foreign investment', in Charles P. Kindleberger (ed.), *The International Corporation*, Cambridge, MA: MIT Press, 17–34.

Bartlett, Christopher A., and Sumantra Ghoshal (1989), *Managing Across Borders: The Transnational Solution*, Boston: Harvard Business School Press.

Beamish, Paul, and Peter Killing (1997), *Cooperative Strategies* (3 volumes), San Francisco: The New Lexington Press.

Behrman, Jack N., and Robert E. Grosse (1990), *International Business and Governments: Issues and Institutions*, Columbia, SC: University of South Carolina Press.

Bergsten, Fred C., Thomas Horst and Theodore H. Moran (1978), *American Multinationals and American Interests*, Washington, DC: Brookings Institution.

Bhagwati, Jagdish (1988), *Protectionism*, Cambridge, MA: MIT Press.

Boddewyn, Jean J. (1988) 'Political aspects of MNE theory', *Journal of International Business Studies*, **19**: 341–63.

Boddewyn, Jean J., and Thomas Brewer (1994), 'International business political behaviour: new theoretical directions', *Academy of Management Review*, **19** (1): 119–43.

Brander, James, and Barbara Spencer (1985), 'Export subsidies and international market share rivalry', *Journal of International Economics*, **18** (February): 85–100.

Brewer, Thomas L. (1983), The instability of controls on MNEs' fund transfers and the instability of governments', *Journal of International Business Studies*, **14** (3): 147–57.

Brewer, Thomas L. (ed.) (1985), *Political Risks in International Business: New Directions for Research, Management and Public Policy*, New York: Praeger Publishers.

Brewer, Thomas L., and Stephen Young (1998), *The Multilateral Investment System and Multinational Enterprises*, Oxford: Oxford University Press.

Buckley, Peter J., and Mark Casson (1976), *The Future of the Multinational Enterprise*, London: Macmillan.

Casson, Mark (1987), *The Firm and the Market*, Cambridge, MA: MIT Press.

Caves, Richard E. (1996), *Multinational Enterprise and Economic Analysis*, Cambridge: Cambridge University Press. First edition 1982.

Coase, R.H. (1937), 'The nature of the firm', *Economica*, **4**: 386–405.

Copithorne, L.W. (1971), 'International corporate transfer prices and government policy', *Canadian Journal of Economics*, **4**: 324–41.

Contractor, Farok, and Peter Lorange (eds) (1988), *Cooperative Strategies in International Business*, San Francisco: New Lexington Press.

D'Cruz, Joseph, and Alan M. Rugman (1997), 'The theory of the flagship firm', *European Management Journal*, **15** (1): 403–11.

Doz, Yves, L. (1986), *Strategic Management in Multinational Companies*, Oxford: Pergamon Press.

Dunning, John H. (1981), *International Production and the Multinational Enterprise*, London: Allen and Unwin.

Dunning, John H. (1993a), *Multinational Enterprises and the Global Economy*, New York: Addison-Wesley.

Dunning, John H. (1993b), *The Globalization of Business*, London and New York: Routledge.

Dunning, John H. (1994), 'Re-evaluating the benefits of foreign direct investment', *Transnational Corporations*, **3** (1): 23–51.

Dunning, John H. (ed.) (1997), *Governments, Globalization and International Business*, Oxford: Oxford University Press.

Dunning, John H., and Alan M. Rugman (1985), 'The influence of Hymer's dissertation on the theory of foreign direct investment', *American Economic Review*, papers and proceedings, **75**: 228–32.

Eden, Lorraine (1985), 'The micro-economics of transfer pricing', in Alan M. Rugman and Lorraine Eden (eds), *Multinationals and Transfer Pricing*, London: Croom-Helm, 13–46.

Eden, Lorraine (1991), 'Bringing the firm back in: multinationals in IPE', *Millennium Journal of International Studies*, **20** (2): 197–224.

Eden, Lorraine (1997), *Taxing Multinationals: Transfer Pricing and Corporate Income Taxation in North America*, Toronto: University of Toronto Press.

Eden Lorraine, and Maureen Appel Molot (1993), 'Insiders and outsiders: defining 'who is us' in the North American automobile industry', *Transnational Corporations*, **3**, 2 (December): 31–64.

Encarnation, Dennis J., and Louis T. Wells, Jr. (1985), 'Sovereignty en garde: negotiating with foreign investors', *International Organization*, (Winter): 147–71.

Fruin, Mark (1997), *Knowledge Works*, Oxford: Oxford University Press.

Gerlach, Michael (1992), *Alliance Capitalism: The Social Organization of Japanese Business*, Berkeley: University of California Press.

Gestrin, Michael, and Alan M. Rugman (1994), 'The North American Free Trade

Agreement and foreign direct investment', *Transnational Corporations*, **3** (1): 77–95.

Gestrin, Michael, and Alan M. Rugman (1995), 'The NAFTA investment provisions: prototype for multilateral investment rules', in *Market Access After the Uruguay Round: Investment, Competition and Technology Perspectives*, Paris: OECD.

Ghadar, Fariborz (1982), 'Political risk and the erosion of control: the case of the oil industry, *Columbia Journal of World Business*, **13** (2): 47–51.

Gilpin, Robert (1975), *US Power and the Multinational Corporation*, New York: Basic Books.

Gilpin, Robert (1987), *The Political Economy of International Rrelations*, Princeton: Princeton University Press.

Gladwin, Thomas N., and Ingo Walter (1980), *Multinationals Under Fire: Lessons in the Management of Conflict*, New York: John Wiley.

Goldstein, Judith (1993), *Ideas, Interests and American Trade Policy*, Ithaca: Cornell University Press.

Granovetter, M. (1992), 'Problem of explanation in economic sociology', in N. Nohira and R. Eccles (eds), *Networks and Organizations*, Boston, MA: Harvard Business School Press, 22–56.

Grieco, Joseph M. (1982), 'Between dependency and autonomy: India's experience with the international computer industry', *International Organization*, **36** (3): 609–32.

Grosse, Robert (1980), *Foreign Investment Codes and the Location of Direct Investment*, New York: Praeger.

Guisinger, Stephen E., et al. (1985), *Investment Incentives and Performance Requirements*, New York: Praeger.

Hedlund, Gunner (1994), 'A model of knowledge management and the N-form corporations', *Strategic Management Journal*, **15**: 73–90.

Hennart, Jean-François (1982), *A Theory of Multinational Enterprise*, Ann Arbor, MI: University of Michigan Press.

Hufbauer, Gary C. (1993), *NAFTA: An Assessment*, Washington, DC: Institute for International Economics.

Hufbauer, Gary C., and Joanna Erb (1984), *Subsidies in International Trade*, Washington, DC: Institute for International Economics.

Hufbauer, Gary C., and Jeffrey J. Schott (1992), *North American Free Trade Issues and Recommendations*, Washington, DC: Institute for International Economics.

Hymer, Stephen H. (1976), *The International Operations of National Firms: A Study of Direct Foreign Investment*, Cambridge, MA: MIT Press (originally, Ph.D. dissertation, MIT, 1960).

Johnson, Harry G. (1970), 'The efficiency and welfare implications of the multinational corporation', in Charles P. Kindleberger (ed.), *The International Corporation: A Symposium*, Cambridge, MA: MIT Press, 33–56.

Keohane, Robert O. (1984), *After Hegemony*, Princeton: Princeton University Press.

Keohane, Robert O., and Joseph Nye (1977), *Power and Interdependence*, Boston: Little Brown.

Knickerbocker, Frederick T. (1973), *Oligopolistic Reaction and Multinational Enterprise*, Boston: Harvard University Graduate School of Business Administration, Division of Research.

Kobrin, Stephen J. (1982), *Managing Political Risk Assessment*, Berkeley, CA: University of California Press.

Kobrin, Stephen J. (1984), 'Expropriation as an attempt to control foreign firms in LDCs: trends from 1960–79', *International Studies Quarterly*, **28** (3): 329–48.

Kobrin, Stephen J. (1987), 'Testing the bargaining hypothesis in the manufacturing sector in developing countries', *International Organization*, **41** (4): 609–38.

Kogut, Bruce, and U. Zander (1993), 'Knowledge of the firm and the evolutionary theory of the multinational enterprises', *Journal of International Business Studies*, **24** (4): 625–45.

Kojima, Kiyoshi (1973), 'Macroeconomic approach to foreign direct investment', *Hitotsubashi Journal of Economics*, **14**: 1–21.

Kojima, Kiyoshi (1975), 'International trade and foreign investment – substitutes or complements?' *Hitotsubashi Journal of Economics*, **16**: 1–12.

Kojima, Kiyoshi (1978), *Direct Foreign Investment: A Japanese Model of Multinational Business Operations*', London: Croom-Helm.

Kojima, Kiyoshi (1985), 'Japanese and American direct investment in Asia – a comparative analysis', *Hitotsubashi Journal of Economics*, **26**: 1–35.

Krasner, Stephen (1978), *Defending the National Interest*, Princeton: Princeton University Press.

Krugman, Paul R. (ed.) (1986), *Strategic Trade Policy and the New International Economics*, Cambridge, MA: MIT Press.

Lall, Sanjaya (1973), 'Transfer pricing by multinational manufacturing firms', *Oxford Bulletin of Economics and Statistics*, **35**: 173–95.

Lessard, Donald R. (1979), 'Transfer prices, taxes, and financial markets: implications of internal financial transfers within the multinational corporation', in Robert G. Hawkins (ed.), *The Economic Effect of Multinational Corporations*, Greenwich, CT: JAI Press, 101–20.

Lustig, Nora, Barry P. Bosworth, and Robert Z. Lawrence (1992), *Assessing the Impact of North American Free Trade*, Washington, DC: Brookings.

Magee, Stephen P. (1977), 'Information and multinational corporation: an appropriability theory of direct foreign investment', in J.N. Bhagwati (ed.), *The New International Economic Order*, Cambridge, MA: MIT Press, 317–40.

Milner, Helen V. (1988), *Resisting Protectionism: Global Industries and the Politics of International Trade*, Princeton NJ: Princeton University Press.

Nieckels, Lars (1976), *Transfer Pricing in Multinational Firms*, Stockholm: Almqvist and Wiksell.

Nigh, Douglas (1985), 'The effect of political events on United States direct foreign investment', *Journal of International Business Studies*, **16**: 1–17.

Nonaka, Ikujiro, and Hirotaka Takeuchi (1995), *The Knowledge-Creating Company*, New York: Oxford University Press.

Ohmae, Kenichi (1985), *Triad Power: The Coming Shape of Global Competition*, New York: The Free Press.

Ostry, Sylvia (1997), *The Post-Cold War Trading System: Who's on First?* Chicago: University of Chicago Press.

Perlmutter, Howard (1969), 'The tortuous evolution of the multilateral corporation', *Columbia Journal of World Business*. **4** (1): 9–18.

Porter, Michael G. (1990), *The Competitive Advantage of Nations*, New York: Free Press.

Porter, Michael G., and D. van der Linde (1995), 'Green and competitive', *Harvard Business Review*, **73** (5): 120–34.

Prahalad, C. K., and Yves L. Doz (1987), *The Multinational Mission*, New York: Free Press.

Rugman, Alan M. (1980), *Multinationals in Canada: Theory, Performance and Economic Impact*, Boston: Martinus Nijhoff.

Rugman, Alan M. (1981), *Inside the Multinationals: The Economics of Internal Markets*, New York: Columbia University Press.

Rugman, Alan M. (1991), 'Environmental change and global competitive strategy in Europe', in Alan M. Rugman and Alain Verbeke (eds), *Research in Global Strategic Management, vol. 2: Global Competition and the European Community*, Greenwood Ct: JAI Press Inc, 3–28.

Rugman, Alan M. (ed.) (1994), *Foreign Investment and NAFTA*, Columbia SC: University of South Carolina Press.

Rugman, Alan M. (1996), *Multinational Enterprises and Trade Policy, vol. 2* of *The Selected Scientific Papers of Alan M. Rugman*, Cheltenham: Edward Elgar.

Rugman, Alan M. (1998), 'Corporate strategies and environmental regulations. An organizing framework', *Strategic Management Journal*, **19** (3): 363–75.

Rugman, Alan M., and Lorraine Eden (eds) (1985), *Multinationals and Transfer Pricing*, London: Croom-Helm.

Rugman, Alan M., and Andrew Anderson (1987), *Administered Protection in America*, London: Routledge.

Rugman, Alan M., and Alain Verbeke (1990), *Global Corporate Strategy and Trade Policy*, London: Routledge.

Safarian, A.E. (1966), *Foreign Ownership of Canadian Industry*, Toronto: McGraw-Hill.

Safarian, A.E. (1993), *Multinational Enterprises and Public Policy*, Aldershot: Edward Elgar.

Strange, Susan (1988), *States and Markets: An Introduction to International Political Economy*, London: Pinter.

Strange, Susan (1997), *The Retreat of the State: The Diffusion of Power in the World Economy*, Cambridge: Cambridge University Press.

Stopford, John, and Susan Strange (1991), *Rival States, Rival Firms: Competition for World Market Shares*, Cambridge: Cambridge University Press.

Tyson, Laura D'Andrea (1993), *Who's Bashing Whom? Trade Conflict in High-Technology Industries*, Washington, DC: Institute for International Economics.

Vernon, Raymond (1966), 'International investment and international trade in the product cycle', *Quarterly Journal of Economics*, **80**: 190–207.

Vernon, Raymond (1971), *Sovereignty at Bay: The Multinational Spread of US Enterprises*, New York: Basic Books.

Vernon, Raymond (1991), 'Sovereignty at bay: twenty years after', *Millennium Journal of International Studies*, **20** (2): 191–5.

Vogel, David (1995), *Trading up: Consumer and Environmental Regulations in a Global Economy*, Cambridge, MA: Harvard University Press.

Vogel, David, and Alan M. Rugman (1997), 'Environmentally related trade disputes between the United States and Canada', *American Review of Canadian Studies*, **27**: 4, 271–92.

Westney, D. Eleanor (1993), 'Institutionalization theory and the multinational enterprise', in Sumantra Ghoshal and Eleanor Westney (eds), *Organization Theory and the Multinational Enterprise*, London: Macmillian, 53–76.

Yoffie, David (ed.) (1993), *Beyond Free Trade: Firms, Governments and Global Competition*, Boston: Harvard Business School Press.

8. Overview and public policy reflections

Stephen Young and Thomas L. Brewer

INTRODUCTION

The objective of this concluding chapter is to draw together the ideas of both Caves himself and the other contributors to this volume on the economics of the multinational enterprise, and to provide some observations on public policy and the MNE, focusing upon multilateral policy dimensions. Not only is there a new dynamic research agenda for MNEs and international business activity, but a new agenda for public policy too. Failure to act upon the latter may see the policy pendulum lurching back in the direction of protectionism as new interest groups dominate the agenda setting process.

The chapter begins with a short summary and critique of Caves' work; reviews the contribution of Caves and the other authors in the volume on public policy and the MNE; and comments on some key areas of debate with regard to the multilateral investment regime at a crucial point in the policy cycle.

MULTINATIONAL ENTERPRISE AND ECONOMIC ANALYSIS: A SUMMARY

As the authors in this volume have shown, Richard E. Caves' *Multinational Enterprise and Economic Analysis* (2nd ed., 1996) provides an extremely thorough review of the state of knowledge on the economics of the multinational enterprise, with emphasis on the fields of industrial organization and international economics. In commencing this overview chapter, it is perhaps useful to summarize what Caves concludes from his transaction-cost approach to the analysis of the MNE:

1. *The multinational enterprise as an economic organization.* The existence of the MNE is explained 'by identifying it as a multiplant firm that sprawls across national boundaries' (Caves 1996, p. 23), where for

transaction-cost reasons dispersed plants are brought under common ownership and control rather than trading independently in the open market. This approach explains the horizontal MNE particularly, but also the vertically integrated firm (including offshore production in low labor cost locations).

2. *The MNE and models of economic activity.* Considering choices between investing abroad and exporting from the home base, there is evidence of value-maximizing locational choices by MNEs, taking account of production and transport costs, scale economies, and production differentiation and other demand-side factors. Tariff barriers, market enlargement (for example, European Union) and exchange rate changes all influence the investment decision. Generally MNEs' exports and foreign investments are jointly determined. Elements of international trade theory help to explain the distribution of foreign investments among countries. However, two-way foreign investments and the importance of a country's human capital as an attraction factor for FDI limit the predictive power of the standard trade model. Similarities and affinities between countries are important for explaining international patterns of FDI, since they reduce transactions costs. On the other hand, pure production cost factors are dominant only in FDI in export processing facilities. From a source country perspective, factors generating national firms' proprietary assets include rapid national economic development, the presence or absence of particular resources, successful agglomerations in certain industries, and, indeed, fortunate accidents of institutional development. The product cycle model is one useful approach to understanding the origin of MNEs and their international spread.

3. *Organization and growth of the MNE.* The risks of FDI are apparent in the evidence of high turnover rates in overseas projects; and initial investment in familiar, low-risk foreign environments is indicated. Subsidiaries in unfamiliar or unstable environments may be left to operate alone, whereas others will be integrated into the parent's administrative structure. Nationality differences in the latter reflect the diffusion of organizational innovations from the USA and the persistence of family control. The evidence on factors influencing acquisition versus greenfield entry is mixed; within host countries the stock of local companies and the frameworks of corporate governance are influential variables. The propensity to undertake joint venture activities varies greatly: the possession of appropriable proprietary assets or extensive intra-corporate component flows limits joint ventures; whereas new and small MNEs, and those undertaking market diversification are more likely to undertake joint ventures. The life of joint ventures is on average short. Finally, it is argued that the 'so-called new forms of cooperation and

alliances among MNEs in many ways resemble joint ventures and supply agreements between buyers and sellers' (Caves 1996, p. 82).

4. *Patterns of market competition.* The transaction-cost model of the MNE implies its existence in industries with high levels of seller concentration, a market structure characteristic that may also produce high entry barriers. While there are high correlations between the sources of entry barriers and sources of FDI, causal relationships are not direct. However, rivalrous behavior in loose oligopolies tends to encourage foreign investment. Within host country markets, the existence of new MNEs reduces concentration levels initially, although the pro-competitive effect is weakened by acquisition entry. Empirical evidence on the effects of inter-firm cooperation, collusion or rivalrous behavior is chiefly pre-World War II (excluding the important studies of Knickerbocker [1973] on follow-the-leader, and Graham [1978] on the exchange-of-hostage syndrome). MNEs create problems for competition rules since national policy seeks to maximize national welfare. Even if national competition policies are non-discriminatory as between local and foreign firms, this is still not first-best on a worldwide basis.

5. *Income distribution and labor relations.* A simple general equilibrium model would indicate that capital export by MNEs reduces the real wage, and capital import increases it. However, if the MNE's capital transfer does not lower the home country's or raise the host nation's stock by the full amount, then wages will be less affected. Similarly, a complementary relationship between investment and exports weakens the predictions of the general equilibrium model. In a partial equilibrium context, studies show that MNEs pay higher wages to acquire better quality labor, especially in developing countries. There is some evidence that MNEs face more strikes; but they are also responsible for labor innovations, without transforming national labor relations systems. Based on admittedly sparse and dated evidence, it is concluded that international trade union coalitions are unlikely to succeed.

6. *Investment behavior and financial flows.* MNEs make investment decisions on a global basis, and so capital expenditure falls in one country when expected profits for investment rise in another country. In respect of patterns of investment and borrowing, there is evidence that MNEs enjoy opportunities for international arbitrage of funds linked to borrowing costs and expected exchange rate behavior. For the subsidiary, relationships among local borrowing and investment, dividend repatriation, and so on, indicate that 'MNE is a present value-maximizer operating in completely integrated international capital markets' (Caves 1996, p. 161). Survey evidence indicates that MNEs do not operate as pure speculators, but neither do they completely avoid

exchange rate speculation. In consequence, MNEs' financial decisions may conflict with government policies, especially those seeking to defend fixed disequilibrium exchange rates. Public reporting requirements for MNEs may clash with internal evaluation and control procedures.

7. *Technology and productivity.* MNEs are commonly found in research intensive sectors. They allocate R&D activities between parent and subsidiary according to the relative pulls of efficient supervision at headquarters and scale economies in R&D; as well as other factors such as foreign market requirements and the availability of local resources abroad. Studies on US MNEs indicate that they would undertake less research if they could not extract rents from their R&D in overseas markets. Competition among suppliers of technical knowledge tends to lower rents, and there is also some leakage of proprietary know-how (although this risk seems to be taken into account in licensing and technology transfer decisions). MNEs' proprietary asset advantages are reflected in higher productivity levels than local competitors and higher market shares. However, the productivity of competing domestic firms also increases with the presence of foreign subsidiaries.

8. *Taxation, MNEs' behavior and economic welfare.* Within industrial countries, the national welfare effects of taxing foreign income violate global welfare criteria, at least to some extent. World welfare requires that all nations impose the same tax rate, whereas there are country variations, albeit with some bunching. MNEs' decisions on investment, raising and repatriating funds, allocating R&D, and so on, are sensitive to taxes. Transfer price manipulation is related in part to tax rates: manipulation is less common among smaller companies, and those with decentralized internal control systems and operating in more competitive environments.

9. *Multinationals in developing countries.* There are significant differences between MNE subsidiaries which serve the domestic market primarily as compared with producing for export. The latter are more likely to be wholly owned by their parents and less reliant on local capital markets. Export-oriented investments are footloose and determined largely by unit labor costs, although incentives in the form of tax holidays and infrastructure investments can affect locational choice (as does tariff protection for domestic market-oriented – import substitution – investments). Behavior patterns tend to be similar to those observed in developed countries, given market structure conditions, although MNEs pay higher wages than domestic enterprises. Some adaptation of technology takes place in response to factor conditions, such as using second-hand machinery, or may occur as a result of designing facilities

for small-scale operation. In respect of the effects of MNEs on economic growth in developing countries, the author concludes that '(The) possible causal connections are numerous but speculative and ill-defined in terms of economic models. Empirical investigations . . . have yielded no trustworthy conclusions' (Caves 1996, p. 242). Third-world MNEs possess proprietary assets suited to developing company conditions. They invest chiefly in neighboring countries and operate on a small scale in collaboration with local partners.

10. *Public policy.* Neoclassical welfare economics supplies rules about what economic policies will maximize real income. The assumptions under which its conclusions apply are that:
- each national government seeks to maximize real incomes, taking other countries' policies as given;
- income distribution decisions are made separately;
- each enterprise has a national citizenship and maximizes its profits in terms of one currency and price set;
- MNEs' proprietary assets mean they face downward sloping demand curves for their outputs, while the host nation faces an upward sloping supply curve of MNE resource commitments;
- each country makes policy decisions in its role as either source or host.

Given these assumptions, Caves' conclusion is that FDI indicates arbitraged resources and therefore a presumption that the allocation of MNE resources is efficient. The problem that arises is that policies to maximize the income of source countries, host nations and the world as a whole are not identical. Conflict is thus expected in the principal areas of policy, namely taxation, natural resources, competition, and knowledge creation and transfer. These generate multiple market distortions, and create difficulties in analysis, leading to second-best policy prescriptions. A behavioral approach to policy is reviewed and the case for international regulation is also recognized as a means of eliminating conflicts that arise between policies maximizing national welfare and global welfare. In this respect, foreign direct investment poses many more policy problems than trade, since the GATT rounds of trade negotiations have been able to spread the global gains fairly evenly among participating countries.

The 1996 edition of Caves' book contains just about twice the number of references as the 1982 first edition, a reflection of the growth of the subject and also of the thoroughness of Caves' work. Yet one conclusion that might be reached is that 'little has changed'. Chapter 1 of the new edition introduces a section on multinationals and service industries, and Chapter 9 discusses third-world multinationals. There is an acknowledgement of the growing importance of organizational issues, both in the comment concerning 'the sharpness of the distinction between close (centralized) and open (localized) subsidiaries' (Caves 1996, p. 66),[1] and in the inclusion of organizational capacity as a fourth type of entry barrier and basis for FDI (along with advertising outlays, capital cost barriers, scale economies, and research and development). The conclusion that pure production cost factors dominate locational decision making in the case of export processing operations only is an important change compared with 1982. At this time Caves observed that 'countries become important hosts if they are the low-cost locations for doing what MNEs do' (Caves 1982, p. 67). In respect of policy, the recent literature (reviewed by Krugman 1989) is included on countries' opportunities for strategic profit-shifting policies in global oligopolies. This has relevance for competition policy, although Caves concludes that the policy prescriptions are not obvious.

There are two inferences to be drawn from the observed similarities in the two editions of Caves' *Multinational Enterprise and Economic Analysis*. The first is that the subject area is maturing, and hence the conceptual foundations are fairly well accepted and are backed up by supportive evidence, even if hard and fast conclusions are lacking in many areas. This understanding, however, is limited to conventional forms of multinationality (namely wholly-owned subsidiaries and joint ventures as opposed to strategic alliances), and to the multinational as an enterprise with operations in foreign markets, rather than a corporation which invests, operates and competes as a globally or regionally integrated enterprise.

This leads to the second inference, which is that the second edition failed to capture many of the fairly fundamental changes taking place in the international environment, in the behaviour of MNEs, and, therefore, in the consequences for public policy. This is partly a reflection of timing, since much of the analysis relates to work in the 1980s. But it also reflects the adherence to a virtually unchanged structure for the two volumes. This creates a straightjacket which means a focus on issues which may no longer be of significance (for example, strikes in MNEs),[2] and the omission of new and important issues and associated research which are the focus of the chapters prepared by the distinguished authors of this volume. In turn these omissions stem from a strict definition of the boundaries of 'multinational enterprise and economic analysis', and in the methodologies applied to analyse the phenomenon. Thus a good deal of the interesting research on the dynamics of firm-level organization and behavior has been captured by scholars in strategic management and other fields.

THE CONTRIBUTIONS OF THE AUTHORS IN THIS VOLUME

All authors recognize the limitations of Caves' very focused, largely static transaction-cost approach to analysing the economics of the multinational, and in their various ways, they introduce new and dynamic themes, agendas and methods of analysis.

In their introductory chapter, Guisinger and Brewer highlight the major topics in the emerging research agenda, distinguishing different levels of analysis. Considering the emphases of the different authors, Richard Caves himself proposes various avenues for future research, including the bases for FDI (where the nature of proprietary assets in some new types of FDI, such as investment in utilities or 'commodity' industries, is viewed as puzzling; and foreign investment in supplier or customer firms, and intra-corporate globalization processes are also under-researched); MNEs and competitive processes (including issues such as explanations for intra-industry merger waves, and turnover in FDI related to closures and sell-offs); financial flows and business behavior; development and technology transfer; and strategic alliances.

For Peter Buckley and Mark Casson, the emphasis is upon the characteristics of the current era which have created unprecedented uncertainty and volatility in the business environment. In turn, these have produced a requirement for flexibility in the external environment of the firm, and in the boundaries and internal organization of the enterprise. On the other hand, greater flexibility means higher transaction costs as firms need to engineer trust in customers and suppliers, in management and in the workforce. The implications they draw for modeling this 'new' dynamic research agenda are discussed further below.

John Dunning also highlights a number of features of the changing world scenario for international business activity, namely the knowledge economy, globalization and the global/local paradox, and alliance capitalism. He then focuses upon location and the changing role of location-bound assets, and their implications both for the global competitiveness of firms and for government policies. Sylvia Ostry's work likewise revolves around globalization (where information and communication technologies (ICT) are both an enabling factor and a driver); and assesses some of the technology and productivity dimensions which have important implications for research and for the nature of the policy agenda. Interestingly, Ostry identifies two issues scarcely mentioned elsewhere in the volume, that is, e-commerce and standards competition. Both have significant implications for the organization and behavior of the firm and for policy. It is noteworthy that recent issues of the *Journal of International Business Studies* have a series of articles from symposia on 'Multinationals: The Janus Face of Globalization' (Vol. 32, No. 3, 2001) and 'Electronic Commerce and Global Business' (Vol. 32, No. 4, 2001).

The themes emerging in the chapters thus emphasize quite strongly the influence of external forces, particularly globalization, trade liberalization and technological innovation on multinationals and the worldwide integration of business activities. Ostry views the growth of electronic commerce as providing a new impetus to integration processes, arguing that at each stage of integration 'the ubiquitousness and influence of the MNEs has increased'.

The contributions in this volume, however, develop notions and insights which extend well beyond the themes reviewed above. Two issues are of particular note. The first relates to methodology in international business research and the encouragement of methodological pluralism. Historically, one of the weaknesses of a narrowly economics-based approach to research has been the almost exclusive focus on quantitative studies. In this volume, Caves himself highlights some of the problems in undertaking international business research, and bemoans the lack of longitudinal databases, such as the Harvard Multinational Enterprise Project which tracked US MNEs from their beginnings to 1975 (Curhan et al. 1977). Given that such databases are so costly to develop and maintain, more use could be made of survey research, and case studies have considerable value too. Although generalization is often difficult from such qualitative research, the problems of quantitative studies have already been alluded to.

The second, and related, contribution of the authors pertains to the subject of models of the multinational enterprise. Reflecting the dynamic and volatile nature of present-day internal and external environments, Buckley and Casson argue the case for alternative methods of analysis, extending Caves' static view of international business. Their solution lies in modeling, an economics approach they contrast with the frameworks commonly applied in strategic management. Their notions of a global systems-oriented view are developed more fully in the volume by Casson (Casson 2000). The criticisms of frameworks (including Dunning's OLI paradigm) are that they can become overly complex and descriptive, and, therefore, do not provide detailed advice on research design and hypothesis testing. Such criticisms are probably overstated and the approaches should be regarded as complementary rather than competitive. In any event, the discussion of innovative approaches to methodology in the volume is welcome, and a further dynamic perspective is provided by Edward Graham, who takes a game-theoretic approach to attempt to understand the dynamics of competition among MNEs.

One issue which readers may find disappointing is that, while a number of the volume's authors criticize the transaction-cost theory which underpins Caves' volume, few alternatives are proposed. Yet there has been significant theoretical innovation over the last two decades, with the distinction now being made between governance perspectives (internalization and transaction-cost) and competence perspectives (the resource-based view and related models, including evolutionary theory, and dynamic capabilities' approaches) in research (Williamson 1999), and extensive discussion of their complementarities and contrasts (Buckley 1994; Langlois and Foss 1999; Tavares 2001). Some authors welcome the diversity, considering the dominance of the transaction-cost model unsatisfactory (Pitelis and Sugden 2000), while others are concerned about fragmentation, even, for example, within the competence perspective itself (Foss 1997).

What is particularly welcome are the efforts seriously to assess the relative contributions of the perspectives. Both, of course, have similarities in terms of their underlying roots in economics. For example, the influence of Penrose (1995) in the competence and knowledge-based perspectives is widely acknowledged. And while the competence perspective is now primarily associated with strategic management, the development of some branches of this approach is associated with economists. This is the case, for instance, with the technology accumulation perspective (Cantwell 1989, 2001).

Scholars from the disciplines of economics and strategic management are seriously probing the relative merits and demerits of competing theories. From the side of economics, Dunning (2000) dissects the notion of competitive advantages, which is a feature of all perspectives. He distinguishes between three types of competitive or ownership-specific advantages, namely those relating to the possession and exploitation of monopoly power (Caves 1971; Porter 1985); those which reflect the superior technical efficiency of a firm, derived from unique and sustainable resources and capabilities (from the resource-based and evolutionary theories); and those relating to the competencies of managers of enterprises, especially stressed by organizational scholars. Coming from a similar economics background, Kay (1997) has followed the agenda set by transaction-cost theory to develop a resource-based perspective of the firm. His conclusion on the MNE is particularly interesting and controversial: '[f]irms will typically prefer to specialize, diversify, or export before they are tempted into the weak-linked multinational option' (Kay 1997, p. 174).

By contrast, in the *Journal of Management*'s Special Issue (Vol. 27, 2001) on the resource-based view (RBV), papers address both the RBV and economics, and the RBV and international business. In the latter vein, Lockett and Thompson (2001) suggest that the RBV has had only limited influence on economics, except in the understanding that inter-firm variations in performance are as important as inter-industry differences, and in the incorporation of the notion of path dependency into economics-based research. However, the authors identify potential areas for future research, including policy questions concerning the RBV and antitrust. Peng (2001) suggests that the three research areas of international business that have been especially propelled by the RBV are strategic alliances, international entrepreneurship and emerging markets; but one might also add the growing area of MNE subsidiary research. By comparison, Peng (2001) regards the identification of international knowledge (as a unique resource that differentiates winners from losers and survivors) as the most significant contribution of international business to the RBV. On the question of rivalry or complementarity, his view is that 'the key seems to lie in how to differentiate firm-specific resources at the core of the RBV from transaction-specific resources at the core of TCE [transaction-cost economics]' (Peng 2001, p. 820; Madhok and Tallman 1998).

There are thus rich research opportunities in the further development of theoretical approaches other than transaction-cost per se, which will in turn provide opportunities for widening the research agenda as recommended by the authors of this volume.

MULTINATIONAL ENTERPRISE AND PUBLIC POLICY

Most of the authors in this volume call for more policy-oriented research. As Wells notes: 'Although one can . . . tease some policy implications out of the research reported in Caves' book, the many gaps in our knowledge mean that a great deal is still judgement and guesswork. Informed policy awaits more research.' Of course, the difficulties of undertaking this research should not be underestimated, as Caves (1998, pp. 6–7) shows in his observations on 'isolating the effects of policy choices'.

Caves' limited but incisive comments on public policy have been presented in the summary above (see also Rugman and Verbeke in this volume), focusing on the efficiency aspects of MNEs derived from neoclassical welfare economics. And a number of scholars have their own observations in this book. The view of Dunning (1998, pp. 57–60) is that for many of the cross-border activities undertaken by the MNE, there is no external market, and, therefore internal markets may provide higher coordinating benefits and/or lower transaction costs than arm's-length activities. In such cases the MNE is not a second-best substitute for the market, but 'a partner with the market to promote first-best allocative efficiency throughout and across value chains' (p. 59). Since cross-border markets will likely be more imperfect than their domestic equivalents (at least in industrialized countries), MNE activity is welfare-enhancing by overcoming market failures; and, indeed, Dunning argues, 'MNE activity *may* be more welfare-enhancing than multi-plant activity within an economy' (p. 59). This, of course, assumes that there are not other market failures deriving from collusive and monopolistic behavior.

There are many implicit and explicit references to public policy in the chapters in this volume, mostly focusing on the national level of policy. Wells quite rightly draws attention to the problems in devising public policy. Essentially the answers to basic questions facing policymakers, namely 'Is FDI good for the country?' and 'How can government policy make the impact of FDI more favorable?', are not widely agreed.

One major challenge in policy formulation relates to the problems in determining the relationship between FDI and economic growth, and, at the micro level, in the assessment of the benefits of FDI for host (and home) countries. In a recent article, Lipsey (2000) confirms the difficulties in macro studies, which derive from the close association between FDI and other potential determinants of growth, creating difficulties in disentangling the directions of causation. His regression analyses show the ratio of FDI inflow to GDP, in combination with the level of schooling, to be the most consistent positive influence on growth rates; however, such equations leave most of the differences in growth unexplained. (For a recent review of the literature, see Lim 2001.)

There are difficulties also at the micro level, recognized by Caves (1996, p. 244) in his criticisms of the benefit–cost techniques of development planning, where the approach is commonly limited to listing items which incorporate 'poorly defined economic benefits and politically defined costs'. In Chapter Six, Wells is even more critical, arguing that almost no investment agency regularly uses tools such as benefit–cost analysis; and project-by-project screening associated with the award of investment incentives has led to corruption, especially in developing countries.

A significant problem, however, is that conventional measures of evaluating the benefits of FDI may no longer be appropriate. This was accepted by Dunning (1994) when he redefined the contribution of FDI in a host nation in terms of the improvement of the competitiveness or the productivity of resources and asset-generating capabilities within its boundaries. While the definition is open to debate, much of the commentary in this volume relates to issues of national competitiveness. On the other hand, trying to generate measures of contribution to competitiveness is exceedingly difficult. Contributions are increasingly qualitative as opposed to quantitative, for example, the presence of a small design and development unit in a foreign subsidiary may generate very limited benefits in conventional terms, but may be important for the long-term competitiveness and security of the facility; or, again, how is it possible to evaluate the contribution of global performance benchmarking in MNE subsidiaries? There is significant evidence that FDI efficiency spillovers exist, but no strong consensus on their magnitude (Blomström, Globerman and Kokko 2000; Lim 2001). At the micro level, moreover, little is known, as Wells indicates, about the number of employees trained by MNEs who then leave to work in indigenous enterprises or to establish their own businesses. In truth, there is not even a readily identifiable set of dimensions by which to judge economic benefit, as between, for example, quantitative and qualitative, direct and indirect or short-term and long-term contributions.

In respect of policy implications, Lim's (2001) review of the literature on foreign investment and growth suggests that an emphasis on non-tax deficiencies (infrastructure problems, regulatory and legal barriers, macroeconomic instability and economic impediments such as trade barriers) are the most efficient way to attract FDI. In respect of improving the contribution of FDI, however, much of the recent policy debate at the national level concerns competitiveness enhancement policies and the promotion of localization within an increasingly globalized world economy (Dunning 1997, 2000; Hood and Young 1999). The encouragement of national innovative systems, industrial clusters, skilled and flexible labor and public infrastructure, and coordinated macro-organizational strategies are all discussed at various points in this volume. Evidence is still lacking, nevertheless, on the relationship between MNEs and the locations in which they operate. This requires greater integration of the literature on economic geography with that on MNEs (in this regard, see Nachum 2001). How does the local milieu, for example, influence the behavior and performance of the MNE? Conversely, how do MNEs affect the localities in which they operate? Models of the dynamic region focus upon the creative region (Andersson 1985); the learning region (Saxenian 1994); and the regional nexus (Cooke and Morgan 1998); while empirical work has identified hierarchies of regional locations (Cantwell and Iammarino 2001). By contrast, there is a strong literature stream focusing upon the MNE as a differentiated corporate network, comprising subsidiaries with distinct strategic roles which may evolve over time in response to internal or external influences (Birkinshaw 2001 reviews the recent literature). Such influences include the ability to tap into local sources of knowledge, either formally, through inter-firm networks, or informally, through spillovers.

The chapter on public policy in this volume by Alan Rugman and Alain Verbeke, integrates a wide range of international business and related literature and provides new policy perspectives. Their approach reflects the dynamic insights brought by the authors in this volume rather than the conventional static efficiency-based economic analysis. The focus is on business–government relations, but they introduce symmetries between inward and outward FDI (the norm in most developed countries) on the countryside, and the global dispersion of firm-specific advantages within MNEs, as well as other issues. The frameworks presented by Rugman and Verbeke are valuable both for the national government seeking policy prescriptions and the multinational looking to define its approach to business–government relations. This approach is consistent with that of other authors in international political economy (for example, Stopford and Strange 1991) and international business (for example, Dunning 1993), but it leaves unresolved questions concerning the optimal (or in this case second-best) policies for enhancing global welfare. The conclusion of the authors is that the symmetry of FDI positions at the national level and the dispersion of ownership-specific advantages at the firm level suggest support by both sets of actors for multilateral trade and investment liberalization.

TOWARDS A MULTILATERAL INVESTMENT SYSTEM

In reading Caves' book, one is disappointed by his failure to pursue the logic of his policy analysis' – which is multilateral investment rules; this is despite the acceptance of a divergence of national welfare from global welfare in a number of major policy areas. In the field of taxation, for example, this divergence derives from varying effective tax rates, interactions between taxes on capital and tariffs on trade, and the involvement of the MNE itself through its transfer pricing decisions. In respect of competition, world welfare requires competitive markets (in the absence of other distortions); whereas each nation gains if it can monopolize its sales abroad (exports and foreign subsidiary sales chiefly) and monopsonize its foreign purchases. Lacking the policy instruments to achieve these goals, the optimal solution for the country is, as Caves notes, to encourage an intermediate degree of competition in both foreign and domestic markets. In a similar manner, the country has an interest in dealing with foreign monopolists, for example, MNE-dominated sectors in the domestic market where excess profits exist. The outcome again is conflict between national and global interests.

Caves essentially writes off international regulation because of the practical difficulties of trying to ensure that the benefits of international policy coordination are spread proportionately among participants. In the case of the multilateral trade regime, countries' interests are relatively similar given the symmetries of imports and exports. These two-way movements are becoming more important with FDI too, but there is not the same degree of concurrence as with trade. Negotiations on tariff barriers are easier than with investment and related barriers because the former are readily identified and isolated, though the emergence of non-tariff barriers highlights the difficulties in trade policy liberalization. And identification and quantification of countries' gains and losses is more straightforward in the case of trade impediments as well.

Caves' views on international regulation are also perhaps conditioned by the experiences of the 1970s and 1980s. At this time the emphasis was on international codes urging national governments and MNEs to behave in particular types of ways. The timing of Caves' book meant that the first steps in multilateral investment liberalization through the Uruguay Round and the World Trade Organization were omitted. While very preliminary and partial, the commitments on investment-related measures in the Uruguay Round Agreements will have a significant impact (as is becoming evident in the early results from the WTO's dispute settlement mechanism – see Brewer and

Young 1999). Progress in liberalizing both trade and investment through the General Agreement on Trade in Services (GATS) and via industry-specific agreements such as telecommunications, means that the WTO is likely to be an increasingly important player in the public policy arena in future (although it is true that its weaknesses in areas such as environmental policy are also being exposed).

As with Rugman and Verbeke, Wells suggests that MNE managers are increasingly likely to support international accords. However, the latter makes the valid point that we have little research evidence as to how existing agreements are working; and 'we do not even know whether bilateral and regional, or possible global agreements really matter in the decisions of MNEs.'

In earlier work, Brewer and Young (2000) presented a case for multilateral investment liberalization which parallels that for multilateral trade liberalization, basically the equivalent of the gains from trade argument. The general conclusion is that, as with trade, international flows of FDI should be encouraged since they generate both global and national benefits. Growth would be stimulated through more efficient production and prices lowered through stronger competition. In broad agreement with Caves, the application of unilateral national policies to achieve this goal is not necessarily optimal, hence the requirement for multilateral cooperation and a multilateral investment regime.

The 'new dynamics' of multinational business as outlined in this volume provide further arguments in favor of a multilateral approach to policy:

- Multidomestic firms were by definition host-country oriented, and hence, in part at least, were amenable to national policy measures; global firms, with operations integrated across frontiers, are often not. Accepting that there may be benefits for some enterprises from localization and close geographical linkages at the subnational level, for many others there is no longer any significant association with locality. The so-called 'death of distance' (Cairncross 1997) requires multilateral policy coordination, and further consideration between issues of trade and investment.
- The growth of mergers, acquisitions and alliances allied to MNEs' flexibility of operation has the potential to restrict competition and lead to the abuse of market power.
- In a similar vein there are dangers of a national 'race to the bottom' with increased competition for FDI; and a bidding up of incentive offers at the national level, in turn making it more difficult to invest in infrastructure and other public goods which might assist MNE embeddedness in host countries.
- There are a wide range of issues – loosely associated with the new business dynamics and with globalization – which could lead to backsliding

into protectionism. For example, shortening product cycles and generally a faster pace of corporate change means faster global restructuring, which could encourage host government restrictions. More generally, globalization has prompted debate about whether it tends to exacerbate inequalities between rich and poor countries and between skilled and unskilled workers, as well as raising new environmental and ethical issues.

It is not difficult to develop a scenario within which the failure of multilateral policy to deal with the issues above leads to a reversion to protectionist national policy measures. Investment policy may be viewed as a pendulum which has oscillated from liberalization in the 1950s and 1960s, to regulation and control in the 1970s, and back to liberalization in the 1980s and 1990s; and now threatens to lurch towards protectionism again. One new variable is the emergence of additional players on the world stage, particularly the wide range of non-governmental organizations loosely united around their opposition to multinationals, a liberal multilateral trade and investment regime, and the World Trade Organization. By themselves pursuing a multilateral approach through the Internet, they have been able to publicize their views among many segments of global public opinion. MNEs have been on the defensive. The work of the WTO too has failed to appeal to the public at large, not helped by very public and protracted disputes between the two major players, the USA and the EU, and their failure to show leadership. The analysis of such processes, in which multilateral policymaking becomes a contest to influence global public opinion, is the domain of international political economy rather than international business or international economics. Nevertheless, aside from issues such as environmental policy (see Rugman and Verbeke 2001 for a review of the literature) which are outside the scope of this paper, there are a number of areas of public policy where international business scholars have a contribution to make, as discussed in the following section.

KEY AREAS OF DEBATE IN PUBLIC POLICY

Competition Policy

Caves' volume provides an extensive review of the evidence relating to multinationals and competition issues. This research probably substantially underestimates the potential influence of MNEs on patterns of market competition. First, regional and global integration is associated with higher levels of intermediate and intra-firm trade. This creates problems for measuring concentration levels meaningfully at the national level and identifying anticompetitive practices. Secondly, and linked because of globalization, competition problems increasingly transcend national boundaries. Examples include international cartels, export cartels, restrictive practices in international services such as air or sea transport, world-scale mergers and the abuse of a dominant position in several major markets (European Commission 1995, 1999). Thirdly, the increasing range and complexity of relationships within and between firms means that collusive behavior is difficult to establish and investigate, and it is therefore also difficult to judge the procompetitive versus anticompetitive effects. Fourthly, national competition authorities are ill-equipped to deal with cross-border competition problems, and multinationals can play off one jurisdiction against another in competition policy cases (as in other matters).

Reflecting these and other arguments, there is little doubt that competition policy as currently implemented by national authorities is inadequate. The economic arguments are straightforward. Effective competition policies implemented by individual countries may maximize national incomes taken separately. World income may not, however, be maximized in the presence of MNEs with global market power, and there is also the potential for conflicts when welfare is redistributed internationally. A variety of issues arise at the practical level (European Commission 1995). First, MNEs are subject to different competition rules across countries. The transaction costs, deriving from different procedures, time scales, and criteria, can act as a barrier to the expansion of FDI in trade. Secondly, distortions may result from the fact that competition policy is more lax (either in terms of standards or of enforcement) in one country than another. At the extreme, tolerance of anticompetitive practices could prevent market access. As barriers to inward FDI are reduced in developing countries, competition policies (which might not exist at all) are necessary to ensure that the positive effects of investment are not offset by MNEs' restrictive practices. The WTO (1998, para. 116) noted that privatization and deregulation in a number of countries had failed to produce their expected benefits. This was a consequence of the lack of competition policies to prevent the abuse of market power by privatized firms (both those acquired by MNEs or operating as joint ventures with MNEs) with dominant market positions. Similarly in East Asia, the lack of market openness, which was one factor underlying the financial crisis in the late 1990s, was partly attributed to the absence of robust competition policies. Thirdly, the national policies of some nations contain extraterritorial provisions by which competition policy rules extend beyond the boundaries of the domestic market.

The case for internationalizing competition policy is unquestionably strong. There are major constraints, however, deriving from the inter-relationships among trade policy, FDI policy, competition policy, and other microeconomic policies. There are also difficulties in defining the types of agreement and restraint on business activity which should be incorporated within competition rules. And, fundamentally, there are the problems of reaching agreement among nations. Nevertheless, progress is beginning to be made in, for example, bilateral cooperation between the EU, USA and other nations (European Commission 1999).

Investment Incentives and Performance Requirements

Linked to investment–trade relationships is the controversial issue of investment incentives and performance requirements (Brewer and Young 1997, 2000). Although incentives are inherently distorting in the context of neoclassical assumptions about markets and competition, arguments on economic efficiency grounds can be made when there are positive externalities or economies of scale. It is particularly where there are positive externalities from technology transfers that governments are prone to use of incentives. In addition, governments sometimes use incentives to offset the costs imposed on foreign investors by constraints on their operations, such as domestic sourcing or export performance requirements. But where investors are considering alternative sites, competitive bidding may lead to a spiralling of aid offers to levels higher than those that are economically justifiable. Aside from the waste and misallocation of resources, competition may be distorted, especially when large-scale capital intensive projects are aided in oligopolistic markets. Moreover, for obvious reasons, even when incentives may be strictly unnecessary to attract an investment project, MNEs will still attempt to maximize aid levels at the point of negotiation with host governments or regional authorities.

The distortions created by incentive bidding for FDI have to date largely been intra-regional as opposed to inter-regional. However, in an era of globalization, it is expected that a certain type of project would become globally, as opposed to simply regionally, mobile. Worldwide competition for such projects could lead to greater incentive bidding both because of fewer constraints (the very limited scope of international rules at present), and the widely varying types and levels of types and incentives (UNCTAD 1996).

A further argument against the use of investment incentives as a tool for investment attraction is that they discriminate in favor of the richer countries. Historically, the main types of investment incentives have been tax holidays and direct subsidies, but incentive competition may extend much more widely to include low-cost infrastructure, low-cost services, market preferences, and so on. As Guisinger (1995) notes, besides increasing levels of incentives, competition has spawned a diverse range of incentives, enabling countries to differentiate their 'product'. At the same time, diversity has served to increase the opaqueness of incentives from competitor governments and facilitates greater discrimination among firms. Hanson (2001, p. 23) has been particularly critical of the value of incentives, concluding that 'countries should be sceptical about claims that promoting FDI will raise their welfare. A sensible approach for host countries is to presume that subsidies to FDI are not warranted'.

Recent work by Oman (2000) has proposed a move away from incentives-based methods of competition (financial and fiscal incentives) to rules-based competition (regional integration agreements, privatization of state-owned enterprises, strengthened judicial systems, export processing zones (EPZs) and environmental and labor standards). The former are particularly costly and introduce a range of market distortions, including an emphasis on large companies compared to small ones, and on foreign over domestic investors, as well as increasing the potential for corruption. Rules-based approaches, by comparison, create more stable, predictable and transparent rules for investors and governments, and lead to better governance. It is true, nevertheless, that some kinds of rules-based competition, such as EPZs, may potentially create problems of a 'race to the bottom'.

It would be misleading to consider investment incentives without also discussing performance requirements (UNCTC/UNCTAD 1991). Local content, trade-balancing and export requirements are the most frequently quoted examples of performance requirements within a wide range of fiscal, financial and other incentives. The linkages between performance requirements and investment incentives derive from the fact that the former may be negotiated as a quid pro quo for incentives. In addition, firms have reported that developed countries used investment incentives with much the same effect as developing countries used TRIMs. Developed countries have argued that TRIMs cause distortions in patterns of trade and investment, whereas developing nations regard them as important tools to promote development objectives and strengthen trade balances. As with the analysis of incentives, under assumptions of perfect competition, TRIMs are clearly distortionary. Under the conditions of oligopoly, however, TRIMs may be employed to shift rents and producer surplus from countries where the investment is located. The conclusion depends on the type of measure, and TRIMs in general represent a second-best development tool.

In the Uruguay Round of negotiations, under pressure from the developed countries, efforts focused upon means of controlling, reducing and prohibiting TRIMs. A balanced approach which deals both with incentives and with performance requirements is clearly an essential prerequisite for further progress in multilateral agreements (Brewer and Young 1997, 2000). However, there is little in the negotiating agenda of the World Trade Organization's Doha Development Round of trade rules (launched in November 2001 for completion by 1 January 2005), to suggest that regulation of incentives will be a priority.[3]

Investment–Trade Relationships

A recent, highly respected study of the world trading system (Hoekman and Kostecki 1995) discusses investment policies (in 2 pages) as one of a number of future *trade-related* challenges for the WTO multilateral regime. By comparison Kobrin (1995, p. 16) regards international production as having replaced trade as 'the "glue" binding international transactions'; and generally it has to be said that scholars of international business tend to downplay the significance of international trade (but see Gray 1998, 1999).

The reality is that the two areas are strongly linked (WTO 1998). From the work of Horst (1972), Swedenborg (1979) and Buckley and Pearce (1979) onwards, there is evidence of complementarities between trade and FDI (see also Mundell 1957; Markusen 1983). Export-generating effects resulted from additional sales of finished goods, components, raw materials or capital equipment; these exports could come from the parent of a subsidiary or they could consist of additional exports from independent suppliers in the home country. Subsequently the subsidiary might begin to export components or finished products back to the market of its parent or to third countries, and to develop new products for export markets. Export-displacement effects, by contrast, occur if output from an overseas affiliate replaces exports from the parent MNE; if subsidiary production replaces exports from a competitor in the home country; if subsidiary manufacture replaces exports from another affiliate in either the local or third country markets; or if affiliate manufacture replaces exports previously undertaken by a third country supplier to the host country.

In the present era, the debate over complementarity versus substitutability is less relevant: investment and trade are inextricably bound together in the global production and sourcing decisions of MNEs; and indeed are linked to other cross-frontier flows of tangible and intangible assets. There is still a requirement for research evidence, including disaggregated analysis of trade and investment relationships in specific manufacturing and service sectors, as well as studies both at the company level, of the influence of global strategies on investment and trade, and at the country level, relating, for instance, to the switch from import-substitution to export-oriented strategies.

The trade performance of multinational subsidiaries is of especial importance for host countries, reflecting the interest in the attraction of export-oriented FDI and its role in economic development; but also the concerns about labor-intensive exports and footloose FDI. On the one hand, MNE-related exports provide opportunities for achieving economies of scale, with positive effects on output and productivity. Similarly there may be positive learning effects from foreign competitors and customers, which, in turn, may spill over to other domestic enterprises (Blomström et al. 1992; Kokko 1992).

In addition, export expansion has beneficial foreign exchange and balance of payments benefits. On the other hand, high-exporting MNE affiliates may be low labor cost, rationalized operations which, by their nature, are footloose; and linkages to the local economy may be very low, with production inputs largely imported. Recent relevant literature in respect of the export intensity of MNE subsidiaries includes Andersson and Fredriksson (1996), Egelhoff et al. (2000), and Tavares and Young (2002). In general, however, the research on export determinants and export performance has mainly been undertaken by scholars in the field of international marketing, focusing upon uni-national rather than multinational firms (see, for example, Bonaccorsi 1992; Zou and Stan 1998).

What is missing, in any event, is detailed analysis of the policy interrelationships and implications, and particularly further understanding of the potentially distorting effects of investment and trade barriers. Included within these are the role of tariffs and non-tariff barriers, including anti-dumping and voluntary export restraints, safeguard agreements and the like. These have been shown to induce tariff and NTB jumping FDI (and 'premature internationalization'), but might also divert investment, say, from developing to developed countries (WTO 1998). On the positive side, trade liberalization is a necessary concomitant to investment liberalization for developing nations attempting to improve their investment climate: reductions in trade barriers would mean that MNEs could import lower-cost or higher-quality inputs, while lowering of export barriers was necessary for export-oriented production (OECD 1988). For MNEs' global or regional strategies, integrated production and sourcing is clearly hampered by trade barriers. However, in respect of domestic market-oriented FDI, MNEs and their foreign affiliates might themselves attempt to secure tariff and other forms of protection (see also the discussion on TRIMs below).

In respect of policy measures, it is accepted that a common approach to investment and trade is not straightforward. For example, the right to trade under free and non-discriminatory conditions is an accepted principle in the trade policy regime, but the right to invest or establish is not so easily defined or implemented. The concept of national treatment is also more complex in an investment context where there are issues relating to both pre-establishment and post-establishment phases of the project (WTO 1998, para. 154). Despite these and many other problem areas, it seems essential that all new multilateral rules should reflect the parallelism that exists between investment and trade, if existing distortions are not to be compounded. In this regard, a WTO Working Group established in 1996 has been undertaking analytical studies on the relationship between trade and investment. To support this, there is also a requirement for a closer integration of the research work of scholars in the international business and international trade fields.

Corporate Social Responsibility

The topic of corporate social responsibility is increasingly becoming a significant component of bilateral and international investment agreements, particularly in relation to issues such as labor, the environment, consumer protection, corporate governance and ethical business standards (see UNCTAD 2001; OECD 2001). Such interest reflects the need for business to dialogue with and address some of the legitimate concerns of developing countries and the vociferous and powerful global civil society.

Among a range of initiatives are the following:

Multilateral level
- UN-sponsored *Global Compact*. Signed in July 2000 by 50 of the world's largest MNEs, this commits the companies to adhere to 9 principles in the areas of human rights, labor and the environment.
- The Organisation for Economic Co-operation and Development's (OECD) *Guidelines for Multinational Enterprises* were first published in 1976 and have been regularly updated since then. The latest set of rules were agreed in June 2000, with strengthened sections on the environment, labor relations and business policies, and attempt to address more effectively the issue of implementation. Like the UN Global Compact, the Guidelines are non-binding and represent recommendations on responsible business conduct addressed by OECD governments to MNEs.

A full review of measures addressing the 'social responsibility' of multinationals in international investment agreements is contained in UNCTAD (2001).

Corporate level
- Corporate codes of conduct. There is evidence to indicate that the majority of large MNEs now have their own codes of business conduct. In respect of coverage, emphasis is on three issues, namely fair business practices, environmental stewardship and fair employment. Recent survey evidence is contained in Kolk et al. (1999), and Gordon and Miyake (1999).

Responses to these initiatives have not been overly encouraging. In respect of the OECD Guidelines, the few studies that were undertaken in the early years after their introduction indicated little interest among MNEs. This was in part because of the climate in which they were introduced, and also perhaps because their philosophy was perceived as being negative to multinational firms. More recently they have suffered by their association with the ill-fated *Multilateral Agreement on Investment* (MAI) initiative within which they were to be incorporated. The OECD as well as the UN proposals have been criticized by NGOs because of their non-binding nature.

In the work of Kolk et al. (1999) on corporate codes, moreover, it was shown that almost one-third of firms did not monitor compliance, while a further 58 per cent undertook the monitoring themselves. The NGOs have been equally sceptical of corporate codes, and are still seeking binding mechanisms to enforce corporate social responsibility; this is despite recent programmes to promote independent verification (Brewer and Young 2000, p. 284).

Undoubtedly, there would be merit in providing a multilateral framework for such standards both to ensure uniformity of treatment and to reassure civil society. However, prospects are not very hopeful. More promising perhaps are localized initiatives by MNEs, developing in the wide range of areas where multinationals and host governments interact constructively at present, for example, joint programs to develop supplier linkages; sectoral training initiatives involving a number of MNEs and the host government; and MNE participation in private sector interest and advocacy groups. Young and Hood (2002) have formalized this notion in the form of a social compact between MNEs and host countries, prepared on an individual company basis as an evolving partnership.

CONCLUDING REMARKS

Using Caves' work and the contributions of other scholars in this volume as a starting point, this chapter has tried to show that the current dynamics of multinational business pose major policy challenges which require multilateral solutions. Agreement on appropriate policy measures is, however, highly problematic, not least because of the variety of new players involved in the policymaking process, and their varying range of interests. In analysing such processes an interdisciplinary approach is clearly called for. Nevertheless, answering the questions posed by civil society would benefit greatly from additional empirical study. This takes us back full circle to the findings of *Multinational Enterprise and Economic Analysis* (Caves 1996) which sets the baseline for what is a very full research agenda.

NOTES

1.   Caves picks this up again in his chapter in this volume, when he comments on intra-corporate globalization and problems of governance and coordination.

2. As Wells notes in Chapter Six of the current volume, in fairness, the pendulum may swing again, as it may with developing countries' attitudes and policies towards multinationals.
3. The negotiating agenda includes mention of negotiations aimed at 'clarifying and improving disciplines' on anti-dumping measures, subsidies (including fishing subsidies), and regional trade agreements. See *www.wto.org*.

REFERENCES

Andersson, A.E. (1985), 'Creativity and Regional Development', *Papers of the Regional Science Association*, **56**, pp. 5–20.

Andersson, T., and Fredriksson, T. (1996), 'International organization of production and variation in exports from affiliates', *Journal of International Business Studies*, **27** (2), 249–63.

Birkinshaw, J. (2001), 'Strategy and management in MNE subsidiaries', in A.M. Rugman and T.L. Brewer (eds), *The Oxford Handbook of International Business*, Oxford: Oxford University Press, pp. 380–401.

Blomström, M., Kokko, A. and Zejan, M. (1992), 'Host country competition and technology transfer by multinationals', Working Paper No. 4131, National Bureau of Economic Research.

Blomström, M., Globerman, S., and Kokko, A. (2000), 'The determinants of host country spillovers from foreign direct investment', Working Paper No. 2350, Centre for Economic Policy Research.

Bonaccorsi, A. (1992), 'On the relationship between firm size and export intensity', *Journal of International Business Studies*, **23** (4), 605–35.

Brewer, Thomas L., and Young, Stephen (1997), 'Investment incentives and the international agenda', *The World Economy*, **20**, (2), pp. 175–98.

Brewer, Thomas L., and Young, Stephen (2000), *The Multilateral Investment System and Multinational Enterprises*, Oxford: Oxford University Press.

Brewer, Thomas L., and Young, Stephen (1999), in Neil Hood and Stephen Young (eds), *The Globalization of Multinational Enterprise Activity and Economic Development*, London: Macmillan.

Buckley, P.J. (1994), 'International business versus international management? International strategic management from the perspective of internalisation theory', *Journal of the Economics of Business*, **1**, (1), pp. 95–104.

Buckley, P.J., and Pearce, R.D. (1979), 'Overseas production and exporting by the world's largest enterprises: a study in sourcing policy', *Journal of International Business Studies*, **10** (1), 9–20.

Cairncross, Frances (1997), *The Death of Distance*, Boston, MA: Harvard Business School Press.

Cantwell, J. (1989), *Technological Innovation and Multinational Corporations*, Oxford: Basil Blackwell.

Cantwell, J. (2001), 'Innovation and information technology in MNE', in A.M. Rugman and T.L. Brewer (eds), *The Oxford Handbook of International Business*, Oxford: Oxford University Press, pp. 431–56.

Cantwell, J., and Iammarino, S. (2001), 'EU regions and multinational corporations: change, stability and strengthening of technological comparative advantages', *Industrial and Corporate Change*, **10**, (4), pp. 1007–37.

Casson, M. (2000), *Economics of International Business. A New Research Agenda*, Cheltenham, UK: Edward Elgar.

Caves, Richard E. (1971), 'International corporations: the industrial economics of foreign investment', *Economica*, **38** (February), pp. 1–27.

Caves, Richard E. (1996), *Multinational Enterprise and Economic Analysis*, 2nd edition, Cambridge: Cambridge University Press. (First edition, 1982.)

Cooke, P., and Morgan, K. (1998), *The Associational Economy*, Oxford: Oxford University Press.

Curhan, J.P., Davidson, W.H. and Suri, R. (1977), *Tracing the Multinationals: A Sourcebook on US-Based Enterprises*, Cambridge, MA: Ballinger.

D'Aquino, Thomas (1999), 'Globalization, social progress, democratic development and human rights', in John H. Dunning (ed.), *Globalization: A Two Edged Sword*, Newark, New Jersey: Rutgers University.

Dunning, John H. (1993), *Multinational Enterprises and the Global Economy*, Wokingham, England and Reading, MA: Addison Wesley.

Dunning, John H. (1994), 'Reevaluating the benefits of foreign direct investment', *Transnational Corporations*, **3**, (1), pp. 23–51.

Dunning, John H. (ed.) (1997), *Governments, Globalization and International Business*, Oxford: Oxford University Press.

Dunning, John H. (ed.) (2000), *Regions, Globalization and the Knowledge-Based Economy*, Oxford: Oxford University Press.

Dunning, J.H. (2000), 'The eclectic paradigm as an envelope for economic and business theories of MNE Activity', *International Business Review*, **9**, pp. 163–90.

Egelhoff, W.G., Gorman, L. and McCormick, S. (2000), 'How FDI patterns influence subsidiary trade patterns: The case of Ireland', *Management International Review*, **40** (3), 203–30.

European Commission (1995), *Competition Policy in the New Trade Order: Strengthening International Cooperation and Rules*, Luxembourg: Office for Official Publications of the European Communities.

European Commission (1999), *European Community Competition Policy 1998*, XXVIIIth Report on Competition Policy, Luxembourg: Office for Official Publications of the European Communities.

Foss, N.J. (ed.) (1997), *Resources, Firms, and Strategies. A Reader in the Resource-Based Perspective*, Oxford: Oxford University Press.

Gordon, K., and Miyake, M. (1999), 'Deciphering codes of corporate conduct: A review of their contents', Working Papers on International Investment Number 1999/2, Paris: OECD.

Graham Edward M. (1978), 'Transatlantic investment by multinational firms: A rivalistic phenomenon?', *Journal of Post-Keynesian Economics*, **1** (Fall), pp. 81–99.

Gray, H.P. (1998), 'International trade: The "glue" of global integration', *Transnational Corporations*, **7** (2), pp. 137–46.

Gray, H.P. (1999), *Global Economic Involvement*, Copenhagen: Copenhagen Business School Press.

Guisinger, Stephen E. (1995), 'Putting an investment code to work: Harmonizing investment policies in the Asia Pacific', in Carl J. Green and Thomas L. Brewer (eds), *Investment Issues in Asia and the Pacific Rim*, New York: Oceana, pp. 157–68.

Hanson, G.H. (2001), 'Should countries promote foreign direct investment?', G-24 Discussion Paper Series No. 9, New York and Geneva: United Nations (February).

Hoekman, Bernard, and Kostecki, Michel (1995), *The Political Economy of the World Trading System*, Oxford: Oxford University Press.

Hood, Neil, and Young, Stephen (eds) (1999), *The Globalization of Multinational Enterprise Activity and Economic Development*, London: Macmillan.

Horst, T. (1972), 'The industrial composition of US exports and subsidiary sales to the Canadian market', *American Economic Review*, **62** (March), 37–45.

Kay, N.M. (1997), *Pattern in Corporate Evolution*, Oxford: Oxford University Press.

Knickerbocker, Frederick T. (1973), *Oligopolistic Reaction and Multinational Enterprise*, Boston MA: Division of Research, Graduate School of Business Administration, Harvard University.

Kobrin, Stephen, J. (1995), 'Regional integration in a globally networked economy', *Transnational Corporations*, **4** (2), pp. 15–33.

Kokko, A. (1992), *Foreign Direct Investment, Host Country Characteristics and Spillovers*, Stockholm: Economic Research Institute, Stockholm School of Economics.

Kolk, A., Van Tulder, R. and Welters, C. (1999), 'International codes of conduct and corporate social responsibility: Can transnational corporations regulate themselves?', *Transnational Corporations*, **8** (1), pp. 143–80.

Krugman, Paul (1989), 'Industrial organizations and international trade', in R. Schmalansee and R.D. Willig (eds), *Handbook of Industrial Organization*, Vol. 2, Amsterdam: North Holland, pp. 1109–1123.

Langlois, R.N., and Foss, N.J. (1999), 'Capabilities and governance: The rebirth of production in the theory of economic organization', *Kyklos*, **52** (2), pp. 201–18.

Lim, E.-G. (2001), 'Determinants of, and the relation between, foreign direct investment and growth: A summary of the recent literature', IMF Working Paper WP/01/175, International Monetary Fund (November).

Lipsey, R.E. (2000), 'Inward FDI and economic growth in developing countries', *Transnational Corporations*, **9** (1), pp. 67–94.

Lockett, A., and Thompson, S. (2001), 'The resource-based view and economics', *Journal of Management*, **27**, pp.723–54.

Madhok, A., and Tallman, S. (1998), 'Resources, transactions and rents: Managing value through interfirm collaborative relationships', *Organization Science*, **9**, pp. 326–39.

Markusen, J.R. (1983). 'Factor movements and commodity trade as complements', *Journal of International Economics*, **14**: 341–56.

Mundell, R.A. (1957), 'International trade and factor mobility', *American Economic Review*, **47** (June), 321–35.

Nachum, L. (2001), 'Review article: The geography of multinationals', *Transnational Corporations*, **10** (2), pp. 161–9.

Oman, C.P. (2000), *Policy Competition for Foreign Direct Investment*, Paris: OECD (March).

Organisation for Economic Co-operation and Development (1976), *Guidelines for Multinational Enterprises*, Paris: OECD.

Organisation for Economic Co-operation and Development (1998), *The Benefits of Trade and Investment Liberalization*, Paris: OECD.

Organisation for Economic Co-operation and Development (2001), *Corporate Responsibility – Private Initiatives and Public Goals*, Paris: OECD.

Peng, M.W. (2001), 'The resource-based view and international business', *Journal of Management*, **27**, pp. 803–29.

Penrose, E. (1995), *The Theory of the Growth of the Firm*, 3rd ed. Oxford: Oxford University Press (First edition 1959).

Pitelis, C.N., and Sugden, R. (2000), *The Nature of the Transnational Firm*, London and New York: Routledge.

Porter, M.E. (1985), *Competitive Advantage*, New York: The Free Press.

Rugman, A.M., and Verbeke, A. (2001), 'Environmental policy and international business' in A.M.Rugman and T.L. Brewer (eds), *The Oxford Handbook of International Business*, Oxford: Oxford University Press, pp. 537–57.

Saxenian, A. (1994), *Regional Advantage, Culture and Competition in Silicon Valley and Route 128*, Cambridge, MA: Harvard University Press.

Stopford, John, and Strange, Susan (1991), *Rival States, Rival Firms: Competition for World Market Shares*, Cambridge: Cambridge University Press.

Swedenborg, B. (1979), *The Multinational Operations of Swedish Firms: An Analysis of Determinants and Effects*, Stockholm: Industrial Institute for Economic and Social Research.

Tavares, A.T. (2001), *Systems, Evolution and Integration: Modeling the Impact of Economic Integration on Multinationals' Strategies*, Ph.D. thesis, University of Reading, UK.

Tavares, A.T., and Young, S. (2002), *Explaining the Export Intensity of Multinational Subsidiaries: An EU-Based Empirical Study*, Strathclyde International Business Unit Working Paper 2002/02, Glasgow: University of Strathclyde.

United Nations Conference on Trade and Development (UNCTAD) (1996a), *World Investment Report 1996: Investment, Trade and International Policy Arrangements*, New York and Geneva: UN.

United Nations Conference on Trade and Development (1996b), *Incentives and Foreign Direct Investment*, New York and Geneva: UN.

United Nations Conference on Trade and Development (2001), *Social Responsibility*, New York and Geneva: UN.

United Nations Centre on Transnational Corporations and United Nations Conference on Trade and Development (1991), *The Impact of Trade-Related Investment Measures on Trade and Development*, New York: UN.

Williamson, O. (1999), 'Strategy research: Governance and competence perspectives', *Strategic Management Journal*, **20** (12), pp. 1087–108.

World Trade Organization (1998), *Report (1998) of the Working Group on the Relationship between Trade and Investment to the General Council*, WT/WGTI/2, Geneva (8 December).

Young, S., and Hood, N. (2002), 'Alliance capitalism, FDI and developing countries', in J.H. Dunning and G. Boyd (eds), *Alliance Capitalism and Corporate Management*, Cheltenham, UK: Edward Elgar.

Zou, S., and Stan, S. (1998), 'The determinants of export performance: A review of the empirical literature between 1987 and 1997', *International Marketing Review*, **15** (5), 333–56.

Index